'Tortillas 1

Motorcycling Mexico, the
Sidetracked by t

B

Sam Manicom, with Birgit Schünemann

'*What is travelling? Changing your place? By no means! Travelling is changing your opinions and your prejudices.*'

Anatole France

'Tortillas to Totems' is dedicated to the memory of David Parkinson, RM, 1944–2009. Around the world traveller by both motorcycle and boat. A courageous man.

A CIP catalogue record for this title is available from the British Library.

www.sam-manicom.com

ISBN 978-0-9556573-3-7

Edited by Paul Blezard
Cover design & text layout by Fil Schiannini
Photography by Sam Manicom and Birgit Schuenemann
Motorcycle Line Art by Jez Cooper and Chard
Line art by Sam Manicom
Printed and bound by The Books Factory
Published by Sam Manicom – Adventure Motorcycle Travel Books
Although every effort has been made to trace the present copyright holders, we apologise in advance for any unintentional omission or neglect and will be pleased to insert appropriate acknowledgement to individuals in any subsequent edition of this publication.

Tortillas to Totems reviews:

'Globe-trotting biker Manicom's a natural storyteller. Although this trip may sound like a standard ride through familiar country, be assured, it isn't.'
Adventure Bike Rider

'You feel it, smell it, you freeze, you sweat, and you see what's before him like you're along for the ride. You are very much there'
ADV Moto Magazine

'Any good travel book must involve the reader as well as inspire and Tortillas to Totems does just that. Sam goes way beyond 'we went here and did this…''
The Rider's Digest

'I enjoyed it from start to finish and would heartily recommend it'
Overland Magazine

'The ordinary guy doing extraordinary things. Great stories.'
RiDE Magazine

'If you want to know why motorcyclists get out into the big world and ride across it then it's all here'
Motorcycle Sport and Leisure

'You could be his pillion, so well does he describe the sounds, sights and smells of the road. If you like bikes, riding and people watching, Sam is your man.'
Daily Record

'Tortillas To Totems'

By
Sam Manicom, with Birgit Schünemann

Contents

Foreword

The Oxford English dictionary says, 'Culture Shock. A disorientation felt by a person subjected to an unfamiliar way of life.' I understood this, didn't I? After all, wasn't this part of the main reason for going travelling on a motorcycle? To experience as many different things and ways of life as possible? To have preconceived ideas challenged?

I was happy with these thoughts, but there was something important that I'd not taken into account. After over six years riding the roads of developing countries in Africa, Asia, and South and Central America, I'd feared that things were going to be too easy. The States and Canada were going to be lands where I knew how things worked. I worried that there'd be few of the challenges or the dramas that had kept my 'guardian angel' working overtime for so many years.

I was wrong to be so concerned, but I didn't anticipate just how different things were going to be. The next two years exploring some of the developed world were going to be just as big a learning curve, and a challenge to me personally. I hadn't realised how much Birgit and I had changed over the years in third and second world countries. Nor had we grasped what a time of great global change this was. (You'll be riding with us through the latter part of the nineties).

The cultures and countries of North America are so varied and so full of surprises that they are just as fascinating, and just as much a challenge to the traveller, as the most rugged countries in the developing world. Being on motorcycles was a key factor. The freedom the motorcycles gave us to roam to our hearts' content through the three nations of this continent was of phenomenal value. The bikes also made it far too easy for us to be sidetracked, and that's where the adventures always seemed to begin...

Author's note

We'd like to thank all the people we met in Mexico, the United States and Canada. In one way or another, you made our journey come alive. You shared your worlds with us in a completely unselfish way. We hope that your example will help us to make any travellers we meet in our own homelands that much more welcome.

Publishing this book has been no solo or dual adventure. There are key people to thank. Paul Blezard has been his usual inspiring and precise self as he has edited with skill and devotion to the task. This book is a far finer thing as a result of his talents. Fil Schiannini has designed a beautiful cover and has dealt with all of the design work for the contents. His tremendous skill and intuition have made all the difference. My sister, the author Ros Woodman, has used her experience and instinct to make invaluable suggestions. Nikki Madan-Schiannini worked with us again on the proofreading and she has made sure that none of my errors have crept through. Thank you both for your care and your reassurance. Elspeth Beard (the first British woman to ride a motorcycle solo around the world) dragged me back from the list of potential titles to 'Tortillas to Totems'. Thank you – you are quite right, this title starts to tell the story straight away. And finally, a big thank you to Iain Harper who has worked wonders with web design and management. He has been a good friend right the way through. Without this wonderful group of people, this book would not have come to life.

I must write words of thanks to all those in the media and the world of retail that have so actively reviewed and promoted my books. You have made it possible for an ordinary person to ride the rocky road of the writer.

You'll find advertisements in the back of this book. I'm drawing your attention to them because if you are dreaming of an adventure, then you can do no better than to start here. All the advertisers are proactive in the world of adventure travel.

I want to say thank you to my travelling buddy and partner Birgit, who has had a lot to put up with over the years. You could say that life around me is somewhat unpredictable. She is an amazing person to travel with. Courageous, kind, insightful, determined and she can be very funny. I am lucky that this adventure allowed our paths to cross. And that it gave us the chance to realise that our relationship was far more than just two travellers passing. We clicked; the adventure would have been far less interesting and exciting without her. This book would not have happened without her encouragement and her enthusiasm. She's more precise than I am so I've been able to borrow many of the facts and figures in this book from her diaries.

Finally, I want to say 'thank you' to you, the reader. Without your support and enthusiasm for my books over the years, I'd have given up a long time ago and would be sitting behind a 'nine to five' desk now instead of sharing tales of the road. I hope that we are all encouraging those who can, to go out and enjoy this amazing world.

We hope you enjoy looking for adventure with us.

Other Books by Sam Manicom

'This story, rich with detail of the terrain, the people, the food, and the circumstances, reveals not only a spirit of determination but also a significant empathy and respect for his fellow man.'

ADVMOTO Magazine

'The word-pictures that bring a good travel book to life are all here.'

Overland magazine

'This is a great adventure and a really enjoyable read.'

Johnnie Walker - BBC Radio Two

'Number 1 in our top ten motorcycle travel books'

Adventure Bike TV

'The deep red of the African earth glows under Manicom's pen.'

Visor Down

'A skyscraper-high stack of experiences. Full of vivid detail of the terrain, people, food and circumstances.'

Adventure Rider Magazine USA

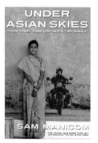

'A unique and wonderful adventure.'

Ted Simon – Author of Jupiter's Travels

'Engaging from the off; a terrific read'

Overland Magazine

'Accessible and well written, this will prod anyone with a bike license to take off and do something amazing!'

Adventure Travel Magazine

'An engaging story of adventure that allows one to escape into the world.'

Adventure Rider Radio

'Why buy it? Inspiration!'

Motorcycle News

'Sam has the skills of the story teller and this book easily transports you into three years of journey across Asia.'

Horizons Unlimited.com

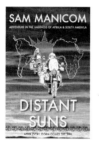

Manicom's storytelling is compelling. With the detailed descriptions of the scenery, people, and events that come and go throughout the trip it's easy to paint the picture yourself.

Motorcycle Monthly

'His descriptions are vivid and precise and he made me laugh.'

Motorcycle Mojo

'Drama, action, passion, disaster and the pure adrenaline buzz of overlanding are all here. '

Overland Magazine

'I was thoroughly impressed'

BMW Owners News USA

'Few travel writers can conjure up sights and smells so provocatively as Sam.'

Daily Record – Scotland

'An epic ride. You are immersed in the sights, sounds, touch, smell and taste of a journey of true human discovery.'

Motorcycle Explorer Magazine

'Author Manicom and his companion are the real thing...'

RiDE Magazine

'Tortillas To Totems'

Motorcycling Mexico, the United States and Canada

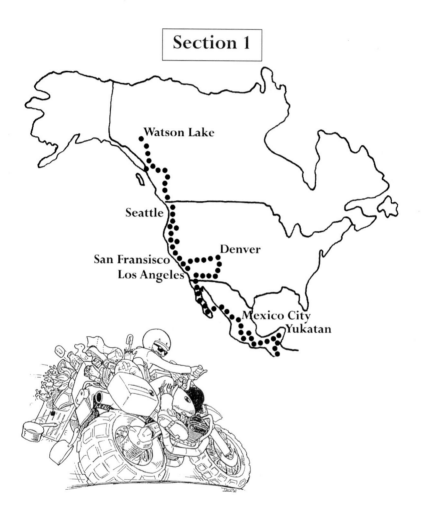

Section 1

Watson Lake

Seattle

Denver

San Fransisco
Los Angeles

Mexico City
Yukatan

Chapter 1

Predators and Border Queens

'Get your motor runnin', Head out on the highway Lookin' for adventure,
And whatever comes our way'

Steppenwolf

The bike and I leapt violently into the air. As we did so, all the thoughts that had been meandering through my mind changed instantly into 'Survive!' My bike's engine screamed as I involuntarily opened the throttle on take-off, this grip of fear almost making the situation worse. As we took off I heard and felt the drive shaft hit the top of the tope with a sickening thump. This just had to have caused major damage. (A tope, pronounced 'toe-pay', is a Mexican speed-bump). But this one was no mere bump. There'd been nothing to warn that it was there. The dusty tarmac had camouflaged it perfectly and the sun, right overhead, hadn't cast even a hint of a shadow. The wheels came crashing back down again, and with a wobble that I was sure was going to throw me off, the bike's suspension bottomed out under the weight.

Somehow the bike leapt sideways and of course, there was a ditch waiting for me to fall straight into. I heaved at the handlebars and for once my instinct made me do the right thing. I opened the throttle wide again and with a wild weave, we somehow managed to stay upright, and on the road.

The day had started back in Guatemala with no hint of trouble. The dawn had been cool and bright with a faint mist that hung around the jungle trees. The sun had tried its best to creep through the gaps and as it did so, its dust-filled misty beams had dappled the road around us. My bike's tyres hummed, all my gear was strapped on tightly and we'd just filled the tanks with fuel from a station that was totally at home with its surroundings. Ancient liana-strung trees surrounded the time-worn crumbling walls, which cried out for some new paint and some TLC. The rough track off the main road to it was heavily rutted by a generation of trucks, and the roadside ditch was filled with that same generation's cast-offs. Paper, bits of broken vehicle, old oilcans and rusting barbed wire were collected together to form an untidy reminder of everyday life. The air was heavily scented with the musty smell of layers of leaf mould, and with the pungent tang from both the fuel and the cigarette that a man was smoking as he poured diesel into the tank of his truck from an old watering can. The cream-coloured pickup looked as if it was being held together by rust, string, and gaffer tape, but mostly by prayer. The wood and silver crucifix that hung from the truck's rear view mirror suggested that this was the greater strength.

The uneven, oil-stained forecourt was time and weather worn, and the pumps looked as if they belonged in the props office of a Hollywood film studio. The pump had clunked and whirred irregularly as petrol sploshed with surprising speed into my tank. The white arm of the gauge had jerked in stages around the crescent moon-shaped dial, and the attendant's eyes had opened wide as litre after litre had flowed into my 43-litre tank. This small Indian man wore beige overalls that looked as if they hadn't been washed for a decade, and he had a jaded look to his face which implied that he wasn't surprised by many things. His deeply lined skin gave me the feeling that he'd seen a lot in his life, but never a bike with a tank that could drink so much fuel. Watching him, I was conscious that he was one of the last people I'd speak to in Guatemala.

As my partner Birgit and I rode the last miles towards the border, my mind ticked over in time with the bike's engine. Around us a sweaty heat began to swirl, and beneath my bike the tarmac undulated with heat heaves that were tricky to ride. Heat and heavy trucks play wobbly games with the road surfaces in this part of the world and my bike's suspension was gently working overtime. Loose gravel on the corners and the frequent potholes kept my mind split between the riding moment, where we had been, and where we were going. Even after more than six years on the road, I still worried about border crossings. This was to be the last in Central America. This day we'd be riding into North America. The border with Mexico loomed. Adrenaline flowed through me at the thought of a new adventure which I knew was going to be very different from those we'd had in the last few years of meandering through South and Central America.

The lush jungle vegetation began to ease away, to be replaced with scrubby bush and an occasional tree. I took the flower-strewn verges as a good omen. The sun was out in full now, and even though the dawn still held a dash of cool under the trees, I began to feel a trickle of sweat creeping down my back. My bike, Libby (short for Liberty as that is what she had given me), ticked and purred as if she too was anticipating a new beginning and perhaps, more gentle roads.

A vast valley dropped us down towards the border. We'd heard no scare stories about this crossing. Central American borders had a million tales of hassle, bribery and corruption attached to them. We'd not found them difficult, but in my eternal search for information I'd always listened too hard to the tales, and had let an edgy tingle creep into me as we'd approached each one. One of the things we'd learnt was never to cross a border on a Sunday. The stories had it that 'fees' leapt up and that many of the crossings were undermanned then. The perverse side of me was tempted to try a Sunday though. If everyone steered clear of borders on Sundays, perhaps it might actually be the easiest day to cross?

Fear of the unknown? No, that's too strong, but the uneasy feelings that slipped in always added an element of wary anticipation that sharpened my senses and gave a valuable burst of adrenaline. Each previous border had been a fresh challenge to be played with. Though similar, each game had its own set of rules and these were normally influenced by an ever-changing combination of people, tradition, poverty, an element of lawlessness, strange customs, the weather conditions on the day, and how we were feeling at each moment of potential confrontation. The latter was a danger if we allowed it to be. For a successful border crossing, we had to be and remain calm, and avoid confrontation if at all possible. If others sense fear or frustration, they can't help but respond to it.

The truth is that most people react in a helpful way when they sense that you are feeling vulnerable, but there are always those who are predators. When they sense your anxiety, they let their own instincts, needs and desires take over. They inevitably try to take advantage of you. We'd learned were to be cool, respectful, and firm. Another key ingredient was to have plenty of time. Start a border crossing early and it didn't matter how many games the predators wanted to play with us, we had time to wait them out. Wait long enough and another potential victim would come along to distract them. The border crossing predators are all chancers. Make life too hard for them, politely, and they soon got bored with us. By playing the innocent and rather ignorant, whilst being overly polite, we found that the predators inevitably couldn't be bothered to work any harder, or any longer, at lining their pockets at our expense.

Luck also plays a part. A moment's good fortune can suddenly blow away a huge amount of hassle. Luck often comes in the form of a helpful person. The trouble is that we were often battling with the scare stories and suspicion so much, that we ran the risk of turning away someone genuine. Judging a book by its cover just doesn't work, as genuinely helpful people come with all sorts of looks, and some very different personalities.

Good humour is the last essential. There's always something mad going on at a crossing and most of the people you are dealing with at borders do their jobs or run their scams, day after day. We'd often find that a little good-natured humour would break their sense of monotony or frustration at their lot in life, and then doors would start to swing open for us. We'd become individuals who could be related to in a pleasant way, rather than just a couple more irritants in yet another boring day.

How often are you going to have to sing and entertain the officials to get them to help you through a crossing? It happened to us. I'm not sure whether my attempt at the Beatles' 'A hard day's night' back in El Salvador was really appreciated, or whether it acted more as an incentive to get us through the system as quickly as possible, but either way, it worked.

Children are a frequent source of fun. One customs officer, who'd been hassling us, got his come-uppance from a child puking on him at just the right moment. The people who'd been watching our attempts to get away without paying a bribe laughed so hard that he promptly stamped our papers in disgust and waved us out to the open road, happy to get rid of us.

But the worst of these rules could be about to change. My optimistic and lazy sides were combining with the gentle rhythm of the ride to ease a tad of complacency into my mood. Surely crossing into the first country in North America was going to take us from lands of uncertainty into a more developed country where things were increasingly familiar and ran according to recognisable rules? It would help that our minds now worked in Spanish, and that the next border crossing into Mexico was still going to be done in Spanish. They say that Latin people have a similar mentality, whatever their country. I was never sure whether it was the language or the heat and conditions that were the common thread that affected how things were done.

The kilometre stones flicked by us at what seemed like an ever-increasing speed. Half of me wanted to slow down and savour the last moments of Central America, the other half just wanted to get on with it; to confront the new challenge, to get the crossing out of the way and to roll our wheels into freedom and on to the next adventure.

Suddenly, there it was – the border. A straggle of dust-stained and water-marked concrete buildings lined both sides of the road. The mood around us changed with those last few hundred metres. Life swirled in a mash of overloaded trucks, people dashing to get their work done before the day's full heat hit, and the inevitable queues of others, as anxious and as confused by it all as we were. Stray dogs hung around, and greasy- looking overweight unshaven men sat in rickety old chairs in front of seedy bars and restaurants. Pack donkeys and running children added to the mix, and scrawny chickens darted among the feet and the truck tyres – all looking as if they were on the run; escapees from the lunch table, or from the cock-fighting pits?

As we pulled to a halt and I lifted off my helmet, the noise hit me with an intense, hot blast. Truck horns blared loudly in competition with doors banging, people shouting, chickens squawking, and dogs barking. Added to this fume-filled mix was the sound of revving engines from the mishmash of beaten-up cars and pick-ups, and from the giant long distance White, Mack and International trucks.

One moment I was rolling along thinking about what might be about to happen, and the next, we were right in the midst of it all. Things were going on at a surprisingly fast pace. Did these people know something we didn't? Was the border closing early this day? The rush was unnatural. Normally crossings are tinged with a 'manana' mood, at least until cash is being handed over!

First call: the moneychangers. Here, for a pretty lousy rate, we changed the bulk of our remaining quetzals for Mexican pesos. We kept a few quetzals for eventualities but having the pesos would mean that we wouldn't be so vulnerable to the money sharks on the other side of the border. Next stop, the Aduana or Customs office. The tang of stale body odour hung in the air around the officers who quickly started the hassle. We didn't have entry stamps for our bikes in our passports. Apparently, when we had crossed into Guatemala, the Aduana should have stamped our passports to confirm that our bikes had entered the country with us. They hadn't done so and we hadn't known that they should. We felt the awful anticipation of a 'fine' coming our way, not to mention the games that these officers could play with us if they were so inclined.

Birgit wasn't having any of it. She told the officers in a firm but friendly way, "It's not our problem. Your officials should be well trained enough to do their jobs properly, and if they aren't, then it's up to you to sort the situation out". The officers looked a bit stunned for a moment and then, seeing the friendly but determined look in her eye, the senior officer gave in. "You are right," he said, "One day these young officers will learn. Please accept our apologies."

This small episode stands strong in my memory because, in its way, it was a very unusual thing to have happened. This was the first time in Central America that a man had had gone so far as to actually admit that he and his male colleagues were in the wrong. Equally, few Latin American men seemed to have the ability to admit they didn't know something, and few would let a woman see that they didn't understand something. Normally, in South and Central America there had been little

16

point in challenging an official in a situation like this. It had always felt a far better option to see if there was another way around that would allow both sides to retain their pride. This time, either the official was an unusually enlightened man, or Birgit had hit exactly the right notes.

Rubber stamps hit our paperwork, and all we had to do now was face the Migración officers. We had the expected demand for money, but we'd done our homework. When we'd been in Guatemala City looking for tyres, we'd stumbled across the Dirección de Migración office, and had popped in to check what we would need for exiting the country. We told the officers that we had done this and that we'd been told there were no fees involved. They gave in straight away. Outside, a young boy was admiring our bikes. Birgit gave him the last of our quetzals, why not? We had no further need of them and it wasn't much anyway. To our surprise the boy thanked us. For some reason this was totally unexpected. Then all of a sudden Guatemala spat us out into Mexico.

Here, I felt confused. There didn't seem to be any clear directions. No one instantly hassled us, asking to help us through the crossing for a small fee, (or propino as it's called). The trickle of sweat turned into a gentle flow beneath my leather jacket. We parked the bikes and looked around for any sign of where to go and what to do.

We saw a board saying Quarantine and thought we'd better check in there first, just in case. We were right to do so. The bikes had to be sprayed before we were allowed to do anything else. I'd once had the same sort of situation in Africa but here the guys knew exactly what they needed to do. The tyres and undersides of the bikes were sprayed, and so were our boots. In Africa, the boots had been omitted. We were told, in a slightly shifty way, that the fee was 30 pesos per bike. Though just $3, this felt like far too much, so we haggled and the price quickly dropped to just 40 pesos for the pair of them.

We found an out-of-the-way spot to park the bikes amidst bits of string, spit splatter marks, a solitary and very battered leather shoe and a mix of bright yellow stringy mango pips. Their colour clashed violently with a pile of discarded orange peel which sat in a jumbled heap next to a concrete step. The dusty step was worn smooth and low in the middle. We set off into the maelstrom, hoping that nothing would be nicked from the bikes.

The customs and immigration offices were full of arm-waving people, who seemed to know that the only way to communicate with the officers behind the metal desks was to shout at them. Waving paper was obligatory. Much of the paper that gets waved about is in the form of photocopies. Borders seem to want an endless supply of copies of just about every document you are carrying – either to do with you, or your bikes. In Central America, little old ladies sit proudly and regally by their photocopy machines, knowing that you will never be carrying the right numbers of copies of whatever the documents are. Therefore, they hold your fate in their hands and they know it. These queens of the crossings had fees that seemed extortionate and we always had the feeling that the women were in league with the border officials. I cynically wondered if most of the copies we supplied ended up as firelighters at the end of the day.

But, you have no choice, and you hope that the photocopy machine is actually working on the day you need it. If it's not, you're faced with a ride back to the nearest sizeable town. That can be a long

journey, which then turns into a lengthy hunt for a photocopier. We always got extras made, as we knew that it was a racing certainty that sooner or later we'd be asked for yet another copy. But you have to strike the right balance at each crossing. Get too many copies and you end up with a significantly slimmer wallet and a wedge of papers to carry for months. Don't get enough and…you're in trouble.

Surely there wasn't going to be a problem with this crossing though? Mexico is classed as being a Second World country. The optimist in me hoped that this upping of status would mean that the customs office would actually have a copier of its own, though I wasn't naive enough to think that we wouldn't have to pay for our potential firelighters. I'd seen a hole-in-the-wall copy shop outside, and I tucked that away as 'Plan B'.

We eased our way to the desk. I focused on one official and tried to think positive, friendly thoughts. This was one of the superstitions I'd picked up on our travels – and sometimes it seemed to work. The official, also sweating in the mid-morning heat, rattled at us in Spanish and gestured impatiently. Fortunately Birgit grasped what he was asking for. She spoke far better Spanish than I did, but even I had got to the stage where I could easily notice the change in accents as we rode from one country to the next. Sometimes the change was so different that we might have ridden in one instant straight from London into Manchester, or from Brooklyn to Houston. Man-made lines on a piece of paper so easily allow these changes to occur. Once a line is drawn on a map, it doesn't matter that there are only a few metres of dusty no-man's land between countries. The differences can sometimes be quite dramatic.

Here we had a surprise. We expected to pay a fee for the bikes to be allowed into Mexico temporarily. Our carnet de passage documents had long expired but that was OK, because officially you don't need these temporary importation documents in the Americas. Paying an entry fee was normal but the surprise came in two parts. First, we could only pay the fee by credit card; cash was no good. And second, neither customs nor immigration would allow us permits for more than 15 days' stay. We needed far more than that. "You have to extend your paperwork inside the country," we were bluntly told by a man who looked like a shrewish, Dickensian solicitor's clerk. He stared at us with a sour expression. There wasn't even a hint of 'Welcome to Mexico' about this guy; we might as well have had the plague!

The official reeled off a list of his requirements and my heart sank when Birgit asked to use the photocopy machine. The official snorted and waved outside. Plan B perhaps? But no, we had to go back in time from a Second World country into a Third. Mexico didn't have a photocopier in its border offices and the one in the shop outside hadn't been working for days! The clock ticked by and the heat rose. As it did so, we hoped that the fact that the mangy dogs were heading for shady spots and getting their heads down didn't mean that we would be faced with a long siesta wait. Sometimes you just have to be completely fatalistic. You've no choice. Railing too much against whatever fate is throwing at you can lead to mistakes – sometimes costly ones. To this date we'd never paid a bribe at a border crossing and we were determined not to do so now. We climbed onto the hot saddles of the bikes, and rode back into Central America on a photocopy hunt. I couldn't resist a little grin at the thought that we'd ridden into a Mexican farce; how easily preconceived thoughts and hopes can be dashed. But in the end, what did it matter? What did matter was that eventually we got through the border.

Then another thought occurred to me. If we were heading north into lands where things were supposed to happen on time and in a firmly set way, would an enormous chunk of 'adventure potential' be disappearing? Yes, Third World countries can be a hassle at times, but each hassle almost always had some fun and a tale to tell attached to it. If we were going to lose this by heading north, did I want to go that way at all? Was North America going to feel horribly sanitised? Should I be sitting down with Birgit for a very serious conversation about what we were doing? There was an awful lot of Central America that we'd not managed to see. Guatemala was fascinating, and in a month we'd only seen a small section of it. I'd love to be able to spend more time in Nicaragua, and we'd not made it to English-speaking Belize at all.

Then we were back into the rush and events took over. Photocopies in hand and into the customs office again; our paperwork was stamped, immigration was easy and that was it. We were finally in North America. I decided to see what the rest of the day would bring. I'd talk to Birgit later. After all, our rough plan was to spend the first weeks in Southern Mexico; we'd never be that far away from the crossings back into Guatemala or to Belize.

Chapter Two
Lost Civilisations in the Dawn

'I soon realized that no journey carries one far unless, as it extends into the world around us, it goes an equal distance into the world within.'

Lillian Smith

The first kilometres of Mexico were easy to ride, almost too easy. I rode the twisting, pine tree-lined road with a slight sense of anticlimax and that put me on edge. It was similar to the sensation I'd get if I'd forgotten to do something important. I had the feeling that we were on the cusp of a monumental change and the more I thought about it, the more I didn't like what we were doing. Why hadn't I had these thoughts before? Why did my brain wait until now for them to creep in? Was the dream to ride up and into Alaska so wrong? After all the years in Second and Third World countries, had I forgotten how to live in the First World? Was this the real fear? Or was it simply an awareness that after so long on the road I was beginning to see the start of the end?

Then I hit that first tope. Birgit had managed to spot the speed bump and had skilfully avoided it. She was looking back down the road to me with eyes wider than the Guatemalan petrol attendant's had been. I sat on the bike and shook. Lucky escape? Too right, but my first thought was the potential damage to the bike. She must have weighed around 250 kilos with her own weight, fuel and water, On top of that were my own 85 kilos and roughly 20 kilos of luggage, tools and spare parts.

On a long journey such as ours, serious damage to your bike can be a real adventure-killer. The costs involved with putting major trouble to rights can be daunting and can dramatically reduce the scope of the journey. If I'd broken the shaft or the suspension, then the bill could well mean that we weren't going to have enough fuel money to make it to Alaska. This tope, so close to the border, could well have just mapped out the next year of our lives in a completely unplanned way.

I leaned the bike over onto its side stand, climbed off and stood shaking for a moment. The fear of the last few seconds had knocked me out of my sense of anticlimax in no uncertain terms.

Squatting down by the bike, I could see the bright shine of a new gouge that had been ripped across the underside of the shaft casing. It gleamed wickedly at me in the sunshine. The bash plate was lined with deep new gouges that made me, yet again, really happy that I'd had it bolted on heavy-duty rubber mounts to the underside of the engine. The impact had been strong enough to rip the top off one of the mounting bolts. The bike's centre stand had collected a new dent, and one foot was twisted slightly to the side. Oil seeped out from the rubber sleeves at both the top and bottom of the drive shaft casing. The impact had been so violent that both sleeves had been jerked loose. This looked like bad news. By now, Birgit had made it back down the road to me. We stood looking at the sorry state before us, both aware that my guardian angel had been with me once again. Behind us, the tope was a lethal twenty-five centimetres high – ten inches – with my new gouge alongside the collection that other unfortunates had previously created.

My guardian angel is another superstition of the road. Over the years I'd been involved in many disasters. I'd got away from them with wonderfully positive things happening as a direct result, so I knew it was more than just plain luck that had kept me alive. I'd been shot at twice, arrested, jailed, hit by a van and suffered dysentery, malaria and dengue fever. My bike had nearly blown up with me sitting on it, and I'd survived an accident that broke seventeen bones in my body and filled my eyes with broken glass. I'd also managed to slip three discs in my back, which was both agonising and debilitating at the time. I suppose that lot doesn't sound very lucky, but the question for me in the end was always, could I still ride my bike, and therefore carry on with the adventure? So far, I had always been able to, so I had to have a guardian angel didn't I?

What to do now? If there was damage and I continued to ride Libby then I could make the situation far worse, and of course it might be dangerous to ride her in this state. The nearest towns were miles away and for sure there wouldn't be a BMW garage anywhere nearby. If the worst had happened then perhaps this would be our chance to meet some of Mexico's Green Angels. Green Angel crews tour

Mexico's roads on the lookout for the likes of us. Each crew has an area of the country and it's their job to help stranded motorists. The crews are bilingual and the work they do helping people out is free. You just have to pay for any parts, fuel, oil etc but they will even give you a tow to the nearest help if they can't sort you out on the spot. We'd been told that a good tip was the only thing that was expected. But I really hoped that things weren't that bad.

We unstrapped the luggage and with Libby now standing 'naked', we eased her up onto the centre stand. The cicadas were in full song in the scrubby bushes and the scents of pine and drying earth surrounded us. With Birgit leaning on the front bash bars, I tentatively turned the back wheel. If there was serious damage, then I reckoned I ought to be able to feel it as the wheel turned. The runs of oil had become worse in the meantime, and I could now see shiny steel for the full length of the suspension shaft. It had bottomed out hard enough to take up the full travel, and the impact had dented the rubber stopper at the bottom.

Inch by inch I eased the wheel round. Not a grind, nor a squeal. No gravelly feeling that would warn of broken bearings, in fact no danger signs at all. I spun the wheel harder. Nothing was amiss, so I started the bike, and with the back wheel still off the ground I put her into gear and gently opened the throttle. The bike coughed, spluttered and the wheel turned with ease. The gearbox sounded fine, the final drive was smooth and the wheel turned with such slickness that I knew I'd gotten away with a potential disaster, again. The only way to see if I'd broken the suspension was to ride her.

Still without luggage, I took Libby for a gentle spin. She felt rock solid, and I could feel the suspension working comfortably as I picked up speed over the bumpy tarmac. With rubber sleeves back in place and luggage back on board, I took her for the real test. A couple of kilometres later I was pretty sure that I didn't have a problem, but I'd have eyes well open for topes from now on!

We stopped for the night in the lovely old town of San Cristobal de las Casas. It felt like a fine halfway house between Guatemala and Mexico. It's tucked up in the highlands and the grid-patterned streets

were lined with old Spanish-style colonial houses. The church was painted a crisp white and trimmed with a vivid bright yellow. The houses were painted an amazing variety of colours and the green of the pine-clad mountains finished off the effect to leave you with the feeling that you were riding onto an artist's paint palette. The surrounding area is famous for being the home of many indigenous Indians who still wear traditional costume. These people are a real draw, but suddenly we felt as if we had hit the 'Gringo Trail' big time. If felt really strange to be strolling the market-filled streets alongside so many tourists. We supposed that this was one of the changes we were going to have to get used to. Mexico is simply that much more accessible for visitors, and there is so much to see that the draw is magnetic.

It seemed logical to take a day or two to acclimatise to Mexico and as San Cristobal was both so pretty, and a good size, we decided to stop. One of the things we always liked to do on arrival in a new country was to find out the prices of the essentials we'd be buying from small shops and the markets. By doing this, there was far less chance of being overcharged. The landlady of our hostel seemed to be friendly and a genuine character who understood what we were up to. In fact she seemed to approve and helped us with our long list of items over a cup of coffee, which of course we paid for. The list covered everything from the price of tomatoes to that of meat, bread and bananas.

A couple of days in San Cristobal would also allow us to check Libby over; the oil leak from the shaft was still there. And Birgit's bike, 'Sir Henry the Hybrid' (because he is made up of parts from so many different bikes, and is an old gentleman) had a problem too. The indicators had stopped working. I was never sure whether anyone in countries such as this ever paid attention to our blinkers when we used them, but for us it was a 'peace of mind' thing. It was also far easier for me to keep up with Birgit if I knew what she was going to do next. She had got really good at indicating a change of direction to me in good time, mostly. When she wasn't able to, following her made some moments potentially dangerous and I might get cut off and we could become separated. That is never a fun thing to have to deal with in a strange town or city. I wasn't daft enough to make any urgent last minute manoeuvres in an attempt to keep up with her, but there was always the risk that I would instinctively do so if I were momentarily distracted.

Thankfully the problem was easy to sort out: dirty contacts on the blinker relays. That was no surprise since we'd ridden so many very dusty roads over the past months, but there was nothing I could do about the oil leak. I had the nasty suspicion that the seal on the back of the gearbox had been jarred. At least I was carrying some spare oil so I could keep topping it up until I could get it looked at. If I'd had a suitable spare seal, then I would have had a go at it myself, but Sod's Law said that of all the seals I was carrying, that wasn't one of them. As I contemplated doing the work, I had a little smile to myself.

I'd had just three months' riding experience when I'd first set off into Africa, and I'd felt as if I was riding an alien being, as if I was some sort of motorcycling accessory rather than the person who was supposed to be in control. The only mechanical things I'd known how to do were change the oil, replace the air and oil filters, and set the valve clearances. The latter was possible if I had the repair manual in one hand and the spanner in the other. Oh, and I thought I knew how to change the tyre. It couldn't be that different from changing a bicycle tyre could it? I'd learned a bit since then, and knowing that was a good feeling.

The other thing we wanted to get sorted as quickly as possible was the time on our entry permits. Neither of us wanted to spend the next days worrying about getting it done and the last thing we wanted was to go over time. The migración officials in San Cristobal were some of the most unhelpful we'd come across in years. Under no circumstances were they prepared to extend the permits until just one day before the expiry date. The officials said they had no idea where else in Mexico we could get the extension done. We reckoned that was just them being very unhelpful. I wasn't going to bribe the information out of them, though we suspected that this was what they wanted. We'd ride on in uncertainty rather than give in. Surely not all Mexican officials were going to be like this? Having changed money at a far better rate than we'd have been able to at the border, we decided that it was time to move on. We'd sort the permits out at the next opportunity.

We cruised on through the mountains on the rough tarmac of roads that Birgit aptly called 'hobbledy bobbley', and we stopped off at waterfalls with names such as Agua Azul. And blue waters they certainly had, but only where pools were being formed downstream. The rest of the time, the water was a churning, seething mass of white water. One of the falls was called, 'The Liquidiser' because several people who were daft enough to try swimming there had been pounded to death by the force of the water against the rounded boulders. We put our tent up, leaving everything else firmly locked onto the bikes, as there didn't seem to be any security at all. Then we went swimming in the calmer warm, turquoise waters of the pools that weren't directly beneath the falls.

In spite of the apparent lack of security, we both slept incredibly well that night. We'd developed the ability to sleep with senses tuned to danger. If a sound was normal, such as the wind rustling the flysheet, then we'd sleep through. But we'd wake up immediately if the sound of footsteps came too close to our tent or the rustling sound came from the direction of the bikes. The dawn gave us quiet murmured conversations from other campers, the rattle of cooking pots and the hiss of camp stoves. And then, behind this mix of waking day sounds, the thin ting-ting of the bell hanging in some nearby whitewashed village church. A cock crowed exuberantly and in my imagination I could visualize the villagers rubbing sleep from their eyes as their thoughts turned to their new day. To feeding their children, to feeding and watering their animals, to getting their produce to market, and to what disasters and delights the day might hold for them as they eked out a living in a hard but beautiful land.

Topes became a bit of a nightmare. The word 'unpredictable' describes them perfectly and we soon became exceedingly irritated by them. Some had rusting signs warning of their presence, some were striped with faded yellow bands but others had no markings at all. Worse still, some were tucked neatly and dangerously just around corners. If you didn't know what the signs were about, the two black, half-round forms could quite easily have been warning that you needed to be wearing a bra, or that a bikini top was required for any sunbathing you might be feeling like indulging in… It must have been the heat that made me have thoughts like that!

The biggest hassle and irritation was that often you'd go through a whole series of the things, sometimes 15 or 20 of them. They were spaced apart just wide enough that you could rarely get out of first gear. If you tried, then you were up and down with the gears like a yoyo on amphetamines. Horrible, and they stopped us from enjoying the magnificent forest scenery that surrounded us.

The next hassle of the road was a never-ending stream of police checkpoints. Mexican cops have six-shooters on their hips and they all seemed to walk as if they'd been brought up on Westerns and Gangster movies. The swagger and the shades were always present. They were abrupt and aggressive in their language too. After a while Birgit began to boil at the way they treated us, but thankfully she kept her feelings locked up. She can be really sharp when she gets totally ticked off.

We were wary of the police. Not only did they look and behave in an intimidating fashion, but they had a fearsome reputation for catching people speeding, and speed limits weren't always clearly posted. They also reputedly targeted tourists, checking for those who didn't have the right paperwork. The problem when you are overlanding is that you are always at the mercy of whoever you dealt with at the border. As we'd found in Guatemala, it's quite easy to end up getting through a border without having all the paperwork you need, without realising. Having said that, the key bits of paperwork for Mexico were our temporary importation documents and a hologram sticker for the bikes, the bike registration papers, our international driving licences, our passports and the all-important entry cards. If the police do stop you and you don't have all of these, they will quite happily fling you in jail. And once in jail, it's up to you to have friends to provide you with food each day. We didn't have any friends! If you have an accident, the police are quite likely to detain you until it's all sorted out and this can easily take two weeks. The best thing, we decided, was to try to sort out any accidental bother before the police got involved. We were fairly sure that if we were unlucky enough to hit a local, they too would be happy to sort things out without the involvement of the police.

We'd also heard that bribery was a major problem. You weren't bribing a cop to do anything illegal, just encouraging him to do his job. In previous countries the police had often stopped us for a chat, to admire the bikes or to see if we needed any help. Hassle was a very rare occurrence and any that had started, had soon melted away with a smile and a polite handshake from us. We were in a different world now.

Birgit and I were on a roll, but gently whenever there were cops or speed signs around. For most of the time the tarmac under us was in pretty good condition. The road builders wouldn't win any awards for getting their roads level, straight edged or for getting the potholes filled quickly, but they were more than good enough to ease along at 45-50mph. We both liked this sort of speed. This pace was slow enough for us to be able to meander along watching the scenery, (which through the mountains of Chiapas was stunningly beautiful) and slow enough to see the next hazard in plenty of time. But it was fast enough to feel that we were getting somewhere. At this speed our bikes were at their most economical fuel-wise too. But topes continued to plague us.

The majority of the population of this area are called mestizos. The name simply means 'mixed'. They are people who have a little Spanish, a little Maya and sometimes a little Negro in them too. The latter, we were told, is more common as you get towards the coast. I hesitate to call them 'peasants' but their clothes were simple and none looked as if they had much money in their pockets. Chiapas is one of the poorest states in Mexico. The bulk of the rest of the population are Maya Indians. These people were quite distinctive. Not from their figures, as just about everyone seemed to be fairly squat in stature, but because of the clothes they wore, with obvious pride. The women wore white cotton tunics which often stretched down to the ground, and these were usually embroidered with flowers and geometric shapes both around the square necks and the hems of the tunics. Some of the men also wore a traditional sort of costume in the form of straight white cotton jackets and trousers.

In part though, these people were a cause for concern. Just about every town or village we passed through had government posters warning about the EZLN – Zapatista Army of National Liberation. The black, white and blood-red posters showed armed masked men, and the warning contained words to the effect of 'Look out! These men are bandits and kidnappers!' A few years before, there'd been a fairly major uprising in which several thousand peasants seized five towns. The Mexican government had sent in the army and hundreds were said to have been killed. More recently, there'd been a massacre.

The EZLN, or Ejercito Zapatista de Liberacion Nacional, claimed to represent the rights of the indigenous population but also saw itself as part of the wider anti-capitalist movement. Historically,

 much of Mexico had been divided up into huge land parcels that belonged to the rich and therefore ruling class. The EZLN claimed to be fighting for the rights and justice of all people but in particular for the poorest people. They took their name from the flamboyant early 20th century mestizo Mexican revolutionary leader Emiliano Zapata, who had fought for "land reform, freedom, law and justice" before being double-crossed and murdered in 1919. There's even a town named after this controversial figure in Mexican history. The landowner system had been pretty much in place since the time of the Spanish conquistadors. The EZLN's manifesto, if it can be called that, says that they don't use arms and that they refuse to use normal channels for resolving matters. They felt that voting or running for public office didn't work and hadn't done so for 500 years. They were a growing threat to the government though and their non-violent marches through the capital had scared the powers-

that-be. Their approach was gathering them tremendous support from the poorer people throughout Mexico, though the bulk of their support was in Chiapas. The EZLN motto was "Enough!" They also supported the separatist movement that had been bubbling for decades through the southern areas of Mexico, and there was no way that the government was going to tolerate that!

The massacre happened in the small Chiapas village of Acteal. How many people were killed depends on who is writing the story. Some reports say 'just' 40 people, and others say more than 1,400 were killed by paramilitary forces that had very close ties to the army and the government. Some say that the paramilitary force was organised by rogue officers within the army, and others say that it was actually sanctioned by Mexico's president at the time, Ernesto Zedillo. No one was ever brought to justice over the massacre and that led to many of the EZLN taking up arms. The posters were aimed at warning people about these guys and the word on the street said that if we had any sense we wouldn't wild camp and we shouldn't stop in remote areas. Back in San Cristobal de las Casas, which was one of the original five towns to be taken over, we'd actually seen Indian ladies selling small dolls dressed to look like hooded bandits.

We didn't really know what to think about the warnings, but erred on the side of caution. Sometimes tourists are vulnerable and can be a major attraction for someone who wants to make a political point at the end of a gun. Even so, over the years, we'd camped many times in places where perhaps it wasn't wise to do so, but we'd always been fine. Sometimes I wondered if it just came down to luck – if you were in the wrong place at the wrong time, then... But we loved to free camp and at times it was a little frustrating not to feel able to pull over in some of the remote and beautiful spots and set up our tent for the night. We'd often only be saving ourselves campsite fees of just $2, but that wasn't the point. Waking up in peace to a wonderful view was something we really valued. In such spots you could start a day on your own terms. I always felt that my senses came fully alive in those first moments of a day. The lack of 'people clutter' meant that we noticed how things smelt and we could easily hear the sounds of the land and the skies. Birdsong and the sound of crickets were clearer and felt, well, free.

One of the fascinations for me in South and Central America was learning a little about the ancient civilisations of the Inca and the Maya. I couldn't help but be in awe of the buildings they had  constructed and the carvings they had sculpted. Their systems for organising their culture and daily life had been complex for their time, and for the vast areas of land that they controlled at the height of their power. The Maya civilisation arose around 600 BC and dominated much of Mexico and Central America for 1,500 years until around 900 AD. Looked at with our eyes, some of the things they did were quite barbaric, but the architecture they left behind is magnificent, and they developed a level of maths and astronomy which rivalled that of the highly sophisticated Hindu and Arab worlds.

It was once thought that the Maya were a peaceful nation, but it's now believed that they were a pretty warlike people who used prisoners for ritual sacrifice. The rulers were the nobility and the priests, and even those of royal blood could be sacrificed, being considered one of the most powerful sacrifices to the gods. All this noted, the people were skilful weavers and their ceramics were stunning. They traded over vast areas without the benefit of the wheel and they didn't use beasts of burden, unless you count slaves. They also had an incredibly advanced agricultural set up. This included fields that were fertilised with fish and the vegetable matter they dredged from their systems of canals. They also terraced their hillsides for cultivation and some of their main tools were made from obsidian. This is an incredibly hard stone of volcanic origin. They would break the stone in such a way that each splinter would have a very sharp edge, keen enough to shave with. We were now riding the land of the Maya and the later Aztecs and Toltecs, and I itched to see and learn more about their worlds. First, we were heading for the Maya ruins of Palenque.

It's a bit of a tourist trap but for the budget traveller the facilities are minimal. For the coach party visitor, a trip to these ruins can be a completely different thing. Sometimes I was envious of the air-conditioned buses, of the tour leaders that were there to make sure everything ran smoothly, of the guides that were organised to take you around such sites, with their informative running commentary in English. On lazy days, the thought of not having to think about where lunch would come from, and being able to sit back and relax on the journey home from a hard day's sight-seeing, rather appealed. As did the thought of not having to stomp around in bike boots, and especially, having a nice hotel to sleep in. In my imagination, this of course would have hot running water, clean sheets, a floor in your room that didn't feel sticky, a bar, and a restaurant that turned out recognisable and palatable food.

But I wouldn't have changed our style of travel for the coach tourists' for more than a day or two. Sure, a couple of days would be a luxurious break, but our style of travel held more fun and more freedom. In fact this sense of freedom was one of the best things about the journey. It was wonderful to wake up knowing that (subject to the restrictions of weather, visas and so on), we could do just about anything we wanted, whenever we liked. We didn't have anyone telling us it was time to leave, to start, to eat, to stop, to look at this, that or the other. We also didn't have to spend our days with people we might not like. As for Palenque, I couldn't wait to get there in the early hours before the coach parties turned up, and I was sure that this ancient place would be another world when the bulk of the visitors had gone at the end of the day.

Sitting amongst the ruins one day, I wondered if I had turned into some sort of reverse travel snob. It wasn't that I looked down on the coach visitors, far from it. In fact I admired them for getting out into the world. They did it in a way that sat well with them, a way that they felt they could manage. The reality is that not everyone is cut out for the life of the budget long distance traveller. The way they were travelling allowed them to see and learn from things that were very different from things in their comfort zones at home. For many, even leaving their own lands was a major adventure. Being dropped into such strange cultures at the end of a long flight took open minds, trust and even courage. It was, I supposed, a little like walking a tightrope, but always with a safety net underneath. So no, I decided, I wasn't turning into anything like a reverse travel snob. It was just that I knew what I as an individual liked at this time of my life. Perhaps I was a little envious of some aspects of their travel style, but my thoughts were far from being based in the cynicism that all snobs seem to have let invade their lives.

The hostels skirting Palenque were real budget traveller stuff, but we knew from them that we had moved into a new style of travel. Some of the hostels and camping sites looked as if they had been there from the time of the hippies. Some of the inhabitants with their 'flower power' clothes looked as if they had arrived in those times too, and had never left. Others were 'new age' hippies. Instead of long plaits in their hair they sported impressive dreadlocks and listened to an eclectic mix of music from Bob Marley to the most up to date alternative bands. To me, there is no stranger sight than to watch the bobbing and weaving dreadlocked head of a stoned, tattooed person who grunts instead of speaks, wobbles instead of walks and seems to have no inhibitions at all.

When this thought went though my mind the first time I wondered if I was getting old. I decided not. Perhaps in fact this was going to be a land of new adventures after all, and the 'gringo trail' was going to be part of it. Perhaps South and Central America had eased me unknowingly into a way of thinking about things and I'd not realised it. Perhaps the bobbing dreadlocks were just a very timely poke in the ribs. I stopped feeling so superior and started to go with the flow, as the nearest dreadlocked guy advised me I should, "man". I took a sneaky look at myself in the flyblown mirror of the bamboo-walled shower stall of the camping site. I had changed and I'd not really noticed. I'd grown a ponytail, but that had started off with purely logical thoughts. If I didn't have to pay for haircuts then I'd have some money spare for an odd beer or two, but mostly it was because the freedom of the road meant that there was no reason why I shouldn't. I was no longer constrained by thoughts of having to fit in with what I always called 'real life'. Perhaps the guys with dreadlocks had started off with the same thoughts. I also took in the bracelets and the necklaces that I'd collected along the way. Each had a story to tell and sometimes they were the only souvenir from a country we'd travelled through. I'd made some of them myself and had bargained for the others. The strangely worrying thing was that with the way I looked, I fitted in perfectly with the people I'd just been thinking sharp-edged thoughts about. Time for a rethink, or a makeover!

We put our tent up under the broad branches of a tree whose leaves reminded me of fig leaves, swatted away an air force of mosquitoes and fell asleep to the crackling sounds of the open fire by the ramshackle bar. Music played gently in the background and voices murmured quietly around us. During the night an enormous storm battered the area. Thunder shook through the humid air with a force that felt as if we were trying to sleep inside a base drum. Lightning sent huge streaks of jagged flashes across the sky and even under the trees. The inside of our tent was completely lit up. The flashes were so frequent that it looked as if the world around us was being strobed. If the flashes had been constant we could easily have read by their light. Rain hammered down and I was glad that we had such a good tent.

We woke with the dawn that rose over a land that seemed slightly stunned from the violence of the night before. Amazingly, smoke still drifted from the fire pit, scenting the damp air pleasantly around us as it did so. Breakfast was instant Mexican coffee powder from a tin instead of a jar, and some slices of completely tasteless sliced white bread that we'd picked up in the town in desperation. At least it was still relatively moist – the heavy, yellow and white waxed paper it came in made sure of that. The just-opened jar of strawberry jam added the flavour we needed, and a bit of a sugar kick. But it made me think again.

At home I'd made a point of eating healthily. Sometimes on the road we just ate what we could find that travelled easily, filled the hole and fitted in with our budget. I didn't feel unhealthy but I knew that the junk we sometimes ate didn't help our general state of health. I made a little vow to myself that in Mexico I'd try to eat more healthily. I wondered if we'd manage to do that when we got to the United

States. A little budget niggle in the back of my mind kept reminding me that we were heading towards a country with First World prices. No longer would we be able to bargain for our food and accommodation. The niggle said that this was going to need a major change of mind-set if we were going to be able to spend any real time further north. I'd not forgotten travelling in Australia though. It's a huge country covering many latitudes, and as a result the 'in season' times for fruit and vegetables would keep happening as I rode. That meant there was always going to be cheap but good food available. I ate well so long as I didn't mind eating lots of whatever was on seasonal offer. Using bulk-bought pasta or rice as a base, I could always conjure up a sauce of some sort to go on top. I did get a bit tired of eating green cabbage for a while, but when I was near a fishing port there was always plenty of interesting food to be had.

Sometimes I'd not even had to pay to eat in Australia. Many of the jobs I'd done were paid in food and with somewhere safe to sleep. Perhaps we'd be able to do the same sort of thing in the USA. I didn't mind the thought of this. Even though being paid cash for labour was very nice, frequently a job was simply fun because it gave me a chance to do work that I'd never done before. I learnt a lot and by this time had had over thirty different jobs. There was a side bonus to working here and there too. When you are on the move a lot you sometimes find yourself falling into the trap of concentrating each riding day on getting somewhere, and not on the adventure of the ride and the things that could happen if your eyes were wide open. It was almost as if having my feet under the same table for a few days allowed my brain to clear from the 'intake overload' of being constantly on the move.

'Intake overload'? Some days are incredibly full and so much happens that it feels as if every sense in your body is being tried and tested. Your brain gets to the stage where, though you aren't physically tired, you are mentally knackered. These are great days, but some had so much going on for so long that I didn't even have time to write my diary. On those days there was no time for anything more than a quick list of key words, and a hope that they would be enough to spark off the memories.

I suddenly realised that I was falling into another trap for the long distance rider. I was worrying too much about what would happen next. If I wasn't careful I'd let these thoughts take over and I'd forget to enjoy where I was right now.

Palenque was worth every bit of attention. Our visit to the site started off with the knowledge that like many things in the world, we have given it a name that doesn't really belong to it. The ruins are what remains of a Maya city-state, whose boom days were between the 7th and 10th centuries. Its real name should perhaps be Baak, from the language of the Maya. The name Palenque comes from the nearby rather grotty town of Santo Domingo de Palenque. The ruined city had risen and fallen, and after the culture declined, the jungle slowly absorbed everything. In fact, much of the jungle still hides ruined buildings. Many of the surrounding hills aren't hills at all; they are vegetation-covered buildings from the original city. It's described as, 'Vast, mysterious and enchanting', and I couldn't agree more. It's certainly one of the most beautiful archaeological sites I've ever been to. But I couldn't help remembering the human offerings that had been made from these temples. When danger had threatened, be that war, drought or some other potential disaster in the making, a high priest would have opened a victim's chest with an obsidian knife and would have ripped out the heart, still beating, breaking the ribs as he had done so. The archaeologists know this from the carvings and from the skeletons that have been found with their ribs broken outwards.

The ruined city is sited amidst steep, heavily-forested hills and there are stunning views out over the dry plains of southern Mexico. This plain stretches right the way to the eastern coast. The buildings that have been cleared from the jungle include pyramids, towers, and temple complexes. Some of them are huge but only 24 had been exposed out of the estimated 500 buildings on the site. You have to be fit to explore the site properly. Some of the steps up the sides of the pyramids were

thigh-high for Birgit and we both struggled to climb them through the sweaty jungle heat. The limestone walls make the city seem to glow in the early morning and late afternoon light. And it's said that this effect would originally have been even more impressive, for its thought that the buildings had once been coated with white plaster and were painted in all the pastel colours of the rainbow. I couldn't help but be amazed at how much the archaeologists had discovered about the city.

Back in Honduras we'd visited the Maya ruins of Copan. There, the jungle had been just as enthusiastic at drawing the city back into its fold, but a gem had been discovered as the huge trees had been cleared. Not a valuable stone, but a quirk of the rulers of those times. Each new ruler, to emphasise his power and dominance, had built his own temple on top of the previous ruler's temple. But they didn't trash the old temple before doing so. This meant that when the ruins were opened up, wall carvings were discovered which still had their original paint on. And because they'd been kept in the dark, in an airless environment, the colours had survived. In Palenque the joy for the archaeologists was that much of the history of the city could be read from the amazing wall carvings and statues, many of which were almost perfectly intact. I had the feeling that I was looking at ancient strip cartoons. I could just about imagine the delight of those trying to solve the mysteries as they uncovered these vast murals; walls that really could talk.

The most famous ruler of Palenque was Pacal the Great. He was still in his tomb when it was discovered. It had escaped the grave robbers of later generations and he was found still wearing his jade facemask. Pacal means 'shield' in the Mayan language and he took power at just twelve years of age. He's thought to have lived until the ripe old age of 80 and during his reign he both expanded the power of the city-state, and commissioned some of the most fantastic Maya buildings ever made.

In the dawn and at dusk the city almost lives. In the dawn a mist hangs gently over the city and the surrounding jungle, and that does much to enhance the mysterious mood. In the peace of the sunset when most visitors have gone, it's really easy to let your imagination run with the mood. For us the place was simply magnetic.

Our stay was made even better by an enviably good-looking American called Zack. Zack was also on a bike, a blue-green Kawasaki KLR 650 trail bike, and he was heading south, all the way south. We settled into some brain-picking and storytelling sessions. We both instantly liked him. He had a wide-open and unprejudiced way of looking at life. There wasn't even the remotest hint of the braggart about him and he had the refreshing ability to be clear-thinking and open-minded about everything. And equally good, he loved being on the road on a motorcycle. The only downside for him was that he was a big bloke, as in American Football quarterback size, and he often muttered about the saddle on the KLR being too skinny for his large American backside – or 'ass' as he called it.

After a couple of days, the itch to move was with us again. The city had given me back my taste for exploring, and the guidebooks said that Mexico was a country full of sights worth seeing. Now we were there though, it slowly dawned on us exactly how big Mexico is. There were over two million square kilometres we could explore in this, the fifth largest country in the Americas. The open road was calling, and there were 118,602 kilometres of those to ride if we chose. I suspected that these roads were going to take us on a roller coaster of a journey through cultures old and new, across plains, mountains and through jungles. And we were hoping to be able to link up with my two Mexican cousins whom I'd not seen since my teens.

Chapter Three

Deep Water

*'I neither look forward, where there is doubt, nor backward, where there is regret; I
look inward and ask myself not if there is anything out in the world that I want
and had better grab quickly before nightfall, but whether there is anything inside
me that I have not yet unpacked. I want to be certain that, before I fold my hands
and step into my coffin, what little I can do and say and be is completed.'*

Quentin Crisp

When I look at a map of Mexico I always think of a hook-billed
fish leaping out of the water, but before covering these first few

kilometres in the country, I'd failed to
realise what a buffer zone it is between the
USA and Central America. Riding the open
road is always great 'thinking time' and
previously disconnected thoughts bubble
into my mind and join together. These often
end with a question mark. Perhaps the fish
that is Mexico isn't trying to leap out of the
water but is actually constantly trying to
leap out of trouble. I guess what I'd learned about the EZLN had
crystallised the thought process.

Mexico has a war-torn history and in the darker parts of its past
it has hop-scotched from being under the control of France, dictators
and even an Austrian Emperor. Civil war ravaged the country on several
occasions. It still isn't at peace and the two centuries since
independence from Spain in 1821 have been stormy. It's also been
greatly affected by its northern neighbour. A two-year war with the
United States resulted in Mexico having to give almost half its land
mass to the US; including Texas, New Mexico and California.

For most of the last half century the United States has been
somewhat paranoid about the spread of communism and Mexico has
been a buffer zone against it. The scars of US foreign policy are visible
throughout Central and Southern America, and I struggled to

understand how the USA could have dreamt up and put into action some of their policies.

Nicaragua is just one example, thanks to the combined and misguided efforts of the Reagan administration, the CIA and Oliver North in their backing of the murderous Contras. (See Appendix 1 for more on this).

Having said that, we Brits haven't been at all clever with some of our own foreign policies. After all, we invented the concentration camp over a century ago during the Boer war and some pretty unspeakable things happened in the dying days of the British Empire during Kenya's Mau Mau rebellion in the 1950s.

And who knows what sort of world we'd be living in if communist influence had prevailed? With hindsight we know that this utopian dream doesn't really work. Numerous examples have proved that it doesn't work because mankind's self-centred instincts tend to quickly undermine the lofty aims of equality. Some would say that true communism simply goes against several key aspects of human nature. I feel that we are all basically tribal creatures and that therefore the idea of communism should work, but I also know that every tribe has its hierarchy and its oddballs. It's these characters, and perhaps I'm one of them, that one way or another tend to undermine a system that is designed for 'the greater good'. We can't forget simple greed of course, but perhaps one aspect of greed is an over-active instinct for survival. We all struggle to feather our nests and to stash away some supplies or money for lean times or an emergency. But when we have created our buffer zone against life's unforeseen slings and arrows, can survival instinct turn into greed? Perhaps.

With the demise of Soviet communism, US foreign policy in this area has swerved to confront the next greatest perceived risk: drugs. Illegal drugs flood north from poor countries, including Mexico itself. They are all countries where the income generated by drug growing and smuggling is far greater than that which can be garnered from farming with antiquated techniques and equipment. In many central and south American countries, existence often means constant hunger and what's on the dinner plate today may well not be there tomorrow. The drugs risk is real and I regard it as a cancer that eats away at a society from the inside.

I'm probably not alone with the thought that if we rich nations took a gamble with our money and helped people in the right way, with no strings attached, instead of using it to kill people, then perhaps the world would be a happier, safer place. A naive thought? Perhaps greed gets in the way of this plan too. It's self-evident to me that having a different skin colour and religion or speaking a different language doesn't make anyone a bad person. Misunderstood perhaps, at first glance anyway. They may well be hungry and without hope, or they may be enflamed into passion and desire by injustice. They may also be bitter at their lot in life. We in the first world are so far removed from what is still the equivalent of our Middle Ages in so many other parts of the world.

And that mediaeval way of living is complicated by having to make headway in a modern world. How must it feel to live in a mud-walled hut, to be hungry and yet to know that other nations have so much more? Can we really blame the developing world's equivalent of our robber barons for behaving the same way that some of our own ancestors have? How many of us do more than glance at other cultures and their people in our day-to-day lives? Shouldn't those of us that are wealthier and better educated concentrate more effort on developing poorer nations? History shows that the downtrodden and disadvantaged will keep on leaping up to bite those they feel are better off and are ignoring or abusing them, often when the powerful nation is expecting it least. The trouble is, in the short term it's cheaper to try to oppress than to aid. If help is left for too long then there is no other choice but to fight. We see this happening all over the world. It seems to be an endless cycle in history. Surely there's a way to break the deadlock? Surely history has taught us something and we should be intelligent enough to act on this knowledge…

This journey of ours across five continents has been a ball most of the time. I've been lucky enough to have had amazing adventures and to be able to ride away from disasters that I really shouldn't have been able to. But, the most wonderful things have always happened because of the kindness and openheartedness of strangers. Surely this simple point alone is enough to support my mobile musings? And yes, it's so easy to criticise others. I constantly remind myself of this fact. But surely if we all get out of our comfort zones and are more welcoming to people that visit our own cultures, perhaps then the world could start to become a kinder, happier, place? The trouble is, the longer we hold off doing this the harder it's going to be to put things right. We will always be on the hunt to find a bigger stick and every time we use it to belt the bad guy we also bruise a lot of innocent bystanders. History shows us that these innocents are liable to become the next guys looking for a big stick to belt us back with.

All of the above thoughts blasted through my mind in a disjointed, jumbled sort of way, as if I was looking at a giant 3D jigsaw puzzle. Hmmm, I'd thought to myself, perhaps I was turning into a two-wheeled political activist. I knew I'd be thinking more on the subject, and hoped that the pieces of the puzzle would slot together in such a way that I could end up with a level-headed, well-informed opinion. I really liked the fact that travel was making me think deeply about things that I'd previously barely thought about at all.

We eased on through the mountains as we headed north and then east towards the Yucatan Peninsula and the Caribbean. Small, dusty villages dotted the roadsides, their buildings low, white-walled and either flat-roofed or laid with uneven slopes of terracotta tiles. The

 white walls were never actually white, but all had been at one time. Any bright colours in the scene came from the sky, bougainvillea and from clothes that hung motionless in the listless, hot air. The walls were stained by the weather and the passing of time and vehicles. Most of the other vehicles we shared the road with were beaten up pickup trucks, fantastically kitted out modern 4x4s with darkened windows, or battered old buses whose giant roof racks held everything from oil

drums to live goats. There was also the occasional cop car looking like an LAPD reject, but the roads were pretty empty.

We left the jungle of the southern borderlands and then meandered through rocky and lightly wooded terrain. Some of the yucca trees had tall stems topped with waxy, cream-coloured flowers that made me think of mini magnolia blossoms just before the buds burst. But these blossoms hung from the tops of the jagged stems in a sort of ice cream waterfall. Long gravel tracks stretched away from the sides, heading out to goodness knows where, presumably to farms hidden away in the gently sloping valleys. We guessed that the locals we saw were mostly people who either worked the land or supplied the farmers.

Down onto the plains we eased along long straight roads and on through towns with exotic sounding names such as Escargena, Silvituc, Chicanna and Xpujil. This was a different world and it was made that way by the geography. On the surface this seems to be a waterless environment and so it is, except in the rainy season. We were riding across a vast bed of limestone. This rock is porous so any water percolates rapidly through it, but then collects underground and the area is veined with underground tunnels and water-filled caverns. In some places the cavern roofs have collapsed and the resulting holes in the ground are called cenotes. The Maya, Toltec and Aztecs all knew about the cenotes and used them not only as a source of water, but also as sites for sacrifice and in some cases as burial sites for their rulers. They considered the cenotes to be sacred entrances to the underworld. They must have seen the water supplies as gifts from the gods, though this gift was obviously respected with a tinge of fear attached. The word cenote comes from the Mayan people and means 'abyss'; looking into the underworld must have felt a bit like standing on the edge of one. Nowadays, as you roll across the landscape, one of the most common sights are the windmill pumps that draw the water up to the surface to irrigate the land and to provide water for the towns. The cenotes are still respected, but now without fear, though I suppose that if you fell into some of them you'd have a hard time getting out!

For a while I actually found this part of Mexico rather sad. For example, the town of Escargena looked like a houseplant that had been left in a home whose owners had gone on an extended holiday. Dust had collected on everything, colours had become drab, and the few plants looked as if they needed a darned good drink. As for the locals, they looked as if they didn't care much about life anymore. It seemed to me that the only reason there was any life there at all was because someone had to feed and water the passing traffic, and someone had to survive there so that petrol could be pumped. The word torpid came to mind. I was glad I didn't have to live there, but I admired those who managed to survive and bring up their families in this environment.

We fuelled up and moved on as quickly as possible, but these thoughts of survival slipped another idea into my mind. I was conscious that if the scientists are right this area is of earth-shattering importance to the origins of the human race. The theory is that around 65 million years ago a huge asteroid, some 15 kilometres in diameter, hit the Yucatan area. The impact would have been millions of times more powerful than those of the atomic bombs dropped on Hiroshima and Nagasaki and it would have initiated a raging fireball right across the earth's surface. Anything that stood in its path would have been incinerated.

The smoke and debris from the fire would have blocked out the sun, creating a global winter. This winter could have killed off more than half the species on earth at the time, including all the dinosaurs (which were of course cold-blooded, like reptiles). The positive side to this mass extinction of so many creatures was that it allowed the smaller mammals to prevail. Without this happening, our ape-like ancestors and homo sapiens would never have evolved. There are still plenty of arguments going on about this theory, but it seems plausible to me and answers an awful lot of questions. These thoughts of apocalyptic mass extinction also gave me a little nudge. A voice in the back of my mind said, "Value every day – appreciate where you are and what you have."

That put the thought of the coast even more firmly in my mind. The idea of being on holiday from the road for a few days became more urgent as we rode across the arid land. We'd covered a lot of ground over recent weeks and perhaps I was seeing the world as dried out and drab because I was letting a touch of 'travel blindness' slip into my days. We needed a break from 'intake overload'. We needed to be in one place for a few days to recuperate. We knew that white sand, beaches, palm trees and warm, turquoise-coloured sea lay ahead. I just hoped that we would be able to find a few laid-back non-touristy spots in between the brash tourist centres such as Cancun and Playa del Carmen.

I'd still not spoken to Birgit about the doubts I was having regarding heading on north into the States. We were almost at the turning point where we'd be heading our meandering way north, but the next day would also see us within striking distance of the border crossing south into Belize. I felt the pressure was on. Until now I'd been able to abdicate from talking things through with Birgit. I'd been quite happy scooting along and soaking up our wonderfully diverse introduction to Mexico. But we couldn't make any mistakes with our funds now; not if we were going to have enough loot to make it all the way up into Alaska, and have adventures along the way too. The thought of blasting northwards, short of money, and doing so just so that we could say we'd been to Alaska, seemed totally wrong.

We just didn't do things that way, though that voice in the back of my mind said that perhaps that was a very good reason to do it. It could be the opportunity to try something completely new. But if we dropped south to explore Belize, money would get very tight; it would be an enormous gamble. Alternatively, we could visit Belize, see as much as possible of the rest of Mexico and then do a straight ride across the USA to New York and hop on a ship heading for Europe.

We found a camping spot on the edge of the very beautiful Cenote Azul. This collection of 70-metre deep pools was the colour

that every holiday brochure aspires to. The turquoise water was so deep and so clear that we felt as if we could see all the way to the bottom. Our campsite was right on the edge of the thin strip of white sand beach and we had palm trees under which to shelter from the heat. Above us, a clear blue sky turned the world into a rich medley of the finest colours nature can provide, and a nearby very friendly village provided some wine, which chilled perfectly in the cool water. The villagers also supplied us with freshly made tortillas in a greased paper wrapper, and fresh salad vegetables. The tomatoes were of the knobbly 'beef' variety and ripened to flamboyantly red perfection. The cucumber was a very fine specimen over forty centimetres long, and the lettuce, once we'd removed the slightly battered outer leaves, was crisp and juicy. All of that lot, when combined with a can of refried beans and some incredibly fiery chilli pepper sauce, made for a feast that was the perfect way to celebrate having made it to this part of Mexico.

We added to the colourful scene by washing every scrap of clothing we had, except our swimsuits, and then hung them up on a washing line made from our luggage straps. Of course we used bio friendly soap to avoid polluting the wonderful water. Mid-week, our spot under the trees was quite deserted. So much so, that a solitary fisherman was actually quite welcome. And so was Zack when he, much to our surprise (as we'd thought he was planning to go south), turned up at the camping spot.

In spite of the beauty that surrounded us, we still had a niggle. We were now at the end of our fifteen-day entry permits. We'd tried to sort them out in Palenque but with no success. Now though, we were very near to both the border with Belize and the Mexican shipping port of Chetumal. Surely we could get the paperwork sorted out there?

We rode to the border and sat looking across the barbed wire and usual border crossing traffic, at a country that had a reputation for being home to fearsome mosquitoes, and I pondered. Was I ready for another border crossing? The alternative to getting our Mexican papers sorted out was to get out of the country. To go, or not to go to Belize? Was all the hassle we'd been having with Mexican officials an attempt by fate to push us in a new direction? I knew that this border was going to be a hassle too though.

Because we'd been through Ecuador we would have to have special health certificates — no one had been able to tell us why. The certificates, as with any form of official admin, would inevitably be a chore to obtain. The ride across the plain had left me feeling somewhat deadened and rather lazy. I shifted uneasily in my saddle, hoping for some sort of guidance. Then Birgit said, "It doesn't look very inspiring does it? Let's get on with our paperwork."

Migración wasn't a problem, though they did only give us 30 more days. "It's a good thing you have come here because you can only do this at an entry point into Mexico, or in Mexico City. You must now go to the Aduana," we were told. On entry we'd been given a permit for the bikes in the form of a hologram sticker. This had to be extended or replaced, so we understood. It made sense.

The Aduana (Customs) officer was yet another unhelpful one. He didn't want to acknowledge that we were there, he didn't want to deal with the extension; he really just couldn't be bothered. Finally, after much gentle and polite encouragement from us, he shoved a scruffy piece of photocopied paper across the table. "Take it, this is the law", he said. "I will not give you an extension because this says you do not need one if your Migración papers are in order." Why on earth hadn't he said that from the beginning? But we were nervous. If we showed this scrappy bit of paper to the police at the checkpoints they'd probably just laugh. If he was wrong then we'd be in trouble. We asked the officer to date and sign the paperwork to prove that it was official. He angrily refused and almost threw us out of his office. I had the feeling that he had no desire to stick his head above the parapet and by signing the paper that was exactly what he would be doing. With no choice, we left, still feeling decidedly uneasy.

On the way out of the border area, the very checkpoint that had passed us through, gave us some really very aggressive hassle. They didn't want to let us out of the restricted zone. Birgit had had enough. No more taking it for this girl. In a rapid fire, very abrupt, steely toned Spanish, she told the men, "We are not terrorists! We are tourists! Some respect towards us would actually be quite nice!" With that she opened her throttle and rode out. I followed as quickly as I could, thinking 'Oops!'

She had stopped and was waiting for me a kilometre down the road. She was still seething and for her, that was unusual. She could be a tad volcanic at times, but an eruption was always quickly over and soon moved on from. Not this time. She was well miffed.

"Let's head back up to Cenote Azul. How about a bottle of wine tonight?" I suggested. Suddenly this felt as if it was exactly the right thing to be doing and when we found our camping spot again, Birgit had calmed right down and I instantly felt as if heading north was the right thing to do. The trouble was, the blasted small voice in my mind had then muttered, "For now". That night, as the stars spangled almost within reaching distance above us, I told Birgit about my worries. She replied, simply, "I know."

Chapter Four

A Bloody Land

*'I travel: to learn and grow, to challenge myself, stretch my limits and foster
an appreciation of both the world at large and the chair waiting in front of
the woodstove back home.'*

Tim Patterson

Being on 'holiday' at Cenote Azul for a few days had given us
the chance to catch up with journals and for Birgit to have a sorting-
out session. She loves to collect things, be they interesting pebbles,
strange seeds, small pieces of driftwood, dried flowers, or dead beetles
(some of which were fine horny specimens). She spent so much time
gathering stuff that her back was deeply tanned, but her face was a far
paler shade of brown. By this time she was carrying several extra kilos
worth of collection but knew she couldn't keep doing so. She laid
everything out on her sarong and set to picking and choosing which
gems would remain in her collection. She handled each piece with care,
and as she did so we went on a trip down memory lane. Each was
special in its own right. She had some hard decisions to make.

The holiday also gave us the chance to learn a little more about
the area. I already knew about the famous beaches and that there were
supposed to be some interesting historical sites to visit, such as Tulum,
Mayapan, Becan and Chichen Itza. I also knew that this was the first
part of what we now call Mexico to be colonised. But I knew little
more than that.

Back in 1511 some Spanish seamen were shipwrecked on the
coast and it was this misfortune that laid the groundwork for Hernando
Cortes when he landed in early 1519. Just the year before he arrived,
'Mexico' had been officially discovered by the explorers Hernandes de
Cordoba and Juan de Grijalva. These men had been sent there by Diego
Velazquez de Cuellar who had also landed there briefly and was now the
governor of Cuba, but their attempt at colonising the mainland failed.

Diego Velazquez was intrigued though and he sent one of his
officers to try again. Cortes, on the back of reports of the Aztec Empire

from Juan de Grijalva, had sold the idea of Mexico being a land of gold and rich natural resources. To get the vast amount of money together to form an expedition such as his, there had to be some pretty significant financial gains involved for his backers, and for the men who would accompany him. Cortes must have had a silver tongue as he was selling the unknown. The trouble was that he and his 400 to 600 men (it seems no one is sure of the exact number) found little in the way of wealth in the Yucatan. No gold, and the people they found were difficult to exploit which meant no one to be captured and sold off as slaves. Cortes and his men had a very hard time of it, but he couldn't give up. His whole life must have rested on making the expedition into a success. There would have been a massive loss of face for him and his followers if they failed. Some of the men had chanced everything on the opportunity to make their fortunes. Cortes founded the city of Veracruz on the Mexican Gulf and repudiated the authority of Velazquez.

Cortes also had another point to prove. Very early on in his plans he'd written to the King of Spain and had told him that the Yucatan Peninsular had been misnamed by Velazquez. The story goes that when Velazquez had landed he had asked the natives what the place was called. They had replied, "Yucatan" which, Cortes claimed, actually meant "We don't understand". Cortes just had to be wrong though, as in the Aztec language the area was called Yokatln.

Furious with Cortes, Velazquez raised another force, estimated to be around 1,400 strong, and sent it under Narvaez to arrest Cortes. Narvaez allowed himself to be surprised and defeated by Cortes, who then persuaded the entire army of newcomers to join his own expedition.

At the time, the country was ruled by the Aztecs and Cortes decided that the only way he was going to succeed was to head inland to the Aztec capital city Tenochtitlán. He'd heard stories of great wealth there, and of a people who dressed in gold. As he headed inland he came across a native group called the Tlaxcalans and these people were sworn enemies of the Aztecs. Without their help, Cortes knew that he was taking a giant risk. The vast territory was largely unknown.

By November of 1519 Cortes had made it to the Aztec capital and he set up a meeting with the Aztec ruler Montezuma. Rumour,  superstition and the fact that he was white-skinned, wearing armour and riding a horse, must have helped him; initially he was treated as a god-king. He and his men were treated well, but Cortes didn't trust Montezuma, so struck first. He kidnapped Montezuma and held him to ransom for gold and jewels. But this was a momentary dominance and the Aztecs had kicked him and his men out of the city by 1520. Not for long though. Driven on by the thirst for adventure, power and wealth, Cortes and his men retook the city and so began the almost immediate decline of the Aztec nation. Soon after, Cortes began to build what we now know as Mexico City. He built on the ruins of the original Aztec capital. By populating it with immigrants from Europe, in particular from Spain, the city grew from strength to strength. It soon became the most important European city in North America.

And Velazquez? Well, he complained bitterly to the Castilian court and obtained an order for the arrest of Cortes, but the Aztec conquest and the resulting riches ultimately spoke louder than legal complaints. A new order came from Spain telling Velazquez to keep his hands off Mexico, and Cortes. Some say that he died a defeated and broken man.

But the story is more complicated than the simple outline above. The land between the sea and the Aztec capital was full of Mayan city-states and the Maya weren't going to surrender their lands to the Spanish so easily. The conquest of the city-states actually took decades of hard fighting. Some of the African slaves also revolted against their Spanish masters and escaped to fight against them. They lived and fought alongside the Maya, and this is why today there is a visible intermingling of bloodlines amongst the local people. It actually took repeated and costly expeditions by the Spanish to finally subdue the area and they didn't manage to do so, officially, until 1546. We'd be riding across a land with a bloody history.

Strangely though, having this new knowledge made me feel more at home and less as if we were skimming across the surface of the land. When we rode on I felt I understood better what I was seeing. Zack had decided to ride with us for a while, so now there were three of us on three bikes. We dipped down to the sea when there was a sandy track to take us there, or just meandered on through the dry countryside when there didn't seem to be a way to get to the water.

Repeated checkpoints were a constant hassle. At some, the men were so pompous and aggressive that I started to watch for signs of a new eruption. Birgit began to get grumpy and I knew that trouble was brewing. Finally she reached the dangerous stage of being totally pissed off with the policemen. Humour? Not a chance, she'd exhausted that option. There was no good reason for their belligerence. We were always respectful. Our papers were in order. We always removed our helmets and gloves and we got off our bikes when we stopped in front of the checkpoints. And we all knew how to greet the men in their own language, with a polite and deferential smile. What else could we have done? Enough was enough and Birgit made herself feel a lot better by roundly ticking off the officers on one checkpoint. She had finished her razor-edged words off with, "Some respect towards us would be appropriate, and I suggest that you say 'please' when you want something. A 'thank you' when you get it wouldn't go amiss either!" The men were stunned and backed straight off. Zack and I glanced at each other with raised eyebrows. Neither of us had good enough Spanish to upbraid them like that and even if we had, we wouldn't have got away with it. But as a small fiery German girl with fluent Spanish Birgit could, and did. Good for her!

The days of exploring eased on by, but I still had the thought of finding a white sand beach to chill out on for a week or so. Finding that without a resort on it wasn't easy. The area's delights had been discovered by mass tourism long ago and some of the resorts looked as if they had been beamed down directly from the First World. Concrete and glass gleamed. Powerboats were moored at jetties and there were adverts for scuba diving everywhere. Bars no longer looked seedy and time-worn, but were showy and slightly tarty. We supposed that they must look better in the dark, but even then they were lit up with neon, and strings of multi-coloured bulbs swayed to and fro whenever there was a breeze. This wasn't for us at all. Looking at the advertised prices I knew that I could blow a whole day's food budget on a single burger.

And talking of food, my vow back in Palenque to try to eat more healthily was made really easy by the food that was on offer. Local cantinas were the perfect places to find a rich range of specialist Yucatan meals, at reasonable prices, served by very friendly people who went a long way to balancing out the brusque behaviour of the policemen. We feasted on poc chuc which is a spiced version of barbecued pork. Or salbutes and panuchos, both of which are corn tortillas filled with such things as lettuce, tomato, turkey and avocado, or with black beans, onions and salad. These were inevitably accompanied by habanero chillies, which

had to be treated with respect and caution – they could be phenomenally hot. And no one should visit the Yucatan without trying cochinita pibil. This is a lush dish based on marinated pork. I actually gained some weight without denting the budget unduly. Such meals would have cost several times as much in the posh resorts.

We found our beach about five kilometres south of the ruined 12th century city of Tulum. The city was well worth a visit. Its white walls perch on the cliffs and it was dedicated to worship of 'The Falling God', or the setting sun. Just about every west-facing door has the image of the setting sun curved into or above it. But boy, was it crowded. We visited Tulum at exactly the wrong time and we should have known better. Actually we did know better but it was just one of those things. Rather than riding on and hoping that we'd make it back some other time, we decided to just bite the bullet and wade into the crowd. We were sweating bucket-loads by the time we'd taken a 'push and shove' walk around the ruins, but it was well worth it. Not only was it an interesting site, but it was fun to people-watch too. I felt that I had little in common with the people that surrounded us, and the Tower of Babel had nothing on the multilingual noise that was bouncing off the remaining walls.

The bumpy but hopeful ride down the coast along the white gravel and sand track was pleasantly cooling, and the thought of setting up camp under palm trees cooled me down mentally. The dusty roadsides were dotted with small shops, little hotels, and places advertising rooms to rent. We also passed a campsite but it looked far too commercial to fit in with the picture of tropical tranquillity that we had in mind. A patch of soft sand violently fish-tailed the bike and I woke up from my musings with a jump. I really should pay attention to where I was going and not just to what was along the roadsides! There'd be nothing more frustrating than having to do my sunbathing and hammock-swinging with a plaster cast on my arm.

Then we found just what we wanted. The building was low and rough with drab paint and dim lighting. But behind it was a stretch of

palm-shaded white sand that led straight onto the beach and when we got there, there was hardly a footprint in the sand to be seen: perfect. For just 30 pesos we had a spot to pitch our tents, a chunk of fallen palm tree to sit on, a hammock, a bucket shower and toilets. No drinking water, but we could get that from one of the shops up the road. The brackish water for the shower came bucket-by-bucket straight from the well. We were set. Once we'd unloaded and put the tent up, I instantly fell into mental 'drop out' mode. Birgit's only complaint was that there weren't any shells for her to add to her collection.

Over the next few days of sunbathing, reading, long walks on the beach and body surfing, we learned a lot more about Zack. His family were a really interesting bunch and at that moment his mother was actually working with the Peace Corps in Turkmenistan. We also discovered that Zack had never learned to cook, so we set about putting that to rights. For all his competence in so many other things, he really struggled with learning the basics. He dropped the onion he'd just peeled into the sand and when he peeled potatoes almost as much potato hit the sand as the inside of the pot. We did get him started though, and we knew it would save him a lot of money on his way south. One night he managed to burn the dish he was supposed to be watching and in an attempt to put things right, he scrubbed the pot so hard with sand that he wore a hole in the bottom of it. His face was a picture when he realised what he'd done. "No worries" we told him, "it's a very old pot".

Evenings were also very special on that beach. Every night there was a clear sky above us and we were gifted with the sight of the Milky Way. We would sit on the warm sands of the beach in shorts and T-shirts, with our bodies bathed by a gentle warm breeze that floated in from the Caribbean. The only sounds were from the waves and the palm leaves rustling in the breeze. We sat for hours, completely entranced by the comets and shooting stars as they flashed across a twinkling backdrop. We could even work out the lazy glide of the satellites as they circled the earth so far above us. It was one of those times when I felt completely free and in total awe of the world that I was lucky enough to find myself living in.

Eventually it was time for us all to move on. Birgit and I had a feeling of real loss as we waved goodbye to Zack. He was heading for Belize. We wondered when, if ever, we would ever hear from him. So often good friends of the moment on the road slip into memory and are never heard of again. Those momentary friends are like gold nuggets found along the way and every time such friendships blossomed, I really valued them.

Months later we did hear from Zack. In his email he let us know what he'd been up to and sounded like he was having a ball. Being an open-minded and kind person, he'd even been able to help others along the way. At one stage he'd come across a person in a really remote area who was critically ill and not expected to survive without hospitalisation. There was no chance of that happening, so Zack had somehow managed to get this person on the back of his bike and, using it as a two-wheeled ambulance, had taken him to hospital. They got there just in time and the man was expected to survive.

The next time we heard from him was in the form of a really sad email, but even through the words of dire disaster, he still sounded optimistic and the road had not succeeded in completely beating the adventurous spirit out of him.

He started his email with a general description of the amazing trip he'd had heading on south from us, though he still muttered about skinny saddles. He then went on to set the scene:

> So you're riding the famed motorcycle through the high
> plains of Bolivia. The day is the same as every
> other day of the season there, the sky is perfectly blue
> and not a single cloud can be seen. The sun is up,
> bright, and tries vainly to warm the countryside.
> These plains average about 4,000 meters / 14,000ft
> in altitude, so it is not warm. Actually traveling
> along on a bike at almost 80km / 50mph, it is not warm at
> all, it is damn cold. You have left La Paz early that
> morning, and you are hoping to make it down to the
> Uni Salt flats for a glimpse at one of the world's more
> bizarre places. Although it is cold, you are
> prepared: you have two pair of wool socks on, your
> big rubber boots, long underwear, your jeans and your
> riding pants, you have your t-neck poly pro plus two
> fleece sweaters under your large riding jacket, on
> your head you have a poly pro balaclava your helmet, and
> a fleece neck gator, on your hands you not only have
> the superdy-duperdy monster "super heater" expedition
> mittens, but you are also wearing liners as well.
> It is cold. With all your gear you are prepared,
> though warm is not a word you would use to describe yourself.
> You have made a few hundred kms from La Paz when
> you pass through a decent size town called Oruro. You
> stop and get gas, then continue on. About 40kms
> more you pass what you hardly even notice as a town

> called Poppo. Still another 5 kms from town you come upon
> a scene you have seen exactly 6,000 times in your
> travels: bicyclists traveling along the side of the
> highway. There is no traffic around so you move into
> the middle of the road to give them room. About the
> time you have just forgotten all about the cyclists,
> you are about 10 meters from them, the lead rider
> decides to make a highway crossing. This is one of
> those things that happens so fast you have no more
> than a spit second to realize what is happening. The
> rider never looks back (probably never hears you),
> never gives any indication of anything until he is
> directly in front of you. In the split second you
> have to react you pull your bike to the left as hard as
> you can and remember thinking to yourself, "don't hit
> him in the center!". The last thing you remember is
> colliding with the front tire of the bicycle carrying
> a 10 year old Bolivian child.
> Much of the next set of memories is very blurry.
> You remember seeing a police officer staring down at you
> ...... you remember wandering around a little
> attempting to pick up your stuff. By the time you
> are conscious, the child is gone, the police are there
> and the people are milling around and helping you get
> your stuff together. You have no idea how long you were
> out on the side of the road, but judging by past
> police response time in the middle of nowhere ...
> it could have been a while. The bike is a bit of a
> blur, but it is definitely mangled. The front tire
> is offset and the basic front clip is mashed.
> The cops get you to a little hospital located a few
> kms away, well it is called a hospital but it is
> really just a white room. Your head is still a bit
> foggy, but the alcohol the nurse pours on your road rash

> seems to wake you up. After a few seconds of that
> you realize you are not alone in the room. After some
> very difficult images and a couple of questions,
> you find the child in the bed next to yours, is indeed
> the child from the bicycle. He is not conscious,
> and sounds very, very bad.
> After a half an hour or so, the nurse decides the
> child needs to be taken to the larger city (about
> 40km) away. They call an ambulance and within a
> half hour the child is being moved. Once the child
> is gone, the room is sickly quiet for a few minutes.
> Then the police from the big town arrive to take
> over the investigation. They question you, and you do
> the best to tell them what you can remember. Every time
> you answer you are not sure if it is true, as it is
> just a flash image that exists in your mind. After a
> while, the police ask you if you can make the trip to
> the bigger town. You answer, "Yes, I can make 40km,
> as long as I don't have to drive them." They laugh
> and you all get into a car and head down the road.
> Little did you know that what you actually said was,
> "Yes I can make the trip and no of course I will not
> need another bit of medical help, hospital, or
> doctor, but thanks."
> Once in the big town you go directly to the police
> station where the endless questions come for hours at
> a time. After about 6 hours of this, they let up and
> one of the cops explains what is going on. "If the
> child is OK in the morning you will be fine, nothing
> to worry about. If the child dies, you are in real
> trouble. Do you have any family in Bolivia?" The
> ambulance drivers happen to be around so you ask how
> the child will be. "He will be dead by morning."
> That night you are put in jail in the Police jail.

> *The jail in the station is not that bad. You are*
> *given your own cell and it even has a bed. The next*
> *morning the child is dead and you prepare for "real*
> *trouble". For the next 3 days you spend all your*
> *time answering the same questions over and over again.*
> *Then finally, they tell you they have completed the*
> *initial report. The initial report has you*
> *completely void of any guilt. The police tell you*
> *that with this the judicial judge will set you free*
> *for sure. You get a hearing scheduled for the next day at 3pm.*
> *3pm, shows up and you are waiting in the courtroom*
> *(actually just a cheap office room). At 6:30, the*
> *clerk says, "Well he is not coming, it looks like he*
> *stayed in La Paz." You think to yourself, well back*
> *to jail. They say the judge should be here early so*
> *you might as well stay in the jail next door. Hmm,*

Zack, in another email, explained how things had then really gone pear-shaped and that after a series of 'requests' for bribes he had no money left, the mood of the police had turned very nasty, and he was beginning to panic. He knew how bad things were. No one knew where he was and there was no one around who seemed even remotely inclined to help him, or to treat the situation fairly. In spite of his fear, he'd not been able to get over the fact that it was him that had caused a death, even though in no way had it been his fault directly. This is the risk that an overlander faces every day he or she rides the roads of foreign lands.

With an incredibly lucky break he managed to jump jail (an episode it's best I don't describe) and made it to the nearest airport. Leaving his bike behind, he escaped, very shaken, to the USA. The last we heard from him he was back on the road and had made it to Africa where he'd got a job teaching people how to white-water raft and bungee jump. After my experience of hitting a man in Tanzania, and of going to jail for that, I knew that Zack would never be the same again. I'd been incredibly lucky not to kill the man I'd hit.

Chapter Five

From Agave to Mescal

'As a traveller you are only ever an observer. Some things you see will instantly break your heart, but then the great kindnesses shown to you by the people around you will mend it just as fast.'

John Mundy

Birgit and I were rolling again. The weather at 6.30am was comfortably warm, and the air between the towns smelt clean and  dustily dry. The bikes felt as if they too had enjoyed their stay by the sea, but that they also were now eager to ride some kilometres. Their engines ticked and purred under us, the way engines do when you've just changed your oils and everything is exactly as it should be. At that time of day the traffic wasn't heavy and both the main roads and the back roads were in pretty good condition. Strangely, some of the towns had no tarmac at all. The road stopped on the outskirts and dusty, bumpy tracks took over until we reached the other side. None of the towns were attractive. They were more like way stations on the road to somewhere else, anywhere else, but that didn't stop the journey from being interesting.

Truck drivers all over the world are a particular breed and all seem to have matching genes. Most seem to be quite happy with being away from home, with the endless hours of driving, with trying to hunt down companies' warehouses in the back of beyond and so on. They don't appear to mind eating bad food or sleeping in their cabs in odd places. But borders apparently make a difference. Even in these times of international travel, the driving styles of truck drivers seemed to change from one country to the next. The only thing that their driving style seemed to have in common was the desire to get 'there' wherever 'there' might be.

In India, trucks and buses are the kings of the road and you just have to get out of their way. If you don't, you end up as a grille ornament and the drivers won't care a jot. They are on a mission and if fate has decreed that you are going to end up as an addition to the flamboyant decorations on their trucks, so be it. In Colombia the truck drivers seemed to have an amazing ability. As soon as they climbed behind the steering wheel of their 18-wheelers, they became trainee grand prix drivers. Overtaking on corners? Not a problem. On the brow of a hill? Why on earth not? Overtaking a vehicle that's driving a kilometre an hour slower? No problem, even if it takes twenty minutes and you send oncoming traffic scuttling for the roadside bushes as you do it. It's a pride thing. In Australia, the giant Road Trains wouldn't even notice if they hit you. Those guys blast across the outback on steroidal autopilot in trucks towing over a hundred tons in three or four trailers in a vehicle over 50 metres long. On a bike, to them, you'd just be another bump in the road. But here in Mexico, what on earth was going on?

The drivers had manners and would ease over to share the road with us. They seemed to be half-asleep most of the time, but still in perfect control of their multi-wheeled giants. As we passed them, the drivers would frequently give us a wave or a toot on their horns. We began to feel as if we were welcome entertainment for them, and we didn't have even the slightest feeling of being some sort of minor being that had to be swatted out of the way. When we parked at fuel stations, drivers would come over to look at the bikes and talk to us. Well, Birgit mostly, as they were all impressed that a small girl was riding such a big bike, and when they heard where she had been on it, I had the feeling that she became an instant mental 'pin up girl' for them. One of the drivers, a tall man whose shaggy black hair and black beard made him look like Captain Haddock from Tin Tin, was enthralled by the idea that she'd ridden all the way from Argentina.

This was all a very refreshing change, but the menaces came in two forms. Firstly, the battered pick-up trucks, which always seemed to be completely overloaded. It seemed that if you were to be a member of the overloaded-pick-up-truck-association, then you had to have at least one knackered spring. If you didn't look like a drunken crab then you weren't going to win any prizes. If your truck didn't have any rust then you'd definitely lose. And the drivers of these four and six wheeled crabs, well, they just had to be dozing or half cut on tequila. Their driving style was erratic. You never knew what they were going to do next, or which part of the road they were going to do it on! You also never knew when some part of a truck or its load was going to fall off. Some of these pick-ups were so completely overloaded that even their manufacturers would have been impressed, or perhaps totally dismayed. These bulging loads seemed to be held on by a mix of luck, bits of frayed rope and bungee straps made from strips of old inner tube. The centrifugal forces applied by hairpin bends were always a challenge to these loads since they were mostly kept in place by the simple downward thrust of gravity. But I'm being too cynical here. It amazed me that these guys could keep their trucks working and on the road at all. There must have been some mechanical geniuses amongst them, and for that they deserved respect.

4x4s with blacked-out windows were another menace. Their drivers were the most arrogant bastards I'd ever come across. And I don't say that lightly. Most drove as if they owned the road — they probably did own the land on either side of it. They drove with mental snowploughs attached to the fronts of their vehicles, but heaven help you if you scratched one of the things. The only occasional bonus was that some of the drivers were women who seemed to have endlessly long legs clad in short, tight skirts. Getting down from the height of the 4x4s was a challenge, but an interesting sight for any red-blooded male. However, we would always get looks of complete disdain, as if we were a blot on the landscape and should never have been allowed to use the same road. The blacked-out windows were sinister and they added to the barrier between rich and poor.

One of the things I loved about riding my bike in these countries was the fact that we had no barrier between us and the rest of the  world. No glass and no metal between us and other people. This made us very approachable, in spite of the fact that we were foreigners. It never mattered what country we were in, the bikes would always be a topic that would start a conversation between us and locals. Where are you from? How far have you ridden? How big is the engine? How old is your bike? We'd always enjoy the questions and with conversation started, it gave us a chance to talk to people about their lives; where they were from and what they did. I used to be a backpacker and even though travelling on buses and trains through a country meant that you were travelling right next to a local, there never seemed to be anything like the connection with them that the bikes gave us. I loved it. The bikes gave us another perfect way to learn and to feel as if we weren't just skimming across the surface of a country, and Mexicans were mostly inquisitive and friendly people.

At first they hadn't seemed to be so though. Most didn't seem to smile much, but I put that down to the rigours of surviving daily life. There didn't seem to be a lot to smile about for many. And, I supposed, we were seen to be very wealthy by comparison. Some people we ended up talking with had been quite shy, and I'd had the feeling that it had taken significant courage for them to start a conversation with us.

I'll never forget someone telling me that it's hard to shoot a person that you've just shaken hands with. I suspect that our habit of always shaking hands had reduced our problems at borders and when dealing with officials. But it didn't seem to help in Mexico. Mexican officials were not, we decided, good ambassadors for their country. I couldn't help wondering why this was. I had a nasty feeling that, as was the case so often with African officials, previous visitors had started the abuse and had set the precedent. A traveller we'd met had told me that he never, ever, learned more than the minimum about any country he was travelling to. He said, "That way I am completely fresh. I have eyes open to everything. My mind has not been affected by what others think." But I wondered how many cultural toes he'd managed to tread on with his ignorance. There has to be a balance but I doubt that even a lifetime of study would undermine the awe that a new country can inspire in the traveller.

My mood changed with the thoughts of how free and how many opportunities being on a bike gave me. With this refreshed sense of freedom in mind, the plains became a traveller's delight and we eagerly took in as many of the ancient Maya ruins as possible. At Chichen Itza we upped our standard of accommodation by camping in the grounds

of the rather swanky Hotel Pyramid Inn. Staying in one of the rooms was way out of our budget, but we still had full run of the facilities. The biggest bonus was the swimming pool. We'd been amazed by the heat, even though technically it was still spring. On the bikes and moving it was easy to ignore it, though we were getting through litres of drinking water. But as soon as we stopped, especially out of the shade, we were instantly sweating buckets in our bike gear. The pool was perfect, even though the water was only just cooler than blood temperature. When we set off to explore the ruins, the sun was already beginning to fall, but that didn't seem to reduce the heat. Birgit wisely took her umbrella to have some shade while on the move. She wryly commented at one stage that she was sweating so much that she no longer had to worry about finding somewhere to pee in privacy. She was pretty happy about that.

This area seemed to be a haven for snakes and we saw plenty, some squashed flat on the road and some which slithered rapidly away when they heard us coming. Some had obviously been made drunk by the sun as they lay still in the sunshine and ignored us totally. We were cautious of them though. We were both very conscious of the creepy crawly critters that abound in Mexico, and even more so after a fist-sized black tarantula spider had crawled down the tree trunk of one of the palm trees right by our tent at Cenote Azul. We always wore our bike boots to do any exploring and Birgit became almost paranoid about making sure that our tent was very firmly closed at all times. A good job one of us was!

Our next target was Mexico City. One of my cousins, Maura, and her family lived there and my Aunt Esmeralda lived close by. I'd heard about the appalling traffic and the frequent robberies. If it hadn't been for my connection with Maura I suspect we would have given Mexico City a wide berth. It sits in a valley formed by volcanoes and mountains, and that makes it one of the worst places to have a major city. In the early days it was quite a sensible spot to put your capital since it had water and protection from the elements. But in modern times pollution from all the vehicles and factories had ruined the air quality. Just over a decade before, the air had been so badly polluted that thousands of birds started to fall dead onto the streets. Kathmandu and Santiago de Chile had been bad enough, but this sounded dire. I've never been a great fan of big cities, though some, such as Cape Town, Buenos Aires and Mombasa had temporarily changed my mind. Maybe things would have improved in Mexico City by the time we got there. I hoped so. The pollution in Kathmandu had provided Birgit with a debilitating lung infection which it had taken her nearly a month to get rid of. She, however, wasn't put off by thoughts of Mexico City. She'd been there before and her friend Quilla lived there. This would be a rare chance for them to link up.

We zigzagged across the countryside on the way to Smog City, taking in the sights of Villahermosa, (which we loved), Acayucan, San  Juan Bautista, the lovely old city of Oaxaca, and Puerto Escondido. We also visited the world famous Acapulco, Chilpancingo de Los Bravos, and Cuernavaca, along with the many small villages along the way. To our surprise, many of the camping sites seemed to be closed in April and the hotels were horribly expensive. Some of those hotels didn't even look clean. In one, when we'd not been able to find anywhere else, we'd been lumbered with a filthy room and sheets that didn't look as if they'd been washed in a decade. Birgit had commented, "They should be paying us to stay here!"

Problems finding suitable accommodation meant that we had either very long days or had to cut them short when we found an affordable option. Some of the sites had no working toilets and cold-water showers. The latter weren't a problem if we showered at the end of a day – then the sun would have been up long enough to take the chill off the water. Mango trees abounded and at this time of year they were heavy with hanging green fruit that made me think, rather romantically, that they looked as if they were crying green tears.

Our riding days started early: we always tried to be on the road by 7am. At that time of the day we had the chance to see the world at its best. I love the dawn light over the land and this time of day also allowed us to get loaded and on the move in the relative cool. We stuck to the back roads as much as we could. These were surprisingly narrow and in many places, passing vehicles had to pull right over to make it by each other. Not that we had this problem; the trucks were still surprisingly considerate towards our heavily laden bikes. The roads took us looping through mountains and dropped us down into valleys that always seemed to be hazy. We soon realised that the smoke was caused by all the wood fires people were using to cook on. One of the most common sights was that of bent-over people struggling along the roadsides with giant stacks of chopped wood strapped to their backs.

Birgit rode with the images taking her to other lands. Some of the valleys had flood plains that were dotted with palm trees and she thought that perhaps this was how the ancient lands around the Tigris and the Euphrates would once have looked. At other times the pinks and oranges of the low sunlight made her think back to our time in India. The smoky air diffused this light in such a way that we could quite easily have been riding the bumpy tarmac of the country roads in northern India.

Oaxaca was a highlight of this journey; I would never have imagined that such a place could exist. The region had my brain ticking, and the city had my heart.

Oaxaca is a rugged state with the city of Oaxaca as its governmental and spiritual base. It's located where two mountain ranges, the Sierra Madre Oriental and the Sierra Madre del Sur, meet. This rocky and mountainous terrain is split by a temperate central valley which is reputed to be one of the most fertile areas in Mexico. The hillsides seem to be largely covered with coffee plantations, and it was no surprise to learn that more than three quarters of Mexico's coffee comes from this area. The remainder of the hillsides are still forested and the shade from the trees is one of the reasons that coffee grows so well. But the mountainous terrain has caused an odd effect on the people. Nowhere in Mexico had we ridden where the people changed so dramatically from one village to the next. It was almost as if each was on a different planet. The buildings were often quite different and so were the clothes that people wore. Apparently there was little in the way of mutual understanding between these villages and this made governing the region a real headache for central government. That was no real surprise, as there seemed to have been very little modern development. Perhaps, we suspected, central government tried to have as little as possible to do with the area.

From time to time I had the nasty feeling that we were riding through a pressure cooker that was about to burst. I'd read that Oaxaca had done just that on several previous occasions. It felt as if this was a classic situation where the government was allowing itself to take its eye off the ball. Previously the locals had become so disgruntled that they had assassinated the brother of President Venustiano Carranza in protest. Federal troops had been sent in, resulting in much loss of life and property. Since that time there'd been very little investment in the region and that, I felt, was going to cause some more grief sooner or later. With the coming of much easier communication, and computers in particular, I had the nasty feeling that when things did go bang, they were going to do so with greater force than ever before. Previously split communities could join forces and that would mean trouble. If I, with broken Spanish and as a tourist was picking this up, why wasn't the government? After all, they were only 500 kilometres away. I wondered if I was turning psychic, or just grumpy!

In the meantime, tourism was alive and kicking, and with good reason. There was a wealth of things to see and to get involved with if we chose. For us, the city of Oaxaca was the key.  The city is packed with monuments, churches, tree-lined squares, markets and beautiful old buildings. At night the squares would fill with people out promenading. The Zocalo is the heart of the town. Its edges are bordered with arcades and there's a bandstand in the centre. The Zocalo and the adjacent Almada de Leon had been closed to traffic and that made them a magnet for people who wanted to stroll and take in the sights, which included us. Another draw was the free music in the square.

Over several days we were treated to a wonderful variety of styles; everything from solo guitarists to mariachi and marimba bands. The soloists played their guitars with vibrant, flamboyant passion. Their fingers were a blur as they flashed across their guitar strings, and though I couldn't understand all the words, I could tell by the body language which songs were about love and which had a message. Historically, a wandering musician would pass on stories of political action or would sing songs that railed against injustice.

The marimbistas were small groups of musicians who played the wooden xylophone that gave them their name, but they were always accompanied by men playing guitars and one of the bands had a couple of trumpeters too. Their sound made me think of music I'd heard in Zimbabwe and I wasn't surprised to read much later that it's thought the style actually comes from the slaves that were brought across by the conquistadors. The Latin influence is very strong though and the combination, I thought, was some of the best music I'd heard in a long time. The mariachi bands were a different ball game, but in the same vein.

Without doubt, the mariachi bands were the more visually flamboyant. They wore a sort of uniform which to my eye was rather like a combination of a gaucho and a pearly king from the East End of  London. The bands were made up of at least two violins, a couple of trumpets, Spanish guitar, and in the bigger bands we could see guys playing guitars that made very different sounds from the Spanish version. At first I thought the combined noise they made sounded like a cross between a cat being killed, a bad jazz band and a set of trumpets that had been jumped on. But the sound is perversely addictive and before long I found myself being swept up into the mood that they managed to create: a real toe-tapping fiesta. It didn't take long before passers-by were dancing. The beat was intoxicating and irresistible. Their songs were about romance, passion and unrequited love. But there is also a side to their music which carries a message. At one time, these bands were employed full time by large haciendas. They'd entertain the evenings away and would be on hand to celebrate births and marriages. But times changed and when the haciendas could no longer employ the musicians full time, they set off to wander throughout Mexico, being paid whenever they could get a booking. In between times they would play just for the hell of it and for the coins that people would throw to them. They added songs to their repertoire that told of political injustice, current events and of revolutionary heroes too, and so became part of the way that word got around.

The music combined with the gentle warmth of the evenings and the hustle and bustle to create a very attractive ambience. Families strolled there alongside young lovers and visitors. People were selling piping hot tamales, ice creams and garish gas-filled balloons which had the kids excitedly tugging on parents' sleeves in anticipation.

I was keen to try the local hooch. It's called mescal and has an interesting reputation. As we'd been riding we couldn't help but note the vast swathes of agave growing in the patchwork fields. Mescal is a spiky plant which is also the main ingredient of tequila. Some versions of mescal are quite drinkable but have a bit of a kick in the tail. Others, you just know are potent from the first sip. They're the ones that have worms floating embalmed in the bottom of the bottle! Something to do with the flavour we were told. The trouble is, this stuff goes down very smoothly and the first time we tried it, we did so on empty stomachs. A shop had been offering visitors free shots and in case we didn't like the stuff we thought we'd try it out. No point in buying a whole bottle if it was horrible, and we were both rather dubious about the worms.

We'd giggled our way back to our hostel, knowing within moments that we weren't safe to be out on the streets. Once in our room, we'd burst out laughing from the combined effects of the potent kick we were getting, and the realisation that we'd just been stupid. Most tourists that get into trouble do so when they are sloshed. But we blamed the Spanish! Originally, the local Indians had brewed a mildly alcoholic drink called pulque, but the conquistadors had wanted something a bit more potent. They had set up distilleries which had gone on to produce both tequila and mescal. The Indians still brew pulque today for their own consumption.

We spent a series of very happy days in Oaxaca, wandering the churches, the Santo Domingo Temple, the theatre, the squares, staring into the jewellery and pottery shops and eating delicious empanadas and tamales. Empanadas are said to have their origin in Spain, though some say that they actually originated in the Arab world. They look rather like the half-moon shape of Cornish pasties but they are normally filled with chicken or cheese. Tamales date right back to the Aztecs. They are a real favourite in Mexico and each region of the country has its own special recipes. We'd seen people eating them for breakfast, lunch and dinner. The pastry is square and can be quite big – as much as 40 centimetres across. The fillings vary tremendously, but the norm seemed to be pork or chicken in a sort of salsa, which can be either red or green and is usually slightly spicy. They make perfect healthy 'fast food'. Corn tortillas were available from just about every street corner too.

At the time of writing my fears have come to fruition and we've heard that the city of Oaxaca is struggling. The violent protests against governmental neglect have been so strong that few tourists now go there anymore. The potters, weavers, tamale sellers, the hoteliers and hostel owners, and all the rest that relied on tourism have either gone bust or are battling to survive. I've even read of one village whose source of income for hundreds of years had been subsistence farming and weaving goods for tourism, has now stopped weaving all together. The situation must be quite desperate there. I just hope that time will heal the wounds and clearer heads will get together to sort the injustices out once and for all. With all the other problems Mexico has, I fear that Oaxaca is not a top priority. Would I go back? Too right I would. Now would be the perfect opportunity to see the city when it isn't full of visitors and if we were to do so, I like to think that we'd be giving the locals a ray of hope. Each visitor in these times must surely help a little.

We simply rode through Acapulco. The number of expensive cars, yachts, modern buildings and flashy women dressed in Mexico's version of haute couture put us straight off the place. The atmosphere felt fake, superficial and completely manufactured. We felt like aliens there and kept on going. Did we make a snap judgement? Yes. Were we right? I still don't know. But at the time, getting out of there felt like exactly the right thing to do.

The road towards Mexico City held a series of surprises for us. One of the most outstanding sights was when we rounded a hillside to find that the road dropped down into a broad valley filled with jacaranda trees in full bloom. We'd seen a lot of these trees in Africa but never so many in one place and we'd timed it perfectly. From above, the valley in full lilac bloom looked as if God had carpeted our way with nature at its best.

But physically, we were struggling. Birgit had woken up with a nasty dose of the 'squits' and she wasn't happy. Her face had gone white and drawn and she soon started to look exhausted. Thankfully there were plenty of spots that she could duck into to hide away for a few moments of urgent relief. But we really needed to find somewhere to stay until she was feeling better. It didn't help that she was concerned about what was going to happen next. The closer we got to Mexico City the more she felt uneasy about linking up with my cousin, especially if she was still feeling ill. She'd not be on form and that meant she'd be a burden and wouldn't be able to enjoy the visit. If she was feeling under the weather and she didn't get on with my cousin and her family, then that would just make the situation ten times worse.

As for me, the constant curves and the very bumpy tarmac were playing havoc with my slipped discs. These had caused us a lot of problems down in Chile and I'd ended up being med-evac'd back to the UK for treatment. At that time I'd been told that I'd never ride a bike again and that I should have an operation which had a 50% chance of putting me permanently in a wheelchair. I'd managed to escape that dire fate with a combination of positive thinking, determination and a severe physiotherapy regime. We'd decided against the operation option. Ever since then, I'd been able to keep the pain under control by starting each day with an hour's workout and with plenty of breaks during a ride. Normally a ten-minute enthusiastic stride out every 100 kilometres would do the trick, but now I was struggling. Birgit looked on, very concerned. For me, it was just a case of trying to find a way to deal with the pain and keep going. For her, it was impossible to tell how bad the pain was and if my back was going to cope. It would feel like some sort of defeat if the trip had to end now. The uncertainty took the gloss off the day for her and her caring nature was frustrated by the thought that there was nothing she could do to help me. We rode on, but more gently, and we stopped every 50 kilometres for me to walk around for half an hour, and for her to visit the bushes.

I'd managed to attract quite a bit of unwanted attention with my exercises – some mornings I should have put a hat out to collect money! Most people seemed to think I was good entertainment but several just thought I was weird. At times, the exercises were a complete chore. I just wanted to get on with the day. But, we'd fallen into a routine. While I did my hour of exercises, Birgit broke camp and loaded up the bikes. At other times doing the exercises was just inconvenient. Biting midges in the dawn light were the bane of my life. I grew to hate them. But hey, I could put up with them as long as I could carry on with the trip.

The next surprise was the sudden lack of signposts. When they were there they often didn't make sense. It was as if someone with a mad sense of humour had been given the job of positioning them. Once he had finished, the local hooligans had come along to twist signs in the wrong direction. Other hooligans, it seemed, had now simply pinched some of the signs. We started off by feeling really frustrated by this but soon relaxed into the thought that we had plenty of time and that each wrong turning had a potential adventure in store for us.

The road started to climb up towards the mountains around Mexico City, but so suddenly and so steeply in one place that the only way to make it up was in first gear. There must have been another way, as we didn't see one other vehicle on the road.

The icing on the day's cake was a town with 152 topes and cobbled streets in between. What a lousy combination. Some days you just know things can't get much worse. But they did. The closer we got to Mexico City the more the truck drivers' style changed. It was almost as if urgency had suddenly infused their systems and as if they had forgotten how to be gentlemen drivers. Perhaps it was something to do with the cooler air, or perhaps to do with the influence of driving in the capital's chaotic traffic. Whatever it was it suddenly wasn't fun. I'm being unfair here though. Some of the drivers carried on with their courteous style and must have been just as niggled as we were, but the remainder drove as if they were in the wrong country. About 5% of them had turned into lunatics. They were so bad that they must have been escapees from an asylum. They bullied, they pushed, they shoved and their 'me first, I'm bigger than you' antics had us scuttling for the verges. Birgit wasn't sure if the rumbling in her stomach was from the squits, or from pure tension.

In front of us were two trucks and a car. The road twisted through the mountains and to the sides the rich green of pine trees lined the way, blocking the view round the corners. The front truck was heavily loaded, the second truck was horribly impatient and the car driver behind them both was frustrated. We were bringing up the tail, working our way uncomfortably up and down between first and second gears. The second truck waited for a blind corner then started to overtake. The car speeded up and closed the new gap. As he did so, another truck rounded the corner heading towards us. Who was going to back off first? The second truck had to as he had gravity working against him. He lumbered back into the closing space and must have frightened the living daylights out of the car driver, who jammed his brakes on and only just avoided the tailgate of the second truck. He'd had enough and while the second truck driver was juggling his gears, the car shot out on yet another blind corner and belted, in slow motion, uphill past the trucks. He made it just as a truck came into view. Horns blared indignantly from all three trucks!

Now it was our turn. Should we sit patiently, clutch hands beginning to ache and engines getting ever hotter, or should we risk a dash for freedom? There was no way we'd both make it past in one go, even though we had heaps more readily available power than the trucks did. The constant blind curves meant that we could be split, unable to see each other for some time. That could be a problem if a turning we needed to take suddenly appeared. I wondered if Birgit was going to wait or 'go for it'. She positioned herself with intent. She weaved Sir Henry in and out, trying to see past the trucks and around the corners. She'd obviously decided that riding blind behind the unpredictable trucks was too dangerous to continue with. The trucks were now travelling so close together that you couldn't have got a football between them. She weaved some more.

Then, with a blast of smoke from her exhaust, she dropped a gear and went for it. There was just enough of a straight ahead for her to make it, if all went well. Her bike hit a pothole, leapt wildly, and then she was past. I felt adrenaline buzz through me just at the sight of her doing it. Now my turn ¬- I copied Birgit's, see-round-the-truck weave, and crashed into a pothole, front wheel slipping sickeningly on the gravel that had been thrown out of it. I'd been too close to the back of the truck to see it. I hung on tight and carried on trying to peek around the trucks. The truck in front changed down a gear with a jolt that closed the gap between us within a second. Too close!!! I'd had enough of this. With my headlight on full beam and my thumb on the horn I pulled out as fast as Libby's engine would let me, just as the road took a dip downwards. The extra burst of speed that gave me was enough to help me down the side of the trucks. I'd almost made it when one of the hated 4x4s shot into view like an evil black tank. It made no attempt whatsoever to make room for me and I was sure I'd had it. It didn't slow down and I swear it actually got faster. The thing was heading straight for me. Now I knew I'd had it.

Then luck took over. The first truck hit the next rise and changed down as he did so, and this allowed me a millisecond to get past. Made it! The 4x4 shot past as if this was just another day on their road. I could see Birgit looking anxiously in her rear view mirror. She'd seen the 4x4 well before me and had known what was about to happen. With hindsight we were daft. We should have just pulled over and been terribly British. There'd been some nice spots to stop and make a brew...

Fortunately Maura lived in a protected housing area in a small town right on the very outskirts of Mexico City, and she was easy to find. Actually, her son Jordi-John found us. We'd just ridden into the town of Ocoayacac and were looking round for someone who might be able to give us directions, when a green Jeep station-wagon pulled to a halt beside us. Maura was on a shopping expedition and Jordi-John had spotted us. Fantastic, it was just the stroke of luck we needed.

Chapter Six
A Tale of Two Cities and Two Cousins
'A traveller without observation is a bird without wings.'
Moslih Eddin Saadi

Even as a kid I'd thought of Maura as being beautiful and to my delight, age had only enhanced her looks. The combination of an English gentleman and a dark-haired Mexican beauty had produced someone who is very easy on the eye. She was now married to an ex-pat from Barcelona and had two children. Her husband Jordi was a real character and he was one of those people that you like immediately. Birgit felt instantly at ease with them. Maura's children, Jordi-John (the John coming from my Uncle) and Jackie were both children who had a dark-eyed inquisitiveness about them. Jordi-John couldn't wait for a ride on Libby, though he was trying very hard not to let any of us see that he was actually rather intimidated by her size. His head didn't even come up to the handlebars. But he loved riding pillion and I suspected that I'd been a bit of a corrupting influence.

Staying with the family was like a refreshing oasis for the travel-worn mind. At times I used to like to think that I was on an extended holiday but the reality is that you are simply living life in a very different way. There are plenty of comparisons to 'real life'. You still have to have a roof of some sort over your head, you still have bills to pay, officialdom to deal with, food to find and, strange though it may sound, you do still have to justify the direction your life is taking. Suddenly landing in Maura's world allowed us to relax and to take stock. It made a difference that for a while we were somewhere safe. We didn't have to think about the chances of being robbed at night, and having someone else do the food shopping and cooking was a treat. It made a massive change to be eating completely different food too. We travelled with one petrol cooker and when we weren't making food for ourselves, we were eating in cheap local cafés and bars, or from the empanada and tamale sellers on the street. Suddenly having well thought-out and well-cooked multi-course meals awoke a part of my brain and appetite that I'd last used in the Yucatan. Suffice it to say that Maura's household produced very good food and they all took really good care of us. We had temporarily upgraded from dusty travellers to normal people, and it was fun.

I'm having a little laugh at myself as I write this. I always seem to be bringing up the subject of food. Why? Well, it's important for several reasons. You've got to eat to stay healthy and after accommodation and fuel, it was often what we spent the most money on. We also spent a significant part of each day hunting for sustenance. At home we can pop into the supermarket and do our full week's shop in half an hour, but on the road it would take far longer. Food would have to be bargained over, item by item, but first of all you had to find the markets. Often, if we wanted something more unusual such as curry powder, we'd have a long hunt on our hands. But equally important, for us it's a vital part of travel. We were always so grateful to our parents that they had brought us both up not to be fearful of unfamiliar food but on the contrary, keen to try new things. Eating the local fare really is one of the best ways to get the flavour of a place and its culture.

Maura and the family took us on adventures down into the city. With Maura driving their 4x4 wagon, we could sit back and enjoy the  view. Normally with city riding we'd be concentrating on following road signs, trying not to hit anything and avoiding being hit by anyone else. That kept us too busy to take in what was happening along the sides of the roads. In Mexico City there was plenty to watch. As with all new places, some of the most important things for a motorcyclist to learn are the rules of the road. Here they seemed pretty basic: "I was here first so I go first" and "I'm bigger than you are so I go first". Maura said the fact that their 4x4 was so big really helped. The wild cards are the 250,000 green-painted taxis, many of which are Volkswagen Beetles. Their drivers are completely fearless and drive like minnows with the brains and characteristics of Great White sharks. It's all very entertaining when you aren't the one with the responsibility of being in control. Maura impressed me greatly with her driving skill. Not even once did we come close to having a prang and she drove as if she'd been fighting with sharks since birth. My aunt Esmeralda's driving style was different. She struck me as being a lady who absolutely knew her own mind. She was feisty and determined, and when she drove there was a sort of aura around her that anyone with any sense wouldn't try to invade. She also knew the city really well and showed us that by keeping off the main drags, the traffic wasn't really too bad. We valued the time she took out of her life to help us get such a good taste of the city.

Maura and Aunt Esmeralda took us to the remains of the Aztec city and down to the water at Xochimilco where the old city had once floated on plant beds in canals. With them we explored museums and the Aztec ruins on the outskirts of the city. They took us to see the anthropological museum to learn about the Aztecs and to see the Diego Rivera murals.

I liked the sound of Rivera. He was pure radical and combined that with an incredible artistic talent. His murals deal with Mexican society and the 1910 revolution. His style is based on bold colours with simplified figures and even without looking carefully you can see how Aztec art has influenced him. But his radical political beliefs and his attacks on the church and the clergy made him a very controversial figure, even within the communist party of which he was a member.

We also dropped into the capital's BMW dealership to ask them about my driveshaft which was still weeping oil. I wasn't too worried about this as the leak had decreased and now it just looked messy. Road dust collected in the thin ooze of oil across the shaft casing and that was untidy, but not a bother. "Better safe than sorry" though. We were also on the hunt for a new regulator and a replacement for Birgit's very worn front tyre. The BMW dealership couldn't help us with the tyre but they very kindly did some phoning around and put us in touch with another dealer, Moto Mundo, who had a Kenda tyre in the right size with off road capability. The bonus was that it cost just $35.

Maura took us for a slap-up meal in a very posh restaurant that had us instantly conscious of our patched and travel-worn clothes. We also went shopping in the arts and crafts markets, where my ex-retailer's brain couldn't help bubbling at the thought of being able to work some sort of business between Mexico and the UK. The mats, pottery, ceramic tiles and woodcarvings were made with impressive skill. In some places we'd been, tourist tat was the name of the game and we'd sniffed at it. But here, oh dear, our wallets came out and we spent money on things for us, and on presents for family back at home. I flung the comment at Maura that at least we could post things back with reasonable safety. After all, we were in the capital city of Mexico. Maura told me not to hold my breath. This was still a Second World country. Hunger and living on the edge were the norm, as was corruption and theft. Even within the postal service.

Sooner or later, the saying goes, all good things must come to an end. I was beginning to look forward to getting up into the United States; we'd serviced our battered bikes, and the open road was calling. We'd decided to head west via Puerto Vallarta and then on to Baja California. We'd be missing out on some of Mexico's more famous landmarks, such as the Copper Canyon, but hey, there was never enough money and therefore time, to see everything. We'd save that for another trip to Mexico. Puerto Vallarta was calling because that was where my other cousin, Leslie, lived. She and her husband Antonio were both doctors there.

We set off, using the smaller roads as soon as we possibly could. Birgit loved the ride. And at last she'd got rid of her spare rear tyre. While fitting her new front tyre she'd decided to put on the spare rear too. She'd been carrying it since Panama City. Avon Tyres had very kindly sponsored us with their amazing Gripster tyres and we'd had sets sent out to Panama. Mine had had to go straight on, but Birgit's rear tyre still had a fair bit of tread left so she'd elected to carry the new one. At times, that extra weight hanging on the back of her bike had caused the front wheel to skip a bit and lugging it into the safety of hotels rooms had been a chore. The bike now handled much better. Birgit hadn't previously revealed that on the odd occasion we'd ridden fast, she'd had a bit of a speed wobble to deal with. She'd not said anything because we didn't normally ride very quickly and she hadn't wanted to worry me.

The smaller roads held some surprises. We rounded one corner at our usual gentle speed only to find ourselves suddenly riding over sticky black tar. A crew was working on the road, dumping crumby dollops of soggy tar and gravel into the many potholes. They were beating the mounds into irregular humps with their shovels and then a truck with a giant sprayer on the back was washing the road surface with a thick layer of shiny wet tar. The undersides of the bikes, our panniers, tyres, tank panniers, boots and trousers were instantly coated, and the heat from the engines automatically sent up the stench of freshly baked tar. I groaned. This stuff would take an age to clean off and we'd get filthy and have to use neat petrol to do it. In the meantime, the crew initially looked bemused, and then slightly annoyed with us for riding our bikes across their work. If only they had put out warning signs. Then a small truck splashed past us, spraying my left trouser leg with black ooze. We didn't stop for a second helping of that and rode off in a cloud of tarry smoke, leaving a few turns of tyre tread pattern on the road as we did so.

That night we found a gem of a camping spot. It was one of those places that you dream about. Tucked away down a long gravel road, the tiny campsite nestled on the shores of a small blue lake. The owner rushed out to greet us. I liked him straight away. He was a small, brown, round and cheerful man with thinning hair. He was shaking our hands even before we could get our gloves off. He showed us to a prime spot right by the shore, and then where the showers were. He was very proud of the fact that they had hot water. He'd rigged up a series of oil drums, suspended over a long fire pit. He told us that at 6pm each day he'd light the fire under the barrels and the water took about half an hour to heat to, "A very good temperature." He was right too. It was blissful and there was something rather fine about showering in a wilderness under water that had been heated in this way. The wooden stalls were only as high as my shoulders and that night we showered to the sight of the sun going down. It fell as a perfectly round orange-red ball until it disappeared behind the forested hills. As a sort of final dash of defiance, the sky suddenly turned a flaming orange which turned the hills into a stark black silhouette. The only sounds came from the rushing shower water and the call of a bird down by the shore. The contrast to the city couldn't have been more profound, and that night we were treated to a sky so full of stars that it looked as if someone had tipped over a pirate's treasure chest.

The further north and west you head from Mexico City, the more the landscape changes. We rode into rugged, tree-lined hills  with deeply sloping valleys and on into a landscape that could have been the perfect set for a western. Giant cacti sprouted all over, either singly or in sociable clumps. As a teenager I'd always been enthralled by images of the dry lands where these hardy plants grew. The cacti stood tall and proud against the elements, but there was a slightly unreal, 'cartoon-ish' look to them. They have the typical outspread spiky 'arms' that stick out sideways and then head upwards as if a pistol-packing baddie had told them to 'Reach for the sky!'. Other huge specimens looked like prickly forests on one stem. I'd seen a very much smaller version of them on a friend's kitchen windowsill. I wondered if he knew how big the thing would grow in time. There were very few other signs of life, apart from clumps of tussock grass on either side of sagging loops of rusting barbed wire strung from sun-bleached, withered wooden posts, The bucking of my bike over the potholes and the humps from the road crew's repairs made it easy to feel that we were some of the last cowboys on the range.

In the distance a train crawled across the dry, cacti-dotted landscape. We lost count of the number of cargo beds the three locomotives were pulling as the train snaked its way around the curves of the beige-coloured valleys. Even at a distance we could hear the roar of the engines, fading in and out as they rounded the corners, and when one of the drivers spotted us he gave a long blast of the lead engine's horn, which he ended with a couple of cheerful toots.

Walking out into the vastness of this cacti-strewn land is like stepping out into a giant's rock garden. Tall spiky shapes surround you, and pale green ground cover succulents and clumpy scrub block your way, forcing you to meander across the garden in an apparently aimless and random zigzag. The sun becomes your friend and your guide; it would be easy to get lost out there. One hill looks much the same as the next and though each cactus bears resemblance to the next, each has its own characteristics and each has been formed as a result of where it has found itself to be living. A large boulder might push it leaning crazily in one direction, or a particularly shallow stretch of soil may have stunted its growth. Strange rustlings emerge from the deep shadows beneath the scrub, reminding you that you are not the only ones passing through the giant's rock garden. This is also the home of lizards, spiders and snakes.

We stopped off in towns which would have been like going back to the 19th century, were it not for the trucks and the inevitable dark-screened 4x4s. Many were bordered with shantytowns. There, the houses, or rather, dwellings, were made of plastic sheeting, wood, reeds, scrapped cars, tar paper and even blankets.

In contrast, the coast road was a beauty to ride as it looped along, following the water's edge as it went. To one side we had the Pacific Ocean, whose deep blue was broken only by the white tops of the rolling waves and by the flashes of white sand beaches in the tiny bays. To the other side, a rich sub-tropical land with farms made of palm thatch. The crops mostly seemed to be rows of small papaya trees, heavy with green fruit. And every so often we'd find ourselves riding past houses and small resorts that were idyllic in comparison to the village shantytowns. Gleaming white buildings with acres of glass looked out over the ocean.

We could feel the heat too. In Mexico City it had been around 24 degrees Celsius, but down here the temperature was a warm 31 degrees (87 Fahrenheit). Riding in this temperature is fun when there are trees that clump out over the road at intervals and it reminded me of one of the reasons I'd grown to love riding the bike so much. Exposed to the world, my senses came alive. Under each tree or clump of overhanging vegetation was a pool of cool shade. As we zipped along, my eyes and body had to deal with the strobe effect of bright light flashes from the sudden bursts of the sun between the pools of shade. My senses were tingling as they were assaulted by the smells of the trees and the crisp salt tang of the sea. Where my face was exposed to the slipstream from the bike's windscreen, I could feel my skin beginning to collect a salty layer from the sea air.

Though we were on the main western highway north, campsites were basic but that didn't bother us at all and out of season as we were, we could usually bargain down the price for the night. Some sites were completely deserted and others seemed to be run by a skeleton staff. Most didn't have all the facilities operating so we felt quite comfortable about persuading the owners to lower the price.

The sensation of time standing still was in my mind. In the longer open sections between the trees I had moments when I felt as if our wheels weren't turning at all, and that it was the landscape that was moving. It made me think of the early days of making cowboy movies. Back then, real action close-ups weren't possible. The cowboy would be filmed in a studio, sitting aboard a wooden horse. This horse would be rhythmically rocked by stagehands and all would be just out of camera shot. Behind him would be a long, hand-painted canvas backdrop which stagehands would pull across the set at a steady horse-in-movement sort of pace. Everyone knew that the cowboy was constantly riding through very similar landscape, but no one cared. Spectators would be too enthralled by the story and the magic of the camera to be bothered about things like that. Beneath me Libby seemed quite happy with our rolling, ever-changing backdrop and she continued to rumble along at a gentle, kilometre-eating pace. As we rode I had another of those glad-to-be-alive moments. Birgit's riding style and my own seemed perfectly in tune, and the sun was shining. It was a beautiful, relaxing day when nothing had the right to go wrong. And nothing did.

Puerto Vallarta was a completely different scene. You ride from a peaceful world into a 25-kilometre long resort city with multi-lane roads. We were now just a couple of days' ride from the U.S. border.

This relative proximity, combined with a superb climate, historical sites, beaches, whale-watching opportunities and a safe harbour, has made Puerto Vallarta a target for holidaymakers from all over Mexico,  and the USA. The new sections of the town were full of concrete buildings, with all that you'd expect of modern tourism. There were scores of hotels, restaurants, car rentals, offices, supermarkets and all the businesses required in a service town. The old town, which was completely dwarfed by the new, was a different world. Its streets were small and winding and often cobbled. In some places the kerbs were so high it looked as if they were designed for giants rather than mere mortals. Many of the old houses had troughs of flowers outside or hanging baskets from which flowers cascaded. But these old streets had also adapted to life as a tourist resort. Brightly-coloured boards advertised boat trips, fishing trips, water skiing, and both Mexican and American-style 'comfort food'. Brightly coloured beach-wraps hung alongside flippers and snorkels, beach balls and buckets. Boutiques sold expensive clothes and an amazing variety of silver jewellery. The latter was tempting, but I was sure that prices would have been set to the pockets of visitors from the north and not for the likes of us. Even though the old town had prostituted itself to the tourist dollar, to me it didn't matter. I rather liked the place. There was a happiness there that far outweighed the brashness of the commerce.

There were also plenty of things which, to my eye, were slightly incongruous. To begin with, one of the main beaches is called Playa de los Muertos, or 'Beach of the Dead'. How on earth did a beach in Mexico's second largest tourist resort get a name like that? Romantic tradition held that this was something to do with the pirates of olden days who had plied their trade from these shores. But the cynics said it was quite simply because there is a lethal undercurrent that rips the unwary and the innocent rapidly out to sea. I wondered if it was more to do with the very obviously polluted water! Weird that they would let that happen on a tourist beach.

My cousin Leslie practised in Puerto Vallarta because she liked the town and because many elderly people from the States retire there, so her skills as a doctor and her fluent English were major assets. She lived with her husband Antonio and their two children in a small apartment down on the edge of the international golf course, not far from the yacht marina. Once our bikes were parked away in their guarded parking lot, we could all start to get to know each other. Leslie had inherited sandy blond hair from her father and it looked mighty fine on her. She stood out from the crowd, even more so because she's a fair bit taller than your average Mexican. And when you are a confident, pretty woman …

Leslie and Antonio made us as welcome as Maura and Jordi had in Mexico City. Their sons, Santiago and Daniel, were full of beans and they attacked everything they did with boyish enthusiasm. Santiago was very shy of us though, and when we first arrived he hid behind Leslie's skirts and covered his eyes with his hand if either of us talked directly to him.

Leslie and Antonio, or Tonio as everyone called him, had a nice surprise for us. They had just bought a house in a complex right on the beach, just to the north of Puerto Vallarta. They'd been renting it out but it was due to become a retreat from the rushing chaos of their hardworking lives and in time might well become their home. Would we like to stay in it for a while? Would we? Too right we would! The tall, white building was kitted out in the crisp, clean lines of a modern Mexican house. We instantly loved the plain, white interior and the cool, brightly-coloured tiled floors, and set to pretending that we were millionaires for a few days. Leslie had even arranged for one of the complex's staff to knock the top off a couple of coconuts and they awaited us on the patio table. The cool milk was delicious.

Between the house and the beach was a small swimming pool whose turquoise tiles instantly took me back to the colour of the water at Cenote Azul. Around the pool, palm trees supplied shade and with another couple of steps we were on a wide, long, white sand beach. The house next door was said to belong to one of the Mexican Mafia. We entertained ourselves by watching, very discreetly, the stream of sinister-looking cars that came and went. The muscled bodyguards made me think of those we'd seen protecting the political candidates at election time back in El Salvador. Mean-looking, gun-toting sods that had probably been trained to behave like pit bull terriers.

The beach was a quiet hub of sociable activity, but it had none of the harsh falseness of Acapulco. Sporadic beach bars further along provided cold drinks for the sunbathers, strollers, joggers, dog walkers, surfers, yachtsmen, windsurfers and the fishermen (from their power boats). In spite of all this activity, the beach was big enough that you never felt even a hint of overcrowding. Such is the life of the better off. We walked the shore for hours, turning even browner, with our hair bleaching in the sun and our feet toughening up from all the sand walking. We swam and body-surfed and we were amazed by the wide variety of sea life that washed up on the shore. We found sand dollars, starfish and even comic puffer fish. There were enough shells and pieces of driftwood to keep Birgit happy and we read every book we could lay our hands on. Life was very good, but dangerous. We could get used to this. Too soon we'd need to be leaving. Birgit still dreamt of making it to Alaska and if we were going to do that, we had a lot of kilometres to cover. If we missed the season this year, then we'd either have to wangle a way to stay in the USA and Canada for a year, or we'd freeze our backsides off in the attempt to see some of that rugged northern land. In the evenings over glasses of Mexican wine, we pondered the target we'd set ourselves.

The last time I'd set myself a strict time limit was in the first year of the trip, when I'd decided that overlanding was brilliant and that since Africa had cost me far less than I'd anticipated, there was a chance to keep travelling. There really hadn't been a good reason to stop the adventure, so I'd booked myself and the bike onto a container ship from Durban in South Africa to Sydney in Australia. Once I'd booked the passage I'd given myself the time limit. This had been an alien feeling and had affected every decision I made from that time on. I actually hadn't liked the change from the previously freewheeling nature of the journey. But with shipping, you do have to plan in advance so… But the time limit had made me make some risky decisions which, if my guardian angel was on hand and all went well, wouldn't have been a problem. But all had not gone well and my angel had taken a nap. I'd ended up in hospital with seventeen bone fractures courtesy of a pothole in a dust cloud while crossing the Namibian desert.

So if we targeted Alaska now, were we running the risk of making some hasty, daft decisions, and might we not also miss out on some exciting adventures? With a third glass of wine we stopped worrying about it. What would be would be. There was no way we were going to jeopardise the rest of the trip by rushing. It would be a totally alien thing to do. We were going to take our time and carry on exploring as many side roads as we could. Inevitably, the side roads had held most of the best adventures so far. We might be heading up into a land of freeways but we weren't going to let them take us past the very things that we had come to this part of the world to see. If we made it to Alaska, all well and good. If not, then we'd have had plenty of other adventures. And that would be fine too. Just fine.

In the meantime we could enjoy Leslie and her family's company. One evening we arranged to meet up with Leslie and Tonio down at the very swanky marina. The plan was to eat some of the famous Puerto Vallarta soup. It's made with octopus, shrimps and chunks of avocado and spiced with chilli and lemon; an amazing combination. We decided to get as dressed up as we could for the occasion. I put on my cleanest, though still patched clothes, and Birgit wore her only dress. She'd picked up a very pretty stripy brown mini dress in Guatemala and she hoped that with it on we wouldn't look too out of place. We rode two-up into town and when we got to the Marina, Birgit ducked into some loos to take off her bike trousers and pull down her dress (as far as it would go!). Bike boots into a pannier and sandals on, she rode side-saddle to the restaurant where we were due to meet Leslie and Tonio.

Sadly, Leslie got caught up at the hospital and couldn't get away to join us, but this gave us the chance to get to know Tonio a little better. He had a great sense of humour and spoke good English, which for once gave me the chance to join in with a conversation fully. I suspect that being able to speak English all of a sudden, meant that I rather dominated the conversation… After we'd eaten, we strolled along the marina's jetties and Birgit spotted an Italian ice cream shop. "Let's have one" she said. The next thing I knew I was stumping up $7.70 for three ice creams. $7.70!!!! (That's about $20 at current rates). I was gob-smacked when I heard how much, but they were rather good and we all need a treat now and then, don't we?

Now we were ready to move on. Mexico had been really kind to us in so many ways. We'd enjoyed the diverse, rugged beauty of the land and had been fascinated by its history and cultures. Most of the people we'd met had been welcoming and in all, the country had given us the chance to recharge our 'travel batteries'. We'd had little holidays in several parts of the country and with this final one in a state of luxury, we felt ready for whatever would happen next. It was almost as if being in Leslie and Tonio's place on the beach had been a halfway house between the simplicity of the road in poorer countries, and the bright, modern world we imagined was waiting for us over the border.

Chapter Seven

Leave only Footsteps and Tyre Tracks

'Travelling… forces you to trust strangers and to lose sight of all that familiar comfort of home and friends. You are constantly off balance. Nothing is yours except the essential things — air, sleep, dreams, the sea, the sky — all things tending towards the eternal or what we imagine of it.'

Cesare Pavese

Mexico held one last treat for us: Baja California. 'Baja', (pronounced 'Baha') simply means 'Lower' in Spanish. Higher or 'Alto' California was the northern part of California and other present-day western US states which Mexico ceded to the USA after the war of 1845-48. Baja California is a long narrow peninsula over 1,200 kilometres long but only 100kms or so wide for most of its length. It's attached to the rest of Mexico by an even narrower strip of land between the US border and the equally long and narrow strip of water known as the Gulf of California or 'The Sea of Cortes' as it's also known. Long after Cortes proved it to be a peninsula, map-makers persisted in drawing Baja California as an island off the coast of Mexico.

I was itching to see this part of Mexico. The peninsula is pretty much desert and mountain range and I love those landscapes. I'd read about its tiny, tucked-away coves that can only be reached by boat, or trailbike. Then there was the beach called El Coyote, which sounded like paradise, according to a guy called Ben that we'd met years before in Nepal. A giant overlander on a BMW, Ben had raved about a stretch of soft white sand on a jade-coloured sea where sand dollars would wash ashore and no man would bother you. Then there were the tales I'd heard of the famous Baja 1000 desert race. The peninsula sounded like it was a dirt bike rider's dream. All these things combined to make Baja California unmissable for us.

The Baja 1000 is an off-road race that's open to all sorts of bikes, buggies and trucks, and it has attracted famous motorcyclists and film stars alike, including Paul Newman and Steve McQueen.

McQueen actually competed in the event on both two and four wheels. The first race was held way back in 1967 from Tijuana on the US border, to La Paz and was actually closer to 850 miles than 1,000 (1,366-kilometres). Then as now, the course ran over rocks, dry lakebeds, sand washes, mountain passes and some sections of paved road. The overall winner is almost always a motorcycle, ridden by a team of three riders. The fastest ever time being an incredible 10 hours and 20 minutes by the legendary Larry Roeseler, Danny Hamel and Ty Davis on a Kawasaki. It requires a near-superhuman combination of riding skill, fitness and observation to ride across the desert at 100mph on a motorcycle...

The course is not the same every year and there are now two types of race – the Baja 1000, a 'point to point' event held in November, which now usually starts and finishes in Ensenada although it used to go right down to the city of La Paz in southern Baja over a 1,000 miles or more. There's also a 'loop race' held in July which also usually starts and finishes in Ensenada; it used to average over 800 miles but is now closer to 500, hence its name, the Baja 500.

As if the terrain itself weren't a big enough challenge for the drivers and riders, there are other very unpredictable hazards in the form of sabotage or booby-trapping courtesy of the spectators. The aim isn't to damage the competitors and their machines but to make the spectacle more entertaining. Under cover of night, people sneak out onto the course and set up hidden jumps and other obstacles. The only warning a competitor may get is if an unusually large crowd has collected for no obvious reason on the course. Then there's the wandering livestock... I couldn't help but admire the people who compete in such a race and I hoped we'd be able to ride part of the course. I knew though that our BMWs, with all our kit, weren't really set up to attempt the whole course, even at a snail's pace.

There's a mountain range that runs up the centre of the 800 mile peninsula. It's a sort of backbone, and it helps to provide both a unique landscape, and some types of vegetation that aren't found anywhere on the 'mainland', as the locals call the rest of Mexico.

This mountain range, or Sierra de Baja California divides the state into four weather zones. In the south, at the foot of the mountains, the weather is incredibly dry. Often rivers would form only when the rainstorms of a hurricane swept in. A large section of the area is called the Vizcaino Desert. There are some amazing succulents in this area and they survive in part from the coastal fog that rolls in from the Pacific Ocean.

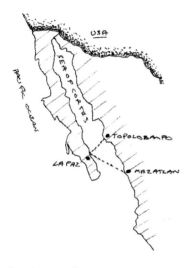

To the east of the Sierra, is the Sonoran desert, which leads down to the jade waters of the Sea of Cortes. This dry region is in contrast to the west and pacific coastal areas because the mountain range forces the clouds high and they tend to drop the moisture they've collected from the Pacific onto the western slopes. The centre of the state holds a collection of narrow, higher altitude valleys and these have sufficient rainfall to be fertile – quality grapes are grown there. In the northwest, the weather is rather Mediterranean and this attracts large numbers of retirees from the USA. As you'd expect, it's far cheaper to live in Mexico than in the States and I even heard of people who lived in the Mexican border towns and commuted to work in San Diego every day.

But we still had to get to Baja California from Puerto Vallarta. The obvious route was to take a ferry, either from Mazatlan or Topolobambo – both could take us across the Sea of Cortes to a port just to the north of La Paz at the southern end of the peninsula. We settled on Mazatlan, since it was much further south and because the ship left at 3pm and the crossing would be 16 to 18 hours long. (The duration all depended on the weather conditions). A night crossing would save us the cost of accommodation and this route would also save us the extra fuel required to ride further north to Topolobambo.

After one last lingering breakfast on the patio overlooking the beach at Leslie and Tonio's house, we loaded the bikes and set off north again. Kilometres of roadworks dumped us onto gravel and sand surfaces, which we were forced to share with cars, trucks and buses, all of whom were delayed and frustrated by the stop-go-stop conditions. By the time we all made it to the end of the roadworks, everyone's patience had frayed and there was a mad scramble for the open road. This scramble never seemed to die away. It was 'dog eat dog' stuff. Every second seemed like a duel on the road. We were the small fry and therefore, very much third class road users and we felt horribly vulnerable. It would have taken just one second of distraction or one moment of bad judgement from anyone to cause a disaster. As it was, I was amazed that no one actually hit anyone else. The driving style was fast and erratic, and completely unpredictable. We rode on adrenaline all the way up the beautiful coastal route to Mazatlan.

It was on this road that we came across our first Recreational Vehicles or 'RVs' as they are called in the US, for short. These lumbering, 'palaces on wheels' were often driven by elderly people who didn't look as if they had the eyesight or co-ordination to drive anything bigger than a Mini on a disused airfield. I admired them for getting out of their home environments though, and respected them for the strength of desire that they must have had to make them prepared to negotiate such lunatic traffic in a foreign land.

The brightly-coloured hoardings on the outskirts of Mazatlan proclaimed it to be a wondrous and tourist-friendly place, but the road signs were absolutely hopeless. Mostly they didn't exist and as for finding a sign to the ferry port, well that was just funny. It was almost as if once the city had you, it didn't want you to get out. We resorted to asking the way. By this time we'd pretty much worn ourselves out and following our compass we headed north out of the city, hunting for a campsite. We found a cheap one and bought some large bottles of ice cold Cerveza Pacifico. The beer went down a treat and we celebrated making it through the day. We hit the sack early, which was a big mistake.

Even though we were out of the main holiday season, the campsite was full, and Mexicans live on a very different internal clock from ours. We were still in the mindset of getting up with the dawn and going to bed at sunset. Mexican life seemed to start with the sunset, and around 8pm the site around us got busy. Just as we were nodding off, music was turned on, and party noises began. Children seemed to be allowed to run riot and the smells of barbecuing food soon began to float through the air. As it was still hot at dusk, we'd gone to bed with the flaps of our tent open and just the mosquito net to keep the bugs out. That did nothing to stop the smells of cooking steak from collecting in our airspace. Since we obviously weren't going to get any sleep, we got up again and watched the Mexicans at play. They played enthusiastically until four in the morning. Then all of a sudden the world went quiet as if someone had just unplugged the power leads to the stereos. We slept like the dead.

The hazy, pale yellows and greys of the dawn saw the start of a long day. Having fuelled up in a gentle warmth that was already just beginning to hint of the heat to come, we set off through Mazatlan's street maze to try to find the ferry port. The ferries run every day except, we'd heard, for a few times a month on the days when they were shipping 'Carga Negra' or 'Black Cargo'. This means such things as dynamite for Baja's mines, petrol, diesel and so on. I was happy not to keep company with that sort of cargo.

Down in the port, it was as if the staff in the ticket office were speaking another language and if it hadn't been for the kindness of a woman standing in the queue with us, we'd have been totally confused. "First you have to go to get your bikes weighed and measured." She said. "This is how they calculate the cost of your motorcycles. Once you have the weight certificate you can get your motorcycle tickets here. Once you have them, you can go and get your personal tickets from the office over there." Ahhh.

It took two hours to get the weight permits. Sir Henry, with 9 litres of water, a full 26-litre fuel tank and Birgit's luggage, weighed 265 kilos. Libby, with 43 litres of fuel, more of water, food and my kit weighed 325 kilos. Why so much water? We were heading to an area where water was at a premium and we were planning to wild camp as much as possible. It was interesting to find out how much weight we'd be lugging around the dirt tracks of Baja. This was the first time the bikes had been weighed since we'd negotiated the price to fly the bikes and our kit from Colombia to Panama. The difference there had been that food, fuel and water hadn't been on board.

It took another hour to get all the tickets organised and by then it was really hot. The concrete of the port roadways and the buildings seemed to magnetically attract the sun's rays and there was very little shade. The road itself was an angular track through the buildings and it carried a layer of air above it that shimmered with heat haze. No one simply crossed the road; everyone scurried across as fast as they could go. We used part of the waiting time to repack for the voyage. The price for the most basic cabin was double the price of two seats in the 'salon', so to save money we'd booked ourselves salon seats instead. The seats cost 209 pesos per person and the bikes fell in the 499 pesos price bracket. The exchange rate still hovered at around 10 pesos to the dollar so this felt like an enormous amount of money to be spending.

As we didn't have a cabin we separated out our sleeping bags, mats and the groundsheet from the tent. With luck we'd be able to find a spot to lie down somewhere. My tank panniers were filled with food and drinks for the voyage. Our thermos flask was topped off with some fresh and very strong coffee.

The next few hours on the hot quayside passed slowly, but at least we were on the loading ramp where there was plenty happening. Truck after truck was loaded through the vast stern doors of the ship. Tug trucks pulled fully loaded artic trailers aboard, RVs were loaded and then the cars. Finally it was our turn and we bumped up the ramp into the ship. With some very efficient arm waving by a deck officer, we were directed over the damp and buckled steel deck, to a spot next to a truck with a big sign saying 'Bimbo' across its side, in big red letters. No it wasn't carrying a load of dumb blondes; it was just a cargo of sliced white bread on its way across to La Paz. Bimbo being the brand name for the Mexican equivalent of Mother's Pride. If only they knew… When we'd repacked on the dockside, we'd slipped off every ratchet strap we had and used them to tie the bikes down. We wished we had more but felt a little easier when a couple of crewmen arrived with some greasy ropes, which they used to strengthen what we'd already done. The Sea of Cortes has a reputation for being rough in the spring, so we didn't want to take any chances.

Following the mass of other people, we made our way back out of the ship and then boarded through the passenger entry point – a strange system. At first glance the ship didn't seem too bad. Everything looked as if it worked and we felt a little more comfortable. We found our salon seats, and then I realised that in the haste to get the bikes strapped down, I'd forgotten to pick up our food. Birgit was very gracious about it, but my stomach wasn't so polite. All we had between us and the ship's inflated food prices, was a few dry tortillas and three slices of dry bread. It would have to do. At least we didn't have to lug the extra weight of our forgotten food around as we went exploring. Our first objective was to find a spot where we could lie down flat for the night. The restaurant area seemed like a good bet.

As the ship dragged itself away from the jetty and out to sea Birgs and I stood on the open deck and watched the mainland disappear over the horizon. The country had been good to us in so many ways and even though we'd still technically be spending the next week or two in Mexico, it felt as if we were heading somewhere completely new.

The restaurant closed late at night, as we'd expected. When everyone had left we laid our groundsheet out under a table, climbed into our sleeping bags and eased off to sleep. A good day. Moments later a torch shone down on us and a voice from the darkness told us we couldn't sleep there. Back in the salon we realised we weren't going to have much luck there either. People were sitting around playing cards, eating, and of course, someone had a radio on full blast – the mariachi band playing sounded as if its trumpets had all been put through a mangle. Those who were either hard of hearing or able to switch off better than us, were slumped fast asleep in their chairs. But they were adding to the cacophony with loud snores which frequently drew looks of amusement from the other passengers.

We headed for the stern deck. We'd seen this spot on our earlier wander round and had marked it down as a potential alternative sleeping spot. A small overhang would protect us from any rain and the area was out of the wind. We were really glad we had the tent's groundsheet with us. The deck was covered in old cigarette butts, spit, bits of food that had been squashed onto the thick green decking paint and there were some suspicious-looking dark dollops that I was sure just had to be rat droppings. Not so good. But it was quiet and from our new bed we could go to sleep with the stars above us. Below us the deck gently vibrated from the ship's rumbling engines. Despite our hunger, we slept well.

By daybreak the ferry was already sailing along the coast of the Baja peninsula. We'd made really good time as the sea was as calm as the proverbial millpond. The ferry port is actually 17 kilometres north of La Paz and has the almost unpronounceable name of Pichilingue. As the sun rose it turned the mountains a slightly surreal and beautiful deep red. It was going to be a good day. We could both feel it.

Down on the cargo deck, trucks were already revving engines and the air in the enclosed space was becoming grey and dense. We hurriedly stripped off the ropes and undid the straps. We'd get out of there as soon as possible. Within moments of the ship docking, the stern doors swung down, letting a blast of fresh air into the cargo area. A couple of trucks were driven out and then it was our turn to bump down the ramp. We were both instantly surprised by how cold it was away from the protection of the ship. Birgit shivered, but at least any officialdom we'd have to deal with would be in the cool. Happily, after a quick check to make sure that our paperwork was correct and that we weren't carrying any drugs, we were done. We rode out of the docks, stopping only to eat and repack our kit properly before we headed for La Paz. The refried beans, tortillas and hot sauce, that should have been last nights dinner, worked very well as breakfast with the fiery heat of the sauce kicking us into action. Riding into the city was fine, we just had to head south, but finding the right way out was another matter, thanks to the usual lack of signs.

We wanted to find our first Baja beach to camp on but we'd not realised how much of a tourist haven the south was. Condos, beach resorts, restaurants and bars abounded. There were a few campsites but we still hoped for a bit of deserted beach. Just past the town of Cabos we found a sandy track that seemed to head in the direction of the sea. The sand was really soft and we rode it with our front wheels ploughing through it rather than over it. With a bit of work we finally made it to the beach. But everywhere we looked there were large signs saying 'No Camping' and 'No Fires'. We decided that it would be rude to risk it so shoved our way back up the track again, glad that it was so cool, because otherwise it would have been a really sweaty exercise.

A little further down the main road, we found another sandy track and decided to give it a go. This one was lined with dwarf date palms and stubby lumps of cactus. It did lead to the sea but dropped us on the coast right next to a campsite. We parked the bikes out of sight and went for a walk down the beach. There was a lot of broken glass and some sections of the sand seemed to have been mined with thorns. If we tried this we could be in trouble, and were we OK to camp there anyway? There weren't any signs to say we couldn't. Back at the campsite, a young American tourist had been watching us. We asked him what he thought about us free camping on the beach. "Weeell," he drawled, "you'll probably be OK. They do check the beach from time to time but they did it yesterday so you ought to be in the clear." That'd do. We'd risk the thorns and the glass. We got the bikes through the ever-softer sand, and managed to avoid both the thorns and the glass. Up went the tent and we went for a walk. Birgit's rating for the beach was three out of ten. "No shells," she muttered. That night, in spite of the bitter cold wind that was blowing in off the Pacific, we slept for eleven hours.

The following weeks saw us meandering our way through an enthralling landscape. Rusty red mountains turned flame-red with sunrises and sunsets. In the daytime they were a misty beige and blue haze. The main roads were in reasonable condition, though most of them were quite narrow. When they weren't running flat and level, they took us whooping through the mountains on curves that must have been designed by a motorcyclist. Better still, the traffic was almost non-existent. We rode tracks whose surfaces ranged from loose gravel to soft sand. We rode the sidetracks when we could and though I've no idea for certain, I'm sure that some of the sections must have been part of the Baja 1000 route. They were fun, even with loaded BMWs. Sometimes they were hard work, very hard work, but each rocky or sandy obstacle surmounted gave us both a glow of satisfaction. I grew to love the giant cordon cacti. These plants grow up to 12 metres high and they are beautiful in a combed, spiky sort of way. Sometimes we were even treated to the sight of small, yellow-centred white flowers sprouting from them. We ate tortillas in small villages and went hunting for fuel far too often. Both our bikes were thirsty beasts and when we were making them work through soft sand and thick gravel, they drank enthusiastically. Sometimes our fuel came from proper petrol stations but often it came from plastic jerrycans or from oil drums with hand pumps. Away from the main road, a fill-up often cost over a dollar more per gallon, but we didn't care. We were glad to be able to find it at all and we didn't mind if someone was earning an extra buck out of us. After all, they had got the fuel to some really out of the way places.

We loved almost every single aspect of the narrow Baja peninsula. When it got too hot down by the Cortes Sea on the eastern

side, the western, Pacific side was never hot. We'd stop in the early afternoon and using our luggage straps and our sarongs we'd create a shade shelter to go over the tent. When we got the angle right then we'd create a bit of extra shade to work

on the bikes or to simply sit and stare at the rugged landscape. Birgit's final drive had developed a fairly nasty leak which was a bit of a worry and was making a mess. We were also keeping a close eye on the level of the water in our batteries. What with falling off and the ups and downs of the tracks, and the heat, both were losing water. Fortunately we were carrying a small bottle of distilled water and that kept them topped up. Sir Henry had a kick-start but Libby didn't so I was always conscious of keeping her battery in top condition. I enjoyed the mountain rides but the coastal tracks on the Sea of Cortes side were far more fun. We liked the fact that it was warmer there, and that the coastline was dotted with tiny white sand coves. Very occasionally we'd see a yacht moored off one of them but normally the only other active signs of human life were the yellow fin tuna fishermen at work out on the emerald green water.

Finding places to camp wasn't hard and we revelled in the peace we found out in the wilds. Sometimes the only sounds were the ticking of the bikes' engines as they cooled down, and from the wheeling, cawing seagulls. My favourite spots were back-dropped by the mountains, where the reddish brown sandy gravel of the Sonoran Desert surrounded us. With shade from our sarong shelter we were at peace with the world. And even when Birgit accidentally broke our trusty thermos, life wasn't spoiled. We'd been carrying the thermos since South Africa and it had become an old friend. Each night, when we were boiling our drinking water for the next day, we'd boil up another batch and fill the flask with coffee for the morning. There's something very fine about waking up in the morning to a hot cup of coffee, and not having to boil the billy meant that packing was easier and we could get under way faster.

The one disappointment was that there seemed to be rubbish everywhere. The main road, the Mex 1, seemed to be lined with Budweiser cans, old carrier bags, scraps of paper and even used nappies. It seemed a complete waste of a beautiful land. Even the most tucked-away of places had streamers of toilet paper hanging from the bushes and whenever there was what looked like a good camping spot, previous occupants had enjoyed themselves breaking bottles. It was sad.

El Coyote beach was just as Ben had described it, 'Stunningly beautiful.' It's the sort of place that you'd spend thousands of dollars to be able to go to, and we lapped up the beauty for days. But Ben obviously hadn't seen a litter problem back when he'd been there last.

No one seemed to understand the concept of leaving nothing but footprints when they departed.

Some of the towns we camped near were ramshackle affairs. Buildings had been thrown up as shelters, but with no attempt at making them attractive. They were purely functional. Many were unpainted, and some looked as if they'd been made from whatever someone else had thrown away. It seemed that many of the villages didn't have mains electricity so at dusk, dozens of generators would power up and in those places we thanked God for earplugs. We'd never have slept without them.

The compensations were many though, and the kindness of the locals to two dusty travellers was one. We were always greeted with warmth and good humour. Some couldn't understand what we were doing. "Ride round the world? Why?" Some were fascinated and wanted to learn more. Others had no interest at all, but were happy to talk and to be friendly. One day, when we thought we'd set up camp far from anywhere, we suddenly heard voices. Two Mexican teenagers had been camping just out of sight around a bend in the cove. They came towards us and explained that they were leaving that day and asked if we'd like some provisions they didn't want to take with them. They gave us half a very juicy bright red and green watermelon and a half bottle of brandy. With smiles and handshakes they headed back to their camp and we never even heard them leave.

Chapter Eight

A New World

'To my mind, the greatest reward and luxury of travel is to be able to experience everyday things as if for the first time, to be in a position in which almost nothing is so familiar it is taken for granted.'

Bill Bryson

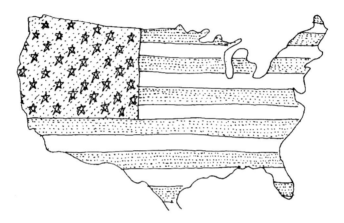

One morning we woke up and looked at each other. Without speaking, we knew that this was the day to start heading for the US border. We'd had enough play-time. We packed, had one last long look at the mountains around us, took a deep breath of the dry desert air and rode the last of the dirt to the main road. We rode with that nervous but eager sense of anticipation you get when something big and new is about to happen. This was the start of a change of life. The kilometres clicked away quickly under our wheels.

The ride to the border changed our mood a little. The world around us seemed to have turned ugly. The closer we got to the border, the busier the road became and the more the roadsides were lined with functional but beaten-up buildings. There were a few campsites but they all looked dirty and unkempt. They made the broken-down villages we'd seen in some parts of Mexico seem like desirable places to live. The fact that the day had turned grey and cold didn't help either. We pulled on extra layers of clothes and rode on with our wet weather gear over our normal bike kit.

We didn't want to stay in any of the border towns. After the freedom of the peninsula, the thought of staying the night in the hustle and bustle of a border town didn't appeal at all. And I couldn't face the thought of trawling around busy streets looking for a hotel with off road parking for the bikes. Leaving them on the street overnight simply wasn't an option. I couldn't understand why no one had invested in a decent campsite close to the border. Surely the location was prime? We passed RV camps which weren't set up for camping at all. Didn't North Americans camp? The owners of these sites told us that RVs are so self-sufficient that they didn't need to provide toilets and washing facilities for the likes of us. We told them that we'd cross our legs and weren't bothered about washing, but still, no deal. At last we heard of a site that might take us. We were just a few kilometres from the border by this time. Yes, they had both a shower and a toilet. The site fee was $17. We were stunned by the high price (I must explain that at this stage of the journey $7 per day covered three meals, fuel and camping costs). Was this a sign of things to come? We tried our best bargaining techniques but the site staff weren't having any of it. "Speak to the Boss," they said. "He's not here at the moment though." Feeling that we now had no choice, we pitched the tent and sat waiting for the boss to arrive. He took one look at us and said, "Of course you can stay. You have picked a good spot. I won't get anyone else into this small space. How about you just pay $10?" That helped.

We started the new day early. I felt as if I was leaving something important behind as we rode the last kilometres of Baja. But I also felt a strong tingle of anticipation. This line on the map was going to see us riding into a new world. For some, these last kilometres are dangerous ones. Tijuana and Mexicali had developed near to the border as a starting point for those who were trying to get US citizenship. They are also kick-off points for those who know that they don't have an earthly chance of getting in legally. These people were in the hands of the smuggling gangs and they faced long, very difficult, high-risk journeys across the borderlands. Others were involved in smuggling drugs into the USA. For some of the migrants, agreeing to smuggle drugs was the only way they could pay the gangs for their 'passage'. We've all heard stories of what happens to many of these people. Some make it successfully across the border, but then are killed by the gangs so nothing can be traced back to them. Some carry cocaine in swallowed condoms. We'd heard many stories of these migrants overdosing as a result of the condoms splitting in their stomachs. Some attempt to drive across the border in specially designed cars with hidden compartments filled with drugs. We were told that every week, several such cars try to get across. To succeed, the drivers not only have to be convincing, but they have to evade the sniffer dogs. One story had it that the containers of drugs would be loaded into bags of coffee in the hope that the drug smell had been disguised enough for the dogs not to get wind of the valuable cargo. Later at the border we saw cars that had been stripped down to their skeletons by the border officials on the US side.

The crossing itself was a shock, even more so due to the previous weeks riding single lane tarmac and the dirt roads of Baja. Twenty-five lanes of vehicles stretched away back into Mexico from the steel and concrete immigration booths. This was the busiest border crossing we'd ever attempted. Our hearts sank at the sight of how slowly the vehicles in front of us were moving forward. The scene made me think of streams of marching ants in slow motion. To the sides, shops selling tequila and mescal stood next to moneychangers and car hire shops. Men and children darted between the vehicles selling small goods from trays around their necks. There were flower sellers, cigarette vendors, windscreen washers and sellers of dancing dolls in Mexican costumes. They all ignored us – we obviously didn't have any money!

Half way down the queue, we realised that we'd got it wrong. This was the queue into the States. There must be another set of buildings for the Mexican Aduana and Migración offices. We still had to leave Mexico officially and the most important part of that was ensuring that our bike paperwork was dealt with in full. The chase around began, but as it did so, I had a little grin to myself. This was the last of the chaos. On the US side everything would be recognisable, organised and efficient. And everything would be done in English. I found myself looking forward to it, but perversely had a little tinge of regret at the thought of leaving border chaos behind us.

Bizarrely, the Mexican offices were only to be found on entry to the Mexico side of the crossing. That meant negotiating all the streams of traffic and a trudge over a bridge. When we got there it was as if Mexico was no longer interested in us. The paperwork was done in double quick time and we handed back our holograms. We spent the last of our pesos on an overpriced bottle of tequila and then we were free to join the queues again. To our delight, this time they all seemed to be moving faster. For once we hadn't joined the one queue that suddenly seemed to be going slower than all the others. Before we knew it, a smartly uniformed, fresh-faced American blonde girl was smiling a warm smile and saying, "Welcome to the United States of America. It's great to have you guys here. Have a nice stay."

'Is she talking to us?' I thought to myself, looking over my shoulders as I did so. No one at border crossings was this nice. Or was this the start of the fabled North American hospitality? I knew from the TV that everyone told each other to, "Have a nice day." I had always wondered if this was said with genuine feeling or whether it was something that was drummed into Americans from an early age, and then spouted with a mechanical lack of spontaneity and a glazed smile.

This genuinely cheerful young woman then told us that we could ride on and pointed towards the open road away from the border. This just had to be too easy. What about the bikes, and didn't we need an entry stamp in our passports?

We were right to think it was too easy. Had we followed her instructions we'd have found ourselves in big trouble much later on. As it was, when we told a very officious customs officer what the blonde had said, she looked at us as if we were the ones who were the idiots. The officer also made it very clear that she didn't like the fact that we'd parked the bikes in front of the customs office. When she had completed the paperwork, she stabbed the chewed end of her ballpoint pen in the direction of another office, saying, "If you'd like, you can go pay over there." But she said it in a voice which implied 'I think you are something nasty I've picked up on my shoe'. Birgit replied, "Well, thank you. But if I don't have to pay then I'll just keep my money. Is that everything done then?" And with such a pleasant tone of voice and not a trace of sarcasm that the officer looked momentarily dumbfounded. She then ripped out a tirade of angry words at Birgit. The tone of which was just as erratic as the bad hairdo the official was sporting. Birgit kept a straight face until the rant had finished and the woman had stormed out of her office. So much for the First World! Officials, it seemed, could be the same in any country. And the blonde girl who'd been so nice, but so misleading? Well, the reality was that she may well never have had to deal with anyone like us before. After all, how often do two non North Americans on bikes head north across the border?

Half an hour later, with our paperwork correct and fees paid, we rode into the United States of America in traffic that scared us silly. It was a huge shock to go from the dirt tracks and crumbling two-lane roads of Baja, to twelve lanes of American freeway hell. I'd read that since 1976 the U.S. has used more oil than it produces. Imports account for 40 percent of use and are one-third of the nation's trade deficit. Road traffic accounted for the greater quantity of the consumption. Surrounded by such an amazing number of vehicles all of a sudden, it wasn't hard for me to believe the statistic.

To make it worse, no one was taking any notice of the 65mph

speed limit and both overtaking and undertaking seemed to be perfectly acceptable. And then, were Americans all jugglers? The giant SUVs and boat-like saloon cars all seemed to have drivers who were managing to drink coffee, eat burgers, talk on their cell phones and hurl their craft around us as if we were mere pebbles in a torrent. We couldn't see what the speeding truck drivers were up to in the cabs of their man-eating road monsters... Our gentle 55mph was far too slow and our assumptions of organised sanity had meant that for a change we'd not taken any time out to learn the rules of the road. Those first moments nearly killed us. I rode muttering, "Give me Mexican potholes any day." We'd always taken it easy for the first days in a new country and since we'd come straight from dirt tracks and quiet Mexican roads it had seemed like a good idea to start slowly in the USA. But it wasn't. It was a scary, dangerous mistake.

We needed fuel and the first 'gas' station held the next culture shocks for us. No one rushed over to pump the fuel as had been the case pretty much all the way through Mexico and Central America. The petrol cost a fortune compared to Mexico, you had to pay before you pumped, and how the hell were we supposed to pay for it anyway? There were 25 credit card options displayed on the pump, but no option to pay by cash.

And none of the credit card options seemed to match any card that we had. We stood by the bikes wondering what the hell to do. The attendant sat watching us from a booth that obviously had plate glass in the windows. The door to the booth looked as if it would be more at home in Fort Knox. The longer we stood looking confused, the more agitated the attendant became. He was obviously beginning to twitch, and why not? We must have looked decidedly weird. I expected him to be pushing on a panic button at any second, and that would almost certainly lead to sirens and guns being pulled. Images of American 'cops and robbers' TV came flooding into my mind. Help! What to do? We couldn't run for it. We had to have fuel or we'd be running out in the middle of the freeway.

As with anywhere else, if in doubt, talk. It's usually a good rule. I approached the booth. The pasty-faced and heavily overweight attendant staggered backwards out of his chair and shrank away from me as I loomed, dust-covered and leather-jacketed in front of him. The road-shocked, got-to-have-fuel, look in my eyes probably made the situation worse. If he could have backed any further away from me he would have. He cringed as I yelled through the glass at him, "Hello, I need petrol. Can I pay with cash?" His eyes widened and it was only then that I realised that he must have forgotten to turn on his speaker system. Instead of understanding my words he was just watching my facial expression as I mouthed words of desperation at him. And anyway, did he know what the lip movements for the word petrol were anyway? The situation was getting out of hand.

Rule two, if in doubt think 'friendly' and smile, use sign language and show money. A smile on its own might have looked evil, but flashing the cash a bit seemed to tone things down a bit. Then I thought, he probably thinks I'm shouting "Gimme da money!" at him. But the money flashing worked.

The attendant edged his bulk back towards the desk and with an extended finger he hurriedly dabbed at a button near the glass. A small electronic voice piped out at me. "What seems to be the problem sir?" Phew, and when I explained, and the attendant had finished laughing hysterically, he took a fifty dollar bill through a slit in the glass and told me to fill up to that amount. If we didn't use it all he'd "Make change for us." Perhaps life wasn't going to be as easy as I'd imagined and being in the USA was going to be as much of an adventure as anywhere else. The only feeling of security I had at that moment was the sense that came from having full fuel tanks.

This was my first ever visit to the USA and I had a set of preconceived ideas about the place, but not all of them were good. I suppose this was partly why I wasn't so sure I wanted to be there. But the other part of me fought against the negative thoughts and wanted to concentrate on the more positive sides to life there. There seemed to be a freedom for people to be quirky and unusual, and I was looking forward to discovering that side of the country for myself.

It seemed to me that California was at the cutting edge of US culture. By that I mean Californians were prepared to be inventive to the point of breaking with traditional norms. Perhaps this state was going to be just the psychological entry point I needed into the USA. I'd seen photos of the nuttier things that Californians had got up to over the years, including motorcycles in the shape of a guitar, and a dress code that meant they could wear anything they liked, and that was quite OK. I also knew that Californians laid claim to being the inventors of such things as skateboards, motels, the Jacuzzi, Barbie dolls and frisbees. They'd also invented McDonalds.

This latter point made me think of an American legend. Don Gorske is known as the 'Big Mac Guy'. By the time we arrived in the States he'd consumed over 8,000 of the things. He subsequently went on to earn an entry in the Guinness book of records when he reached the 18,250 mark. The most he'd eaten in a day was nine, and over his 30-year 'eating project' he'd only missed eating a Big Mac on eight days. You'd expect him to be enormous, but I'd seen a photo and he was quite a normal build. Definitely a quirky guy though.

 With our full fuel tanks, we edged back into the traffic with determination, heading for Los Angeles. I really, really didn't want to be going there. To be honest, I feared it. This multi-laned freeway was bad enough; what on earth was the traffic in the LA Megalopolis going to be like? 'Megalopolis'? We'd heard all the tales, and with a name like El Pueblo de Nuestra Senora la Reina de Los Angeles de Porciuncula, the only thing that sounded simple about the place was the abbreviation, LA. What started as a duel turned into an eyes-wide-open adrenaline buzz. We decided that if we thought big then we'd have no problem. Being timid was never going to work. Think like a London driver and learn the rules of these roads fast. Take control, don't just sit there reacting to everyone else. 'Make them react to you!' I muttered to myself as we ducked and dived through the rush....

LA was on the travel menu for us for some very good reasons. Two of Birgit's friends from Munich, Bine and Jonny, lived there, we needed to organise insurance for the bikes and we needed to acclimatise for a few days before travelling on. For once I couldn't wait to get off the bike.

Bine (pronounced 'Beena') and Jonny made us very welcome. We soon settled down to beers and a traditional German meal that they had put together in Birgit's honour. Jonny is a musician and on returning to the USA from Germany, he'd got himself right back into the music scene and to hear him talk about it was fascinating.

It was the lack of insurance that made me want to get off the bike. We'd not been able to arrange anything in advance, nor at the border, because we didn't have a postal address in the USA. Actually, we'd not looked very hard at the border because as always, we suspected that prices there would be horribly inflated. With Bine and Jonny's address to use, and their home as a base, we started the hunt. What we thought would be an easy task turned out to be a voyage of discovery. My R80GS model was never sold in the US so the insurance companies didn't seem to know what to do with it. The cheaper companies wouldn't even think about it and Birgit's bike was even worse. It was based on an R60/5 600cc machine but had an 800cc engine. "Not original, can't do it" we were told. One company, a specialist in insuring foreign visitors' bikes, would look after us but, when they told us the price... our fingers kept on walking. Eventually we ended up with a year's minimum cover for $354, which would do nicely.

Staying with Bine and Jonny also allowed us to begin to discover things North American. We started to walk around with our mouths open less. We discovered the delights of a food store called Trader Joes. Here we could get a vast array of foods from right across the Americas, but the prices really shocked us.

North American supermarkets were a childish adventure for us. We were like kids in a toy store at Christmas. For the last couple of years we'd done most of our shopping in little shops where squadrons of flies practised aerobatics over the one choice of sardine, shampoo, soap, bread and sometimes even goat or sheep cheese. We'd bought our vegetables from little Indian women, choosing from their displays lovingly laid out on blankets on the ground. Great fun, but sometimes we'd dreamt of not having to bargain for everything. It's a slow process. Now, these dreams were coming true. Ten choices of sardine, fixed price; twenty choices of shampoo, fixed price; but what to choose? And so many different types of bread! The goodies on the salad vegetable bar looked really fresh. We stood admiring them and then were amazed as artificial thunder rolled, lights flashed and artificial rain fell all over the salad from the 'roof' of the salad bar! When cool air floated out towards us I suddenly realised that I was standing with my mouth open, again... No blanket on the ground here, that's for sure.

We realised that people think you are weird if you walk anywhere and that many areas didn't even have 'sidewalks'. The statistics say that the average American male will devote a huge 1,600 hours a year to his vehicle. That's buying it, servicing, parking it and all the other things related to owning a car or truck, but in particular, driving the thing. Why walk when you can drive? We, however, were used to walking to most places in a town, but actually began to feel quite uncomfortable doing so in LA. Curtains would twitch and the drivers of passing cars looked at us as if we were about to do some 'burglarising'. But at least it was easy to replace worn-out travel kit. Our groundsheet was shot and Birgit's Thermarest sleeping mat had developed a large blister, which made it rather like lying on a molehill. We did the tourist thing and explored Beverly Hills and Venice Beach. The beach was just like the movies. There is a boardwalk, palm trees line the sand, bronzed hunks and babes stroll the shoreline, and tanned girls in very skimpy bikinis rollerblade the walkways.

This was a mental challenge. I'd read that the USA is pretty puritanical about nudity and that it's against the law to sunbathe topless. No doubt the French think that's a very weird law. But in the States it seemed that so long as a woman's nipples were covered, and there was some sort of fabric, however tiny, over the pubic area, then that was fine. To me, the oh-so-tiny bikinis were far more erotic than a nude woman would have been. The bizarre thing was that when a woman had a couple of bits of string and a few postage stamps of material on, she could happily walk or skate through the crowds of a shopping area. It was strange. No one seemed to take any notice. Even the men seemed to take no more than a flick of a glance at the girls. Such a sight would definitely create more of a stir in the UK...

Bine and Jonny took us out to a party at a Wildlife Reserve in one of the canyons in the foothills around LA. These hills amazed me.

They are dryly beautiful and houses are sited on the steep slopes, each defying gravity. Yet this is a major earthquake zone. I'd not have liked to sleep in one, despite the stunning views one would wake up to. The Topanga Canyon loop was a ride that introduced us to roads that whirl through the hills just to the north of LA, changing rapidly from double lane to single lane. It's a motorcyclist's dream that had us scooting off down the side roads in full 'explore' mode.

Mollie Hogan's Wildworks Centre is aimed at preserving mountain cats, most of which seem to have been hunted almost out of existence in many parts of the USA. The staff explained that sadly, the cats are much misunderstood. They compete for the land with humans, and horror stories abound about them. They are also considered to be good sport for hunters. How similar these tales were to stories we'd heard about predators in so many other parts of the world. Wild tigers in India? Not many now. Indian Cheetahs? They were hunted out of existence decades ago.

Many of the animals at Wildworks come from captivity and are just too far removed from the wild to be released back into it. But this does give them a chance to survive and to help educate the public about them. The bulk of the people at the party seemed to have bucked the American system. They were all alternative thinkers and many volunteered large portions of time to help the project work.

The party also enabled us to meet one of America's few genuine horse whisperers. Sol Spitz is a tall, lean man whose woolly grey hair shot out from the sides of his head in complete abandon. I quietly thought to myself that he looked as if he had just stuck his fingers in a power socket! I'd heard of the 'Horse Whisperer' movie, though I'd never seen it, so I was able to listen to the guy with a fresh mind and I was intrigued by what he said and soon understood why he prefers the description 'Animal Behaviourist'. I didn't see Sol Spitz at work with the animals but to me, as a mere human, his voice and mannerisms were quite hypnotic. He was treated with complete reverence by the others at the party. I later found out that he'd been the man behind the scenes looking after and 'guiding' the animals in some Hollywood movies.

And there was another bonus to staying with Bine and Jonny. They told us about Golden Eagle Passes. For $50 we could buy a pass and from then on we'd have free entry into the National Parks. As most parks seemed to have entry fees of between ten and twenty dollars it'd only take a couple of visits for us to have covered the outlay.

The final bonus in LA came from a visit to a bookshop. There we discovered two books that were going to save us a fortune over the coming months, and were going to lead us to some delightfully deserted spots. These are two books that every traveller should try to get hold of. Guide to free Campgrounds tells you about a terrific number of free camping spots around the USA. (ISBN 0-937877-27-1). Some of the spots have long drop toilets; some have nothing at all, other than perhaps a circle of stones to make a wood fire in. None have showers, but many are beside rivers or streams. Few are easy to get to unless you have your own transport.

The second book listed cheap campsites all over the country. Most of which were under $10 a night and after our experience near the border, these books made us feel as if we'd discovered gold on the streets of the City of Angels.

The next choice to face us was, to head straight north up the west coast, or to do some meandering in our usual style? We waved our goodbyes to Bine and Jonny, and with an 'Oh, what the hell' thought, we headed inland towards Death Valley. After all, with a name like that, how could we miss it? And by now, we'd got hold of road maps that would get us off anything remotely like a multi-lane freeway really quickly. We'd use the freeways if we felt that somehow we'd dawdled too long somewhere, or if we had no choice because they were the only sensible way to go. The rest of the time we were going to hit as many different types of roads as we could string together. This was going to be fun. We felt really optimistic. The campsite books were going to help our budget, we could stay off the busy roads and the vastness of what was supposed to be a beautiful and diverse land stretched before us. We knew it was a big journey to be had. 'Bring it on' we thought.

Another bonus was that we'd discovered special offers in the supermarkets. Two for one, three for the price of two, and the 'almost out of date' shelves. Fantastic! We stocked up on cheap tuna, discount sweet corn, two bags of pasta, two bags of rice, two packets of biscuits, powdered milk, herbs, and muesli that was packed to the re-sealable closer with brazil and hazel nuts, raisins, apricots, wheat, oats and not a sign of added sugar anywhere. Fuel prices were still a shock after the south, but even so it was incredibly cheap compared to Europe so we had no complaints. We left LA on April 14th and summer seemed to begin. The freeway no longer scared us and with clear blue skies above us, the horizon beckoned. We were on the road again, and free.

Chapter Nine

Wild Horses in the Sunset

'When you travel, remember that a foreign country is not designed to make
you comfortable. It is designed to make its own people comfortable.'

Clifton Fadiman

From LA, we got onto Highway 14 and headed for Death Valley
in the Mojave Desert (Say: 'Mo-Hah-Vay'). This desert covers a vast
area of southern California and spreads across into the neighbouring
states of Nevada, Utah and Arizona – 25,000 square miles of it in all.

Once we hit the dry I started to feel at home. The Mojave is
well known for the famous Joshua Trees that grow nowhere else, and

 these trees made me think of alien beings from
science-fiction movies. The long, stubbly
branches, with their spiky-leaved tops, reach
skywards from the lower sections of the
trunks as if they are pleading to be allowed to
live. And they are under threat. Climate
change is altering the Mojave to such an extent that the Joshua trees,
which can be hundreds, even thousands of years old, are beginning
to struggle to survive.

The Mojave is also well known for its amazing spread of military
bases. Edwards Air Force Base, Fort Irwin, and the China Lake Naval
Weapons Base are just three of the key ones. We skirted the El Paso
Mountains and rode past miles of not a lot. Sporadic clusters of houses,
a gas station and a shop here and there showed that people did scrape
a living from the passing traffic. The road seemed to be another of those
that most people only drove on the way to somewhere else. That suited
us fine. The traffic was minimal and no one seemed to be in a hurry.
That meant we had some great thinking time to ride with.

In a car, I often reach the end of a journey and realise that there
are significant chunks of it that I can't remember at all. That rarely
happens on a bike. A car's glass and metal insulates me from the world
and with that insulation I find it's dangerously easy to be somewhere

completely different with my thoughts. A friend once said to me that to him, driving a car was like watching a movie, but riding a motorcycle was like being in one. I knew exactly what Mark meant and suspected that this wonderful sensation is something that all motorcyclists have in common.

But you can almost ride these sorts of roads on autopilot. This gently undulating road had my thoughts two-wheeling through different worlds. I thought about the relationship I had with my bike. Over the years she had changed from being a feared 'it' to an old friend whom I understood and could read. I knew whether she was happy or not from her sounds and vibrations. On good days she'd have me humming the Beach Boys 'Good Vibrations'. What a great riding song that is. I knew from the way she handled whether or not she liked the road we were on, and I loved the way that we seemed to be in tune. There had been no 'her and me' for a long time – it was just 'us' when we were on the move.

I thought about the relationship I now had with Birgit. When we'd met in New Zealand, neither of us had been on the hunt for a partner, far from it. She was riding a bicycle through the country for six months and as Libby was back in Australia with a broken shaft drive, I was hitching and working my way around for three months. But we'd got on amazingly well and for once around a girl, I wasn't tongue-tied. In fact I actually seemed to be able to say the right things at the right time. But our paths were completely different and we both knew it. At the end of her trip she'd headed back to Germany to take up her first post after leaving university. By that time I was back in Australia and heading north to Indonesia.

We'd stayed in touch though and soon, one of the most important things I wanted to do each day was to write to her. And one of the first stops I made in any town was the post office to see if there was a letter from her. This couldn't go on and I wrote to ask her if she'd like me to fly to Germany for a couple of weeks. In part I just wanted to see her, to be with her and to laugh with her. But I also wanted to see if the way we'd got on together in New Zealand was just a traveller's mirage.

It hadn't been, and when she joined me as a pillion passenger in Nepal and India, we knew we could travel together, and that we wanted to be together. So I asked her if she'd come to South America with me. She replied, "Yes, I'll come with you, but on two conditions: I want to go to Africa first and, I want to ride my own bike."

She'd started our ride in Africa with just 600 miles of motorcycling experience and had never ridden a dirt road before. That was even less experience than I'd had when I started out. It was then that I'd discovered what a determined and plucky lass she is. It'd taken us quite a long time to get used to being together and to be able to complement each other's travelling styles. But when we finally 'clicked' it was as if, all of a sudden, we'd become a well-oiled machine. And we still laughed a lot. I'd actually enjoyed travelling on my own. I'd loved being able to wake up in the morning and wonder selfishly what I wanted to do that day. This 'I' changed to 'we' and I stopped being a selfish two-wheeled hermit. The joy of travelling with someone I cared about and got on well with became ever stronger. And it was a very fine thing to have someone there to help me pick my bike up when I dropped it! But the real pleasures came from planning together what we were going to do next, and from sharing conversations and observations about the amazing things we were getting involved with along the way. Sometimes we needed no words. It was enough to be sitting side by side, staring out at an amazing view together. The looks of appreciation that passed between us were more than enough. We also learned from each other and protected each other. Border crossings were far easier with two people. We spotted danger in advance and avoided, or wriggled out of it faster when the two of us were together. Our natures complimented each other. In many ways we are quite different and between us we always seemed to find the right technique to deal with a situation. We made more friends than I'd have made on my own too. In part because many people we talked to would never have got into conversations with a hairy, bearded bloke who looked travel-worn and probably smelled a bit of road grime. But also because travelling with Birgit gave me a type of confidence that hadn't been there when I was on my own.

The Chinese philosopher Lao Tzu once wrote, 'Being deeply loved by someone gives you strength, while loving someone deeply gives you courage.' For the first time in my life I really understood what he meant.

The freedom of the road also had me thinking about the early settlers who had traversed this desert with their horse, ox or mule-drawn wagons. Our ride must have been a total contrast. I'd read once that these mid-19th century wagon trains often managed no more than a few miles a day. This thought jerked me back to the surroundings. Having seen lots of cowboy and indian movies, and now seeing the land for real, I could easily imagine how harsh life must have been for the people in those wagons.

The history of Death Valley includes many tales of families, prospectors and miners who tried to make it across this, one of the

hottest and driest parts of the US. The most famous is perhaps the story of the Bennett-Arcane party. They had been on their way to California during the gold rush of 1849 and took the valley to save time. Their story is horrific. Unable to find a way out of the valley, this group of a hundred or so wagons, wandered around for weeks with their water and food running out. They ended up having to eat many of their draught animals and some tales say they had to drink the blood of their oxen in the attempt to survive. (The Masai tribe in Kenya would have approved, since their diet consists largely of blood drunk from the necks of their living cattle.) In fact, only one person in the Bennett-Arcane group died and he, by all accounts, was half-dead even before they entered the valley. The name Death Valley reputedly comes from one of this party. She is supposed to have looked back and to have said, "Goodbye death valley." The name stuck. One reason they survived was that they made their attempt in winter when the temperatures normally only range between 18 and 32 degrees Celsius (64 to 90 F) and many of the surrounding mountains have snow. This means that springs form in the bottom of the valley and though often brackish, the water is supposed to be drinkable. Death Valley also contains the lowest point in North America, at a place called Badwater. The spring there, when it exists, is 86 metres below sea level and the guide books say that out of the three million acres of land, nearly 550 square miles of it are below sea level.

We were heading for the free campsite at a place prettily called Wild Rose. Having paid our entry fee into the park and read up a little on what we could expect to find, our plans were suddenly dashed. The campsite was closed. And to add spice to the day, we were told that the very bit of road we were standing on had just been seriously contaminated by radioactivity! What we couldn't understand was why nuclear items were being transported through the National Park, but we supposed it had something to do with the local military bases. To an outsider, doing this seemed odd.

We rode on in a hurry. Before us stretched a long straight road that swooped right down into the bottom of the valley. In the distance, craggy cliffs and canyons gave the whole scene a backdrop of whites and dull reds. Spiky sagebrush struggled to survive on the sand and gravel roadsides and there was a horny lizard who, chameleon-like, raised a sandy coloured foot as if to welcome us.

We knew that at one time this had been an inlet from the sea and then with a change in land mass it had become a lake in which rivers and streams ended up. The combination of these factors had made the valley a source of salts and minerals, some of which were plentiful. Borax was one, but in spite of the occasional gold strikes, there had never been very much there to make man want to live in the valley. Indigenous Indians had survived there as hunter gatherers, but they had retreated up into the mountains during the summers. I didn't blame them. The temperatures could get up to 49 degrees Celsius (120 Fahrenheit). For us, the main reason for being there was to enjoy the starkly unique landscape, and to see the strange effects of salt, wind and heat.

Down by Badwater the land looked as if a mad ploughman had been let loose and the clumps of crusty soil he'd left behind all appeared to have been dusted with frost. In fact, had we not been standing sweating buckets in our bike gear, we could easily have been looking out over a winter scene. It was a 'mind tease' and because of that, well worth seeing. So too were the rocks that move – this is a 'field' where it's thought that the wind is channelled so strongly it actually pushes the rocks across the landscape. As they move, each one leaves a sort of trail, rather how I imagined the marks mini comets would leave if they struck earth a glancing blow. The rocks in the field are so regularly placed and so similarly tailed that it really doesn't look natural at all.

We ended up camping at the Furnace Creek site, which hammered our budget but the bonus was that we met Rudi and Bettina, or rather, Rudi met us. No sooner had we pulled up than he was heading across from his RV with a couple of cold beers for us. Rudi had been a motorcycle traveller before he'd married Bettina, who wasn't at all sure about this travelling lark. They were heading down into Central and South America with their RV. Rudi later told us that it felt very strange but he really wanted to do this trip and if an RV was what it took, then so be it. As he thrust the icy cans of beer into our hands he said, "When I was on my bike, people often did such things for me. I swore that I would do the same for overlanders whenever I saw them. Enjoy!" Excellent. It was almost as if he'd read our minds and the pure generosity of his thought was something that we enjoyed even more than the beer. What a wonderful idea.

One of the things I liked about Death Valley was that the area had helped the United States pull itself out of the great depression of the 1930s. As part of his attempt to create employment and therefore revitalise the economy, President Hoover had set up companies to build 800 kilometres of roads and tracks through the valley, the very roads that we'd been enjoying.

We cut across to Highway 95 and headed for Las Vegas. This was another iconic image of the USA that I had in my mind, so I had to see it for myself. The sensible side of me knew that it wasn't all going to be glitz and glamour but I really wanted to see this desert city of lost souls and pure greed. I couldn't think of any place I'd been to that even came close to having the reputation that Las Vegas has. It represented a side of the United States that seemed to be in perverse contrast to the way that I understood most Americans liked to think of themselves.

At Indian Springs, we had a reprieve though. With the way the day's riding was going, we'd be arriving in Las Vegas at night. This is one of the few loathsome things about overlanding for me. The night makes me feel as if one of my main senses has been lost or at least, significantly dulled. It feels as if I am riding almost blind. I feel disoriented and decidedly vulnerable when I have to ride into a big city in the dark. I can't see what's happening in the shadows, I get dazzled by the lights, I miss the road signs and my sense of distance sucks. Birgit is even worse and on the few occasions when we'd had to ride into a town in the dark, I'd feared for her.

We'd just stopped to fill up with fuel and were wondering how the day was going to end, when a man in a work-worn dull brown pick-up pulled up alongside us. He wore a battered beige cowboy hat

 above a pair of twinkling blue eyes, a close-clipped moustache and a flash of healthy white teeth. "Where are you guys going t'day?" he questioned. Normally I would be instinctively evasive when asked this question by a complete stranger at this stage of a days ride, but this guy had something genuine about him. Every ounce of his body language said that he was a nice guy and no threat at all. So I answered, "Las Vegas, but we are going to try to find somewhere to camp beforehand so we don't arrive in the dark."

"Then I've got just the place for you. I can see you guys don't mind riding on the dirt. If you ride a couple of miles towards Vegas, you'll find a dirt road that heads up into the hills. It'll be just on your right. Follow this for about five miles and then you'll come to a fork in the road by an old house. Go to the right there until you get to the next fork – you'll know it from the burnt tree. Go right again and that trail will take you down to a valley with a stream running through it. It's a great spot and wild horses sometimes roam through the valley." Amazing. That would do very nicely. We smiled our thanks and he drove off in the opposite direction, tipping his hat a little in Birgit's direction before he left. "Ma'am" he said with a nod at her as he did so.

His directions were perfect, though he hadn't mentioned that the final trail was rough enough to be more suitable for lightweight dirt bikes than a pair of heavily laden BMW twins. But the stream he'd mentioned tumbled down through the rolling grassy sides of the valley, and there were plenty of level places where we could put the tent. We found a great spot tucked out of sight behind a small clump of trees and pitched camp. An hour or so later, as the sun was beginning to fall over the end of the valley, turning the violets, sages and greens of the hills into shadowy dusty reds and oranges, a group of horses appeared. The lead horse, a black, white and brown 'paint', pawed the ground and sniffed the air. We were downwind but perhaps he thought he'd heard us talking to each other. I doubt he could see us but he was on his guard as the other horses, a couple of which were wobbly-legged foals, set to grazing the stream's

 banks, or to drinking from the gently flowing water. We held our breath. This sight felt like a pure gift. Never had I imagined that we would be sitting in a place such as this, surrounded by wild horses. The now brilliant orange sun made the perfect backdrop as the milling horses kicked up small clouds of dust as they fed and drank. This was the real Wild West as far as I was concerned. The horses did their thing and we sat silently watching their peaceful movements. It was almost as if, to the horses, we weren't there at all. Slowly they began to head downstream, feeding as they went and before long they disappeared into the deep red that the last of the sun had cast over the land. Then suddenly it was night and the stars were appearing above us. We didn't need anything else at that moment. Life was pretty much as perfect as it could get.

The wild horses hammered any desire I had to see Las Vegas. We still rode into the city the next day but the place held little interest after the previous night. I was much more at home in the countryside than the city. We camped the night on a site on the outskirts of Las Vegas but I couldn't even be bothered to ride the bike, luggage-free, into the city for a look-see. Birgit had been there before when she'd hitchhiked around the States in her teens, so she was in no hurry to go in either. We might have made a mistake, but at that moment, leaving Las Vegas alone felt like the right thing to do.

I still felt a bit confused. I'd thought that Mexico had been big, but the sheer hugeness of the United States had finally hit me. I just couldn't work out how we were possibly going to do our visit justice with the money we had left, and still get up to Alaska. We were still in the late spring so time wasn't short yet but working out what we had time to see and do was a quandary.

I was also having some rather perturbing thoughts that were weighing on me like a dark and heavy sky. It worried me that US policies had such a profound effect on the rest of the world when so many Americans, including their leaders, seemed to be so ill-informed about the world outside the USA. Prior to arriving in the USA I'd sometimes found myself wondering why on earth US policy makers had made decisions that seemed so illogical, but had accepted that I wasn't seeing the whole picture. But this feeling was then brought into mind as a result of some of the people we'd been meeting in the United States. A woman asked Birgit if it was possible to get drinking water from the taps in Germany; another was a man who was certain that all Africans lived in squalor and was convinced that if he went there, he'd be shot, simply for being American. Then there was the guy who was surprised to hear that Afghanistan wasn't located in North Africa. I was baffled by the fact that we seemed to keep on meeting people who knew next to nothing about the outside world.

How could the US decision makers be helped to make the right plans where the future of the world is concerned, if many of the people who had put them in a position of power had such slim and even incorrect knowledge? How could American people judge whether what was being done in their names was right and just, if an apparently large number knew so little?

In my own ignorance I'd assumed that Americans would be well informed about what happened in the world beyond their own borders. After all, they had the ability to influence and even 'police' much of the world. It seemed to me that if there was a crisis going on in the world somewhere, then representatives of the USA would be there, either trying to keep the peace or trying to help. Perhaps I was being unfair with my assumptions. Many people in the UK know little about what really happens around our world, but I was struck by just how many people in the USA knew next to nothing about the outside world.

On the Las Vegas campsite, I asked one of our neighbours about this. Earl was a large man with a rounded face that had once probably  been handsome but now showed the signs of age, and a life outdoors. The corners of his eyes crinkled, which said that his straight and rather hard mouth was more than likely not a true reflection of who he was. Despite the heat, Earl was dressed in heavy blue jeans and a long sleeved cotton shirt. He was wearing heavy, sand-coloured CAT workman's boots and had topped off this outfit with a baseball cap which had an embroidered Coors beer logo on the front. He stood with his feet firmly planted wide apart on the sandy pathway, looking solid and fixed as if he had grown there. He creased his straight lips into a sort of smile and rather condescendingly said, "Son, why should I learn about things outside of the good old US of A when everything I need is here? It would take me more than my lifetime to see everything we have on our own doorstep. And if I think that, why the hell should I waste my time learning about places I have no interest in and have no reason to git to?" I could see his point but what about his responsibility to the rest of the world?

It was the size and wealth of his country that really gave his politicians so much influence in the rest of the world. I asked him,

"But doesn't it worry you that if you don't know what they are doing, then you have no control over your politicians?" "Hell no," he replied. "I vote. That's good enough for me." It seemed that it didn't matter to him what his party was up to, he belonged and if they said something was right, then it must be. He had a sense of duty, but did he understand what that duty was? John F. Kennedy once said, 'The ignorance of one voter in a democracy impairs the security of all.'

It is human nature to take the value of things from the face we are shown, isn't it? And, what doesn't appear to affect our lives directly and immediately, isn't prominent in our consciousness. We'd not seen much TV in the States, but what I'd watched with intent was the news. The programmes had been a real disappointment. After riding the back-roads of countries whose languages I wasn't fluent in, I was hungry for world news. What was happening out there? But all there seemed to be were 'sound bites' of information, a lot of which didn't sit well with what I already knew.

I couldn't help feeling that too many people in the US were living with worldwide blinkers on. I also worried that they weren't the only ones. I thought about some of the people I knew at home, and my mind flicked back to the thoughts I'd had in Mexico about the EZLN 'bandits' or 'freedom fighters' (take your pick). Perhaps this was a problem for all those living in the developed world.

The American journalist H.L.Mencken once wrote, 'The men the American people admire most extravagantly are the most daring liars; the men they detest most violently are those who try to tell them the truth.' Was this a problem for people in the first world in general? We don't want to hear the bad news. Or we hear it and don't take any notice. Or perhaps we are all so jaded by the over-hyped and scandalous way that bad news is presented to us, that we have lost any perspective we had. Perhaps we only hear the news that we want to hear, and only then because it fits in with our pre-conceived ideas.

We'd travelled in countries where the British weren't much liked, but in others where there had been admiration. This contradiction of thoughts from people had applied to the USA too. I'd also found a genuine distaste in some countries towards the politicians of a powerful country, but an open-mindedness towards the ordinary citizens of that same nation. For example, a surprising number of Iranians told me that they'd like to shoot American politicians on sight, but that grass roots Americans would be very welcome. In some countries, the 'Iron Lady' Margaret Thatcher was admired hugely, and in others she was despised as a selfish meddler.

Being in the US, my thoughts were concentrated on Americans. I was beginning to wonder if one day a group of people who had grown fundamentally discontented were going to bite them hard and Americans would be standing there confused and wondering why on earth they hadn't seen the situation coming. (This was two years before the cataclysmic events of '9/11' changed American perspectives forever).

The way I understand it, one of the final stages in the downfall of an empire is that the people turn against the politicians who have led them into a dangerous state of ignorance and misunderstanding. A  climactic event suddenly shocks people into seeing through the greedy, selfish, often self-centred men and women who have gained positions of relatively unassailable power, and they start to trust no-one but themselves and the people they know well. The people's feelings of betrayal combine with ingrained corruption in the system, the vital foundations are eaten away and the empire crumbles. But those who suffer most are not those fat cats who have stashed away huge amounts of cash and long since made escape routes. It's the ordinary person.

It feels to me that several things are required to make a democracy work. People must be participants and not just observers. They must demand a system that does not allow ingrained corruption. The press must be free and must resist selling over-hyped scandal – 'making' the news. And education must be wide and deep.

But I knew that I was missing some points; I wasn't seeing everything that I needed to in order to have a full understanding of where I was. I knew for sure that if I was an American, living in America, having been brought up with very little genuine contact with the outside world, the chances were that I'd be blinkered too. Little did I know that by the time I returned to the UK, I'd find that world news would have been cut to a minimum on television, unless scandal or disaster were involved. Hype would rule and 'celebrity news' would have been inexplicably promoted to having, apparently, world-shattering importance.

It is so easy to stand on the outside of something and look in. It is also very easy to be critical and to believe that you understand what you see and therefore have the right to make comments. The reality is that there are always more questions to be asked. Inevitably there is more to any situation than any visitor can see in a brief period of time. You have to live in a place to have any chance of a real understanding. But when we are in that situation, how many of us do actually question what we see?

I really hoped that when I got home again, I would remember these thoughts and keep them fresh in my mind. One of the problems with the end of a long journey is that too soon, society requires you to swim in the same direction as everyone else. I hoped that before I allowed this to happen to me, I'd be able to take a long hard look at my own country, with the fresh eyes of a visitor. I wondered what I'd learn. How many of the thoughts I was having about the situation in the US I'd be having at home too. I wondered if I'd still like England.

I also asked myself if I was being prejudiced. I'd fought against having preconceived ideas as we'd ridden into the USA. I had hoped that after all the years of travel I was open-minded enough not to let preconceived ideas take over. But now I realised that I was failing. I'd arrived in the USA with thoughts that had been formed by a few personal experiences, and a vast stream of anti-American media-led publicity (the film and TV culture in the US has a lot to answer for. To my mind they paint a very specific image of the country to the rest of the world – drugs, gangs, guns, mobs, corruption, lack of moral fibre…). And not only that, I was expecting human beings to be perfect. I was shocked at how powerfully negative this combination was. I realised that in fact, I was not being open-minded at all, but I was allowing myself to see and hear the negative things that I expected to hear and see. My prejudice was leading me towards them.

I knew that I must not let this way of thinking take over, or the rest of my time in the country was doomed to cynicism and ultimate failure. What a waste that would be.

Standing back from my prejudice, I actually really liked being in the USA, so far. This was a beautiful and rugged land that really  stirred something deep within me. It made me feel wonderfully alive. Also, most of the American people we had talked with by this time had been friendly and apparently genuine. There had been lots of weird things going on, but that's one of the points of travel isn't it, to learn and to experience? I also admired the way that the people would do things collectively.

The whole concept and tradition of 'barn building', for example, was something to be appreciated and respected. If a farmer needed a new barn, then it seemed that it was quite normal for all the neighbours to get together to help build the barn. They'd work for free and make a huge party out of it, knowing that when they too needed a 'barn' to be built, there would be plenty of people to help out and to make hard work into something that was sociable and fun. We'd already seen the equivalents of this tradition on many occasions during our time in the US and I liked what I was seeing. I liked the 'can do' attitude.

I wanted now to be an observer and to learn from the things that I came into contact with, rather than give credence to things that were just loaded with disruptive intent; things that were, perhaps, no more than mere wisps of smoke that had been fanned into flames in my mind.

One of my more comfortable preconceived ideas was that this nation had been founded on good intent, not just greed, ignorance and paranoia. I had the notion that the gene pool of the American people was teeming with hard working and courageous instincts.

 Perhaps this was the reality of current times. Maybe the real face of the United States of America was strong, honest and vigorous. I just had to look for the positive.

With this thought an amazing sense of freedom came over me, as if my own blinkers had suddenly been removed. I revelled in the feeling that I now had the chance to see things without tainted thoughts getting in the way. I felt as if I'd suddenly opened my eyes; really opened them.

I also reminded myself that there were many places in the world where expressing these thoughts in word or speech could have put my life at risk. I was lucky to be able to travel through a country that allowed itself to be discussed openly.

And I could understand my neighbour's point about there being so much to see on his own doorstep. I really didn't want to get to the end of our time in the US and then be saying, 'What if?' and 'I wish we had done such and such....'.

Perhaps the reason the 'what-to-do' decision seemed so daunting now was because the United States of America is just so big; it's overwhelming. Perhaps it would make more sense to think about each state as if it were a different country.

Thinking about the country this way helped. It also helped when we accepted that we weren't going to see half the things that the States had to offer. We'd simply see what we could and take our time about it. I was also suddenly really conscious of the fact that we'd been very lucky to get six month multiple-entry visas from the US Embassy in Panama City. Perhaps I'd understand more and my worried thoughts would settle down with more knowledge and experience of a country that had already impressed me immensely. I already knew that it wasn't just the geography that impressed me so much; it was the resilience and the generosity of the people too.

With those thoughts in mind we thought, "Let's go to Bryce Canyon, the Grand Canyon and Monument Valley. Then let's go and see Joe, Sarah and the kids". We'd last seen them when they were based way down in Chile's capital city, Santiago. They'd moved home to the Denver area while we were riding through South and Central America. Their being back in the States was a big bonus for us. The plan was made and when we ignored Lake Mead, I felt absolutely fine about it.

But we couldn't just ride past the Zion National Park. We would just pop in, we told ourselves. In our ignorance, we'd underestimated how cold this area was going to be in the late spring. We'd been used to full-on heat for far too long to be able to adapt quickly to the chill of these mountain roads. We couldn't afford more bike clothes, so our leather and rain jackets would have to do on the outside, but we could afford some more warm layers on the inside by taking advantage of 'yard sales'. Neither of us had come across them before. They are a simple way by which Americans get rid of items they no longer need and make a few dollars at the same time. This works well for everyone and I couldn't understand why we Europeans hadn't adopted the same system. In England we now do the same thing communally at 'car boot sales' (an idea we have pinched from the US) but in America people often have a sale in their own front garden, or 'yard' as they call it.

All you had to do was to pile everything you wanted to get rid of, on or around a few trestle tables or stacked cardboard boxes, hang out a Yard Sale sign and wait for people to turn up. The beauty of this is that there appears to be no social stigma attached to yard sale shoppers. You are just being thrifty. Well, we understood that concept and Birgit and I rode away laden down with second hand fleeces and plaid shirts; just what we needed. They cost us buttons and we had a great chat with the Yard Salers and their customers.

The next issue was where to camp. The Zion park campsite was full to bursting and several dollars too expensive, but on the way to the park entrance we'd seen a couple of RVs pulled off the road amongst some trees. Perhaps that was a campsite we didn't know about and perhaps there'd be room for us. There'd been no campsite sign by the roadside so we weren't sure, but it was worth a look.

This was how we discovered free camping on State Forestry Commission land. US Law says that you can do this and though there are seldom any facilities, we didn't care a jot. The river would do for

 washing and we knew all about burying our waste so it caused no grief for anyone else, and didn't pollute the land. Tucked in amongst the trees were the two RVs and a scattering of small tents. Perfect, and no one made us feel as if we were invading anyone's territory. The cool, fast-flowing Virgin river was the ideal spot to bathe and we washed wearing our swimming gear so as not to offend anyone.

Zion is an American gem. The winding roads take you through a spectacular cliff and canyon landscape. The sheer, vividly-red cliffs tower above the road, which was surprisingly busy. We shared the roads with RVs, cars, cyclists and hikers. We parked up to do some hiking. This would be the first time we'd done any real walking for a considerable time and I wondered how our bikers' muscles would cope. I'd long realised that I'd developed a set of muscles that could cope with just about anything from the saddle of a bike but hiking was going to be a very different ball game. Fortunately, none of the main trails were too hard going and they took us winding along past a swamp, a petrified forest and waterfalls, and then right up into the canyon's Emerald Pools. The sun shone brightly on us.

Heading for the Grand Canyon we stopped off to use our Golden Eagle pass at Bryce Canyon. It had a spectacular landscape that looked as if God had sat down to embroider the land with cream, gold and pink filigree, but I still preferred Zion. In any case, my mind was focused more on thoughts of the Grand Canyon.

The last time I'd seen anywhere comparable was way back in Namibia. Fish River Canyon is second only to the Grand Canyon in size and I'd been awed by that, so I had high expectations. But the weather was a worry. It suddenly turned very cold and the night before we left Zion, it rained so hard we discovered that our tent wasn't waterproof anymore. The forecast posted on the notice board at Bryce said that the weather was going to worsen and we knew that we'd be heading higher into the mountains as we neared the Grand Canyon. What to do? Suck it and see, we decided. Fingers crossed it wouldn't rain and at least in the tent we'd be out of the wind. I uneasily put off the thought that perhaps we were going to have to stump up for a new tent. This one had kept us safe and dry on two continents. It had protected us from a Force 8 storm, had kept out squadrons of biting insects and had provided us with shady protection from the outside world whenever we'd needed it.

Other campers on the Virgin River told us of a free site on the east rim of the Grand Canyon. To get there we took the turning off towards the Canyon at the Jacob Lake junction, and then rode south towards the north rim. The directions were spot on and we soon found ourselves bumping up a rough dirt track, which, after a few more jinks and turn-offs, led us to the site. Two RVs and three tents were there already, so we knew we'd found the right place. There wasn't a soul around so we picked a spot as far away from anyone else as we could, and pitched the tent within a few metres of the edge of the canyon. "We'd better not sleepwalk here." I said to Birgit. "If you get up in the night for a pee, you'd better have a torch. That looks a very long way down."

By the time we had the tent pitched amongst the pine trees, an icy and very persistent wind was zipping around us. It was so cold that Birgit retreated straight into the tent. What we needed was a hot meal and an early night snuggled into our sleeping bags. Hopefully the weather would change for the better in the night.

I fired up our petrol stove and set about cooking tuna, onions, garlic, mixed herbs and a mushroom soup mix to act as a sauce with our pasta. I huddled over the stove, not caring about the petrol fumes I was breathing in. As I was doing so, we heard a strange sound, strange for this place anyway. Moments later a Harley-Davidson cruiser bumped into the camping area. We'd worked a bit to get our bikes up the track, so how had these guys made it on their low-slung Harley-Davidson Police Special? The bike stopped about 50 metres away, and the riders stared across at us. I felt a little intimidated. Birgit, who had popped her head out of the tent to see what was going on, retreated straight back inside, but still watched as the bike set off again in the direction of one of the tents. The riders were clad head to toe in black leathers. One, a blond girl, set to opening up their tent. The guy though, straightened himself up to a good six foot and started to walk towards us across the clumpy sodden grass. He had jet-black hair and at least three days of stubble under his thick black Mexican-style moustache. He seemed to glower at us as his rolling gait brought him closer. At any other time, this walk would have looked gentle and almost lazy, but now it seemed full with measured, dangerous intent. Not a hint of a smile of greeting crossed his face. Had we offended him somehow? Were we too close to his tent, in spite of our best efforts? Birgit disappeared fully into the tent saying, "It's your turn. You talk to him." With that she pulled the flaps shut and left me to face the guy, who was nearly upon us. He stood above me and for a moment stared straight at me with a look that seemed to read danger. I'd heard about American biker gangs and was absolutely certain that this guy was a gang member. I'd no doubt that we were in trouble.

Then he spoke. With a quiet drawl he said, "Hey, my name's Peter. That's Peggy over there. We saw your bikes. You guys seem to have come a long way. How are you doing?" I breathed a sigh of relief and felt stupid. My blasted preconceived ideas had got the better of me yet again. How could I be so daft? I knew better than this. Never, ever judge a book by its cover! How many times was I going to need this lesson to be drummed into me? That night, after dinner, in celebration of our 'lucky' escape, we downed steaming mugs of coffee laced with brandy. In the morning, Peter and Peggy invited us to join them for breakfast at the Grand Canyon Lodge. There, over an 'all you can eat' breakfast, which they insisted on treating us to, we made a couple of good friends who were to play an important part in our American lives.

During breakfast Birgit kicked me under the table and whispered, "I've done most of the talking through South America. It's your turn now." She spent the next hour saying almost nothing, but putting away a huge amount of food. American breakfasts are legendary and Birgit managed to do this one complete justice. She surprised me at the quantity of bacon, eggs, pancakes, syrup, hash browns, coffee and toast that she managed to consume. Who cared that a cold wind was still blowing outside?

Peggy had an absolutely infectious giggle that slipped out so often that she frequently had Birgit and me laughing along. Peter never seemed to smile or laugh, but in spite of his straight face, he seemed quite happy. We felt a real sense of loss as they climbed on their bike and set off for home.

We spent the rest of the day walking and riding around the various sights and viewpoints. The canyon certainly deserves its title of 'Grand' and in fact the cold was just a bonus for those of us who were stomping around wearing bike kit. Perhaps these lower temperatures weren't so bad after all. But in the night it snowed.

We woke with the 5am dawn to find the tent sagging oddly and then we realised that the world around us seemed strangely quiet. The wind had gone and the heavy fall of snow was muffling everything in a slightly surreal way. I felt as if my ears needed to pop, as if I'd just dropped down from altitude.

Chapter Ten

Dinosaurs and Ghost Towns

'When the going gets tough, don't give up.'

Ray Mears

We needed to get down to lower roads and fast. We were just not kitted out to deal with these sorts of conditions and I dislike the cold intensely. I don't seem to function well in freezing temperatures; my body wants to hibernate, I don't think clearly and the joys of life seem a long way away. But Birgit was revelling in it. She's the sort of person who wants to leap around and make snowballs and snow angels. I'd not heard of snow angels before but watching Birgit having fun in the snow made me smile. To make an angel she laid down on her back in the snow, with her feet together and her arms by her sides. Slowly she brought her arms up above her head, scooping the snow across the ground as she did so. Then she moved her legs outwards. These two movements altered her outline in the snow to add on wings and an angel's skirt.

Birgit sees a beautiful world that is made up of soft, brilliant, white and contrasting dark shadows. She notices spiders' cobwebs that have collected frozen snow, turning them into giant, multi-stringed snowflakes that hang in limbo, never seeming to fall to earth. She sees the setting for traditional Christmas cards and seems to have a mental log fire burning within her that keeps her impervious to the cold.

The cold makes me behave like a grumpy old man, or worse still, a petulant child. I don't like myself very much when it's cold. I stomped around shaking snow off the tent with increasingly frozen fingers. Even climbing into all my bike kit inside the tent didn't seem to have helped me to retain much warmth. I was sure that the dirt road back to the tarmac was going to be a slippery, rutted hell that my frozen fingers were going to make a pig's ear of. I knew I was going to fall off, but Birgit didn't seem to give a hoot. She mouthed, "Bring it on", to me with a cheeky smile.

I didn't fall off and neither did she, but the effort of keeping upright warmed me up enough that by the time we got to the end of the dirt I felt a little more at one with the world. My feet were the only things that were really warm though. For once the heat that radiated from the horizontal cylinder fins of the BMW's boxer engine was a blessing. In hot countries my feet were often bathed in sweat. Every cloud has a silver lining.

But the day didn't get any better. The Bryce Canyon forecast had been right. The cold weather was here to stay for a while. We stopped to pull on every layer of clothing we had and even Birgit had soon pulled on her silk balaclava. Our boots were wet through from the constant rain on the lower roads – the carrier bags we'd wrapped around them had ripped to shreds in the wind, and we were getting covered in mud every time we took a detour onto a track. We stopped regularly to warm our hands and gloves on the cylinder fins but within moments we were back into wet, cold, miserable riding. I couldn't remember the last time I'd felt so miserable. Even riding on black ice in the Turkish mountains in the middle of winter hadn't been as bad as this, had it? To make it worse, a strong wind was lashing the rain at us from the side and our misery was compounded by the effort of keeping the bikes heading in the right direction. My hands were hooked like claws around the handlebar grips and my teeth chattered horribly. Even singing Monty Python's 'Always look on the bright side of life…' didn't help. The thought of making it to the end of the day and having to climb wet and cold into a tent that leaked, lowered a cloud of pure gloom over me. I tried laughing at myself. "Come on you wimp, you've ridden nearly all the way round the world, you are tougher than this! Don't let it get to you." The last kilometres to Monument Valley were a grey disappointment. The bit of the valley that we could see from the road looked nothing like the pictures we'd seen, and the park's campsite looked like a windblown stretch of the moon that someone had dumped rubbish onto. At that moment, life sucked.

Being in the 'wrong' season for motorcycling was one of the new challenges we had to learn to deal with. Before North America we'd mostly been able to ride in front of the rains. We'd managed to be in most countries in their summers. We had copped the wrong weather in parts of South America when we'd had the enforced break in the journey because of my stint in hospital, but that blip had seemed insignificant. In the north I was growing to hate the cold, clammy feeling that came with the struggle that wet bike gear always enforces.

Feet disobediently get trapped on their way down soggy bike trousers, as if the insides of the trouser legs have been smeared with glue that never dries. Gloves are always a challenge. Pull off wet gloves and the finger linings always seemed to turn themselves inside out. Trying to get cold and numbed fingers to get those linings back into place was always a source of frustration. There were times when I was so frustrated by this hassle that I was tempted to ride without them. But I knew that would have been plain stupid.

In the morning I felt like a complete fool. Had yesterday really been as bad as all that? It had stopped raining just before we'd put the tent up, and the battle to get it up in the wind had rapidly warmed us. Our sleeping bags were still dry and the blasting flame from our cooker was strong enough to make it through the wind to cook a giant meal of rice, chopped up salami and sweet corn, washed down with an endless stream of piping hot cups of coffee. We'd finally warmed up and the world didn't seem so bad after all. We'd slept like the dead, able to completely ignore the wind's efforts to send the tent flying towards the horizon with us in it. The dawn gave us a day that had clear skies, the first warm rays of sunshine, and the sight of another biker. Patrick gave us a grin and a thumbs up as he was getting his big black Kawasaki Vulcan ready for the day's ride. Hot muesli for breakfast set the mood and soon the three of us set off into the valley to explore. The photographs we'd seen of the park beforehand simply had not done justice to the stunning landscape. To appreciate this place you just have to have a view all around and up and down!

Within moments of dropping down into the valley we were surrounded by tall, steep-sided, orange-red, mesas and buttes. I knew something about these proud, enduring, ever-changing formations from schoolboy geography lessons. Geography had been one of my favourite subjects and I'd always been fascinated by mesas and buttes. These giant structures are two of nature's marvels and riding amongst them made me feel quite insignificant. It had taken thousands of years for wind, rain, heat and cold to all play their part in creating them. The key was the layer of hard rock that had once covered the whole of the area. With land movement, cracks in this layer had appeared and then the elements had got to work. Over the years the sides of these cracks had been eaten into by the elements until small surface 'plates' of rock remained as caps to the free-standing towers of rock and sandstone.

I wasn't a biker anymore. The landscape had transformed me into a cowboy. There I was on my trusty steed cantering across a world that was red sand and blue sky with just a tinge of purple to the distant  towers. The only other colour was the vivid green from the occasional clumps of sage. The first time I'd seen this landscape was in the John Ford movie Stagecoach, but many Westerns since then have used sections of the valley for filming. I loved it. Feeling so insignificant seemed to allow me to retreat back into childhood. It really wasn't so hard to imagine that I was a lone rider trotting gently across the red sands.

I suddenly realised that I was singing. The song from the band America had popped into my head:

'I've been through the desert on a horse with no name

It felt good to be out of the rain

In the desert you can't remember your name

'Cause there ain't no one for to give you no pain

La, la …'

I couldn't remember all the words, but that didn't matter. I sang away to myself in the bubble of my helmet. Good job Birgit and Patrick couldn't hear me over the noise of their engines…

Patrick decided he'd like to ride with us for a while, so we set off together towards a road junction called 'Four Corners'. It was fun to have the three bikes riding as a mini convoy, and as we rode I sat watching the flickering, elongated shadows that the bikes threw across the tarmac. Each bike formed its own completely different shadow and I became so entranced by their speeding wavering shapes that I nearly hypnotised myself into falling off!

Four Corners is the only place in the USA where four states touch, those states being Utah, Arizona, New Mexico and Colorado. A brief visit felt like a notch to be etched into my newly-imagined gun belt.

We split up there, with Patrick heading south into New Mexico, while we turned north into Colorado and headed along Highway 160 towards the small town of Mancos. This town sits just 13 kilometres down the road from the entrance of the Mesa Verde National Park and as the park was on our roughly thought-out route towards Denver, it was on our list of 'must sees'.

Riding into the Mancos Valley made me think of travelling through the mountain-backed meadows of Switzerland. The town itself brought home to me just how young a nation the USA is.

Cattle ranchers didn't start to settle the valley until the 1870s, and it wasn't until 1894 that the wooden boardwalks were built along the main street, and laws were passed which outlawed such things as riding your horse fast, or driving your wagon at speed through the town.

1870 was also the date of the first international football match, between Scotland and England and the year that State Education was made free for every child in the UK. What a contrast.

Death Valley and places such as Mancos made me strongly aware of the huge leap forward that Americans had made in a very short space of time.

Mancos began to prosper and to develop when the Rio Grande Southern railway company built a station there but even now there are fewer than 300 families living there. It's a town with a real difference though. We didn't find any of the big shopping chains we'd already come to expect. Instead we found family-run stores, bakeries and artists' galleries. Mancos has the reputation of being the home of a large arts community and we liked it straight away. To learn more, we stopped off at the tourist office and there we met one of the most helpful Americans we were to come across. Bob, a tall slim man whose hair was just beginning to turn grey, had a gently lined face which gave you the instant feeling that he was a kind man. The clear-eyed and very intent gaze he settled on us showed his interest in the unusual. It was quickly obvious that Bob was passionate about the arts and a fringe way of life, and he made us feel at home right away. His manner was so warm and open that he made us feel as if he'd welcomed us into his own lounge at home, rather than just the tourist office. And he did actually end up inviting us back for dinner at his own house. How often does that happen to complete strangers? This town seemed like a great place to celebrate my birthday.

It was from Bob that we discovered that Mancos is the home of Western writer Louis L'Amour, whose books I loved and whose stories I'd had in my mind when we were riding through Monument Valley. Bob also told us about Boyle Park. This is a centre of activity for the town, where such things as the farmers' market is held and baseball games played. We could pitch our tent there and no one would mind at all. Perfect.

It had become rather urgent to find somewhere to stay too. Birgit's bike was giving her some real hassle. The ignition points on the bike just wouldn't settle down. She'd been having intermittent problems with them ever since Colombia where the bike's backfiring had become so powerful that it had blown the battered ends off her exhaust pipes. That time the only place we'd been able to find to stay had been a brothel. The 'madam' had been highly suspicious of us. She had then become interested in our mechanical efforts, but tried hard not to look as if she was, and then had become openly friendly in her own prim way. I say prim because she reminded me of a starched Victorian maiden aunt, which struck me as decidedly incongruous in her line of work.

Sir Henry was back to popping and blasting again and Birgit was battling to get him to produce an even ride. He lost power several times when it was quite dangerous to do so. Battling with the wind, as we had been for days, had become a real chore and it was all taking the gloss off the adventure for her.

With a safe place to stay, the sun shining and a workshop or two nearby if needed, we had the right conditions to try to sort the problem out. Birgit was carrying several spare sets of points and condensers and when we realised that the points on the bike were badly heat-pitted, the only thing to do was to replace them. Birgit burnt herself badly doing this. The part of the engine that houses the points and condensers is right between the exhaust pipes. The bike was still baking hot when she set to work and at just the wrong moment, her foot slipped on the gravel car park. Instinctively she grabbed the nearest thing to stop herself falling – she'd have smashed her face into the side of the bike if she'd gone over. Unlucky, she'd grabbed the exhaust pipe and it must have been like squeezing a hotplate on an electric cooker. The smell of burning skin instantly filled the air. Grabbing our water bottles I poured every drop straight onto her hand. She stood stunned, her face a picture of agony, her right hand holding out her injured left hand as if it was a wounded bird, or a hand that belonged to someone else. But she didn't shed a single tear. We bandaged the flaming red part of her hand with a sterile dressing from our seldom-used medical kit, and gave her paracetamol. Without a further word she got back to working on her bike. She never complained, not once. Not even when we were riding the bikes, which must have been really uncomfortable. Happily, her skin hardly blistered. We must have got the water on it fast enough, but this was a sobering moment – a very lucky escape. It took nearly two weeks for her hand to heal completely.

The heat-pitted points on Sir Henry weren't the cause of the backfiring problem, just a symptom, and therefore replacing them was only half the solution. The thing we battled with the most was getting the timing right. We weren't carrying a strobe light but had rigged up a length of wire with a light bulb attached. With the use of this simple tool we could get pretty close to the ideal timing position. But even that seemed to do no more than temporarily solve the problem. We scratched our heads. Was there a pattern? Was it the length of a day's ride that caused the problem, the type of fuel, a particular riding temperature? It was a mystery. We decided to explore the area for a few days and monitor really carefully what was going on. We still wanted to see the Mesa Verde anyway.

Mesa Verde is a knob of land that sits 2,621 metres above sea level and we could feel the temperature change again as we rode up from the valley. This time we were prepared and were already wearing every layer of clothing we had, including the new gear from Zion. I felt rather like a semi-inflated balloon as we staggered around. I couldn't get my arms to touch my sides all the way down, so I was walking rather like a penguin. Birgit looked even funnier – at least my long legs stopped me looking too daft. But we didn't care how we looked so long as we were warm!

The first thing that struck us was the stunning view out over the valleys and canyons towards Four Corners, but what we really wanted to see were the cliff dwellings. Built into the sides of the cliffs of Mesa Verde, they have walls of stone block and dried mud. It's believed they were inhabited until about 1200 AD, but no one really knows the true history as the people left no form of written record. I found it quite amazing that the buildings had remained in such good condition, and that they had been built with such skill. It wasn't hard to imagine the world of these hunter-gatherer people, who had also farmed the top of the mesa. We could tell that they'd struggled with the cold as much as we did because all the structures had sections of blackened walls inside where fires would have been burning permanently through the harshness of the cold months. Much of what is known about the people comes from their rubbish. This they'd just tipped over the side on the cliff to collect in mounds down below in the valley. Not so different from our world then, but perhaps their bones and pottery were kinder to it than our chemicals, plastics and metals.

For once I was enthralled by a museum. This one had been put together superbly and displayed the mass of information so that it was really easy to take in. It was also a chance to get out of the wind, and to our dismay it was snowing again. With every minute that passed the snow fell stronger and the risk involved with riding the twisting forty-five minute road down to the park entrance in the valley increased significantly.

Back in Mancos after a miserable ride that felt like an achievement, we stumped frozen into the Visitors' Centre to grab a coffee and the chance to warm up. The ride down had been a slippery affair with visibility often down to no more than five metres. The poor visibility hadn't bothered the SUV drivers and they hadn't seemed to decrease their speed at all as they twisted their way through the multiple bends.

Bob took one look at us and, kind soul that he was, took us to his book-filled home, fed us hot sangria and then poured us into his shower which had an endless torrent of scalding hot water. Later that night, he visited us at our tent and gave us a card with an Indian traveller's good luck symbol on it. He also gave us a verse that he'd written for us:

'May the long time sun shine upon you.
All love surround you and the pure light within you guide your
way.
Your spirit has chased the clouds from the morning.
Ride with the wind.
The shield and sword of your joy and courage
will take you through the dark hours.
And the wrap of your web of human goodness will shelter your
days.
Work for peace.'
Brother Bob

Until that moment, we'd no idea that Bob had been having the same sort of thoughts about us that we'd been having about him. It felt rather strange, but in a good sort of way.

Being in one place for a few days gave us the chance to inspect our tent for damage. Bad news. The waterproofing had come off our tent's fabric in several large patches and the seams had opened with the constant use in wind and temperature change. It made us feel vulnerable. If we had a warm sleeping bag, a good sleeping mat, an efficient cooker and a decent tent then we felt we could cope with anything. The leaking tent was a worry. The tent was our home and our protection.

Birgit and I had never had a static home; I wondered sometimes what that would be like. Perhaps half would be chaotic and half would be ordered. On my side of the tent, I liked to have everything where I could find it in a hurry, or in the dark. So, my book, torch, wash gear, boots, socks, dry clothes, bike kit, helmet and so on all had a place where each always goes. In stark contrast, Birgit seemed to just bung her stuff in. She swore she knew exactly where everything was, even though her 'house' arranging seemed to vary every day. I have to admit that somehow there was some sort of system to her chaos and the only times she had a 'can't-find-it' panic-stricken moment was when she couldn't hunt out her bike keys.

The damage to the tent was a real worry though, but a man camping next to us at Boyle Park advised us that silicone spray was the best quick fix we could make. It was worth a try and to our amazement we also found rolls of stick-on seam-sealer. If these two things worked then perhaps our trusty home would last. It felt wrong to be even thinking about discarding our old friend.

We'd had fun hunting down the hiking and camping shop in the next town Durango. When we asked the old lady at the service station for directions she looked at us as if we'd asked for directions to the moon. I kept on forgetting that on the outside, to many, we must have looked quite alien, though so far in the US we'd never had anyone cross the street to get away from us. Leastways, not that we'd noticed. That had happened to me several times in the UK and once in a waiting room in a hospital Birgit had stood up to give a seat to an elderly gentleman, who had just about had a heart attack at the sight of her! It's that book and cover thing again. I made a mental note to myself: 'Must try to tidy my appearance.'

The Rocky Mountains run for 4,800 kilometres, dividing the Western side of the North American continent. To get across them we could either head north towards the town of Silverton and then skirt Red Mountain on the southern tracks, or we could head a little further east through Pagosa Pass and try to get over via Wolf Creek. With the recent snow in mind we watched the weather forecasts carefully. Wolf Creek it would have to be. More snow was on the way and some of the roads up around Red Mountain were reported to be closed by previous snowfalls. In a way that was a shame because our AAA (Automobile Association of America) map said that the roads that way were stunningly beautiful. Well, we'd just have to save those for another time. The Wolf Creek pass looked as if it was going to be challenge enough. We were going to be climbing another 5,000 feet to get there and the road is a famous one, in part because of a country and western song written by Bill Fries and Chip Davies. It's about a couple of truckers making the attempt to get over the pass with a load of chickens. The aging truck runs out of control and the song goes something like this:

> "I looked at Earl and his eyes was wide
> His lip was curled, and his leg was fried.
> And his hand was froze to the wheel like a tongue to a sled in the middle of a blizzard.
> I says, "Earl, I'm not the type to complain
> But the time has come for me to explain
> That if you don't apply some brake real soon, they're gonna have to pick us up with a stick and a spoon..."

Thankfully it wasn't so bad for us, though we quickly realised why this beautiful area is dotted with ski resorts. Strangely, it wasn't horribly cold. The air was crisp and clean, and the cold was windless and dry under a hazy sun. Snow had settled thickly on the roadsides and the mountain slopes were glaringly white, but the tarmac was completely clear and totally ice-free. We were lucky, but still glad when we started to drop down the other side of the pass towards Rio Grande and Del Norte.

 We'd had enough of the snow and cold so carried on all the way down to Highway 285 and the town of Chaffee. After the cold this busy but easy-to-ride road gave us a chance to warm up and to open up the bikes. Sir Henry seemed to be behaving himself but this was the chance to see whether it was a constant quick pace that had somehow been causing the problems.

The higher speed didn't seem to make any difference, but both bikes seemed to revel in being back down at a lower level. Our old bikes had traditional carburettors rather than self-adjusting fuel injection so the thin air at altitude was potentially more troublesome. I'd read all about the need to change the carb jets but we'd never previously had to do so, even when we were high up in the Andes. However, there was a noticeable difference here and the bikes seemed to enjoy having the proper mix of fuel and air.

At Chaffee we eased on eastwards through the foothills and passes before the town of Woodland Park. Camping spots were very easy to find and several of them were tucked away in flower-strewn meadows alongside streams full of clear ice water. My favourite was at a place called Trail Creek in the Pike National Forest. As it was spring at these heights, flowers were everywhere and with new buds on the trees it was as if the world was slashed and dotted with every colour I'd ever seen.

Joe and Sarah, our American friends from Chile, had settled in a place called Evergreen, to the west of Denver and the easiest way to get there took us rumbling along quiet roads through the towns of West Creek, Buffalo Creek, Pine Junction and Conifer. We arrived in Evergreen buzzing with the good fortune we'd had of being able to ride our bikes through this part of the world. I was absolutely delighted with the way the journey was going and I was really surprised by the welcome people gave us along the way. We'd got used to people in third world countries coming over to chat and ask questions, but I hadn't expected this to happen so often in the States. The battered, travel-worn state of the bikes was always the initial draw and the foreign number plates the clincher. When people saw us without the bikes there was still a real sense of reservation, but when we were with them, it was completely different.

Arriving at Sarah, Joe, Hannah and Emily's house was like coming home. It seemed more like a week than the year that had actually passed since we'd seen them last. Year-old conversations seemed to start up again, almost exactly as we'd left them, but we all had new stories to tell and the girls greeted Birgit with big happy hugs.

The family inspired us and we felt in a rather strange sort of way that we'd known them all our lives. We had a lot in common and that had helped the budding friendship to blossom in Chile when we'd first met them. Joe, a dark-haired man with a gentle face and a twinkle in his eyes, was a passionate geologist and he and Birgit (who studied geology as part of her degree) instantly shot off into conversations about Joe's work. When we'd met he was a director of a company that hunted the world for mineral development possibilities. This meant that he and the family had ended up travelling and living in some really interesting places. Sarah, a slim blond woman, was a freelance graphic designer and a fine watercolour artist, besides being Mom to Hannah and Emily. She's the sort of person who listens very carefully to everything, makes her mind up and then acts decisively. Both she and Joe were ardent travellers and were not like any other Americans I'd ever met. The two girls were blond like their mother and just as inquisitive as their parents. I liked them a lot, in part because they didn't seem like other children I knew. They had an absolute fascination with everything around them and would far rather go out and hike up a mountain than sit at home and watch TV. When we were with the family I couldn't help but be impressed and enjoy how they were together. They all obviously liked and respected each other.

They threw me a belated birthday party, before which Birgit had said, "You behave yourself this time." We'd celebrated my last birthday with them in their house in Santiago and Sarah had generously, but perhaps mistakenly, brought out a prized bottle of vintage cognac. To Birgit's embarrassment, I drank the lion's share of the whole bottle.

The next morning, with my tail between my legs and a sore head, we'd headed off into the city to try to find a replacement. "Don't you dare do that this time," Birgit had muttered at me, nudging me under the table to emphasise the point!

The next few days were a combination of laughter, exploration and work. Both bikes needed a thorough clean and desperately needed to be serviced. Having a garage to work in out of the weather was brilliant. All our clothes needed washing and most of them needed repairing. On some, old patches needed new ones on top. Birgit's trousers were beginning to look like cast-offs from the set of Joseph and the Amazing Technicolor Dreamcoat. But we also had money to make.

On our way through Africa we'd regularly bought locally made stone and ebony pendants. Malawi and Zimbabwe had been great shopping countries for those sorts of things. We'd bought carved faces, fish, weather-worn bits of wood that had been polished to a high gloss and strangely-shaped bits of stone in colours that ranged from reds to greens to blacks and rich browns. Each time we'd made a collection we'd parcelled them up and posted them to Birgit's friends Joe and Nancy in Chicago. In South and Central America we'd added to the collection, but more importantly we'd bought plaited leather thongs and reels of silver wire. They'd cost us buttons and we'd had great fun visiting the markets to buy them. Each purchase told a story and they could have all made great souvenirs. But that wasn't our intent.

We knew that we were going to be short of money on the journey through the States and the plan was to make the carvings and stones into pendants which we'd try to sell along the way. We thought that they'd also make great gifts for people who either helped us or made us welcome in some way.

 So we spent the following days drilling holes, threading leather, twisting silver, joining plaits and making clasps. We'd no idea how much to charge for them but Sarah advised us. If her pricing was right and we actually managed to sell them all, we would earn nearly $2,000. That was a hell of a lot of travel

money. All in, our daily costs were averaging out at around $12 to $15 each. This was double our average in South America but here, at worst, the earnings would still give us funds for nearly two and a half months of travel. Fantastic, and by selling the things we'd get the bonus of being able to talk to loads of people. That was just going to add another layer of quality to the adventure. Excellent.

Joe and Sarah suggested where to head for next. Joe said, "My sister Caroline and her husband George own a vineyard in California. Their son Damian is the winemaker. Their other son Rick and his family live just down the road. We think you guys would all get on really well. Why don't you call in on them?"

A vineyard in California? Family of Joe and Sarah's? What a great idea. This sounded too good to be missed. That night over a couple of bottles of wine, we all settled down to scan our maps. Joe and Sarah were both very experienced travellers, so we were very happy to let ourselves be guided by them.

The Rocky Mountain National Park roads had just been cleared of snow, and that had opened up an enticing route. "Why don't you ride up through the park and then loop down to join Highway 40. You'll find some beautiful scenery and there are some great camping spots tucked away along that route. You'll also be passing through quite a few old mining towns from the days of the gold rush. You can even sign up to go panning for gold. Just keep going along Highway 40 and you come to places like Steamboat Springs and Craig, but whatever you do, don't miss out on the Dinosaur National Monument. It's fascinating. A lot of the route is at low altitude so you'll steer clear of the snow but you will have the mountains on either side of you."

We couldn't have had better advice and rode the next days stunned by the magnificent scenery. But it had been hard to leave Sarah, Joe and the girls. Birgit and I knew that in reality we might never see them again. For me it's still one of the saddest things about overlanding. Every so often you make some really special friends, but then you move on. As with Zack back in Mexico, paths cross momentarily, rich with value, but the call of the road is inevitably there. However, fate can play happy games with life as well as sad ones.

The AAA had provided us with a really good selection of maps, but the ones that helped us most were those we picked up from State Tourist offices. They were much more detailed, showing most roads,  sites of interest, and National Parks. The Bureau of Land Management areas and State Forests were also marked. One map brought home to me the huge cultural mix that makes up the population of North America. The back of the Colorado State map listed all the Colorado Transportation Commissioners' names. There was a Garcia, a Mirelez, a Haight, an Anderson, a Buescher, a Morrison, a Guillermo and a Vidal, amongst others. I was fascinated by this. Europe has many similarities to the US and one of the things is the historical wariness of other nations. How could immigrants from Europe, with this background of wariness, have melded together so quickly? I understood that in the early days individual nationals had set off in groups to explore and to colonise this rugged country. This meant that some regions had their foundations built by immigrants from a particular country. On our maps we'd seen towns with names such as Fortuna, Rhinelander, McLaughlin, Choteau, Buhl and Portsmouth. I'd read that some cities were split almost into ghettos – there'd be an Irish area, a German area, an Italian area, a Scandinavian area and so on. I'd also read that next to Warsaw, Chicago has the largest population of Polish people in the world. Now, seeing the mix of origins on the back of the map, it made me realise that common aims and pure survival can rapidly rub out many of the rough edges that being different gives. I still bore in mind how young the country is. The change into nationhood had happened in quite a rapid way. But I wondered how often we'd still find people putting their origins first when making a decision that affected the whole nation.

The United States seemed to be fighting a 'losing battle with illegal immigrants from the south'. (I've borrowed that quote from an article in the US press at the time).) I wondered how this would change things in a country that was founded on immigration – a country mostly populated by people whose ancestors were in search of a better life. I'd read somewhere that it was estimated that within 50 years the main language in the US was going to be Spanish rather than English. Interesting, if hard to imagine, since it appears to under-estimate the desire of immigrants' children, born in the USA, to make English their 'mother tongue'. It's worth remembering that if the Seven Years War (1756-63) had been won by the French then in all probability the whole of what is now the USA and Canada would be French-speaking. There's also a much-repeated urban myth that German nearly became the official language of the US in 1795. What is true is that a third of the population of Pennsylvania was German-speaking in the 1750s and many millions of Americans are descended from native German speakers.

Now, as the new Millennium approached, how flexible could the people of the United States be to the migration from Latin America? Would they welcome the change as a situation to be appreciated and be guided forward positively, or would a potentially destructive border battle commence? I knew from England that initially, immigrants had not been welcomed en masse, but that within a couple of generations, change had been pretty much accepted and was lived with comfortably – in most places. But it would take several more generations though before the new additions to the gene pool were fully integrated and no one thought twice about it. And of course, during this time, more change would happen that would need to be accepted and integrated.

Perhaps every country just has to accept that modern times are very different from those of a hundred years ago. Or perhaps things are actually the same, but just of a different ilk. Heady stuff that, I decided, as we were cruising along soaking up the scenery. I simply wasn't well informed enough to be able to work out solutions myself. I was actually rather glad that I didn't have to, but it reinforced the thought that when our adventure finished and I returned to England, I'd be looking at things around me there with much more curious and analytical eyes.

Using the possibilities given to us by the State map, we free camped by roadsides or in the parks and Land Management sites. None of them had facilities but we didn't care. We carried everything we needed, streams gave us water to drink and to wash in, and local shops in small towns supplied our food. By this time we'd discovered that, as in developing countries, you can bargain for your food in the US stores. I'd loved the expressions on people's faces when we tried this. Amazingly, most times we tried it, we'd get money off whatever it was we were buying. Sometimes pure cheek and originality are a great combination. I guess we were good entertainment value for the staff too. Doing this became a fun game that usually had a great result. I could just imagine the conversations at home or in the bar that night.

Fuel was never a problem. Between us we could carry nearly 70 litres; that's 15.4 Imperial gallons or 18.5 US gallons. The whole ride was crisscrossed with side roads and tracks, most of them dirt and many without gates. We slipped off the main road to explore at just about every opportunity. Elk and deer seemed to roam quite freely and though they were quite skittish, they were happy for us to watch them from a distance.

I loved each opportunity to take the bike onto the dirt tracks and I loved the mind-teases the gravel and sand played with me. I liked the fact that there was no way I could ride on 'autopilot' and my thoughts could only be on what the track was going to try to make Libby do next. I got a real buzz when something unexpected happened and I had to react without thinking. It might be a patch of soft sand or mud that suddenly had the back tyre fishtailing and scrabbling for grip. I always got a zap of adrenaline at those heart-stopping moments when the bike was almost at the point of disaster and then, yet again, its momentum, balance and power kicked in to carry me to safety. I also had a real sense of satisfaction when I emerged from the other side of each of these moments with the realisation that I'd survived on intuition. The bike and I had dealt with the hazard almost as one being. I'd learnt a bit over the years, but I've never forgotten the fear with which I rode my first countries through Africa.

Being outdoors all the time gave us a grandstand view of the ever-changing skies. We always rode on a high when the sky was blue, with a dash of tension when the changing colours threatened a coming storm, and a feeling that combined fatalism and vulnerability when that storm actually did come crashing through the air above us. I was awed by the unexpected shapes that formed up there. And I was enthralled by the astonishingly beautiful colours that would either ease across the sky, or flash across it with an urgency that always held a hint of danger. A high point from a day's ride often came from stopping the bikes, lying on the ground wherever we were, and watching the sky. It never looked the same and lying there on my back always made me conscious of the freedom we had.

One night, Birgit and I found a small valley to camp in. We'd ridden tracks through rolling grass-covered hills for hours and towards the end of the day, just as the land around us began to be hazed by subtle tones of yellows and oranges, we found a perfect spot to camp. It was out of sight of any but the closest passersby, and was sheltered from any wind that might blow up in the night. When we turned off our engines all we could hear was the sound of the warm breeze blowing through the dry prairie grass. Within moments we had the bikes parked, the tent up and the billy on the stove. We unpacked, and then as the hills around us changed from a glowing orange to deep red, we sat sipping tea with the flickering glow of the stove lighting up our faces. Above us, the sky slowly turned into that majestic midnight blue that always forms the perfect backdrop for the bright white of the stars. A sharp edged sickle moon hung crisp and clear, with the dark side of the moon a round deep blue-purple outline against the star-spangled reaches of outer space. We lay back in the grass to watch, quite awed by this gift of a sight. Birgit and I didn't need to say a word…

Before arriving in the USA I'd often wondered if we'd find ourselves riding through any 'three-horse' towns. I'd kind of liked this description for a small settlement, which in the UK would probably have been called a hamlet. There were plenty, and in one of them, we had a run-in with the law. Well I did, as Birgit managed to keep out of the way, although she was the one that got me in trouble!

We'd been happily meandering along, watching the scenery and then within a few seconds of passing the name board at the entrance  to a town, we were rolling gently down a wide street that had a feed store, a hardware store, a few picket-fenced houses, a diner and a gas station. The street was wide enough to have turned a stagecoach and full team of horses around in it, and I guessed that perhaps this had originally been the reason for it being so wide. There were a few dusty old cars and pickup trucks parked at 45 degrees to the walkways, but there was no other sign of life. No people, no dogs, no cats and not a single horse, never mind three. Birgit was leading as usual, and must have been momentarily distracted from watching the signposts; the main highway turned left in the middle of the town and she'd missed the turning and gone straight on. I beeped my horn, then made a 'circling wagons' type of motion over my head when she looked back and she realised what the problem was. She looked back again to make sure no one was creeping up on her, and pulled a U-turn.

With a quick look over my shoulder, I carefully one-point-turned the bike and followed her back up the highway. Just before she disappeared around the corner, I heard the 'whoop, whoop' sound of a police siren. The black and white police car, lights flashing, held two cops, one of whom was motioning me vigorously to the side of the road. I had a small sinking feeling moment. What had I done wrong?

"Would you step away from your motorcycle please sir," the first cop said to me as his right hand slipped down to the gun that was holstered on his belt. His voice was icily firm, but respectful. It also held a hint of a question in it.

The second cop was now out of the car, which he'd parked nose to the walkway in front of me, the lights still whirling lazily on the roof. He stood on the other side of the 'hood', with his hand hovering over his gun. "Oh dear", I thought to myself, "this doesn't look good." I'd still not worked out what I'd done wrong. I stepped away from the bike, gently pulling my gloves and my helmet off as I did so. "Good afternoon, officer." I said to the first cop.

"You sir, have just broken the law. Please keep your hands in front of you where I can see them!" I could see Birgit looking at me from a safe distance on the corner. She'd wisely decided not to get involved. If something went really pear-shaped then she'd be free to try to sort things out. This was something we always planned to try to do when we were in South and Central America where so many police were supposed to be on the take. But I still had no idea what I'd done wrong.

"Your licence plate is not American," the cop said. "Where are you from?" "Um, the UK," I replied. "Damn" the cop said. "I've never pulled over someone from England before. You pulled a yooie. You just cain't do that here. Where's your licence?" By this time both he and his partner had relaxed and I thought, "Perhaps this isn't going to be too bad. I wonder how much they are going to fine me?" Birgit still stayed safely up the road.

The flashing lights on the car went off and I suspect I was probably a welcome break from three-horse monotony for the next ten minutes. The guys wanted to know all about the trip. They also wanted to know how much trouble we'd had with the law in Mexico. When I told them about all the checkpoints and the arrogant behaviour of the cops in the south, these two pulled themselves proudly up to their full height and said, "Yeah well, it's dangerous down there. Glad you survived. You have a nice day now, and don't be pulling any more of them U-turns. You be careful." I climbed back on the bike, and mindful of every element of Highway Code I could remember, I set off slowly, well within the speed limit, to join Birgit, who was still looking worried. We got out of town and at the next chance to stop, she nearly fell off her bike laughing at the thought that she was the one that had got me into trouble with the law.

Very early on in our travelling together, we'd slotted into the routine of Birgit riding in front. Initially it had been because she was so much more inexperienced than I was and her bike was not as easy to handle as mine. Being in front meant that she could ride at the pace that suited her best for the conditions. As for me, I enjoyed not spending so much time looking in my mirrors to see if she was OK. It was then that I'd also discovered that she likes to make decisions, and that she's good at it. Knowing this sort of thing is a real asset when you are travelling as a team. Having two people trying to be in charge when you are riding doesn't work. It just causes grief, misunderstandings and tension. By this time Birgit had turned into an exceedingly competent rider and there was no reason why we should change the routine we'd settled into. I just hoped she wouldn't miss any more signs...

We'd seen very few other bikers along the way but all of a sudden there seemed to be a rushing tide of Harley-Davidsons. We'd stopped one day by Granby Spring Creek and were working on Sir Henry's points, again, when a bunch of them pulled over to see if we needed any help. Not used to this, we were a little taken aback at first, but we soon got into conversation. No, there wasn't anything the guys could do; we were playing with an old problem. And where were they all off to? There was a big bike rally going on over in eastern California.

Another of the culture shocks for us in the USA was the average size of the motorcycles we were seeing. In the far south most bikes were around the 125cc to 250cc size, so to have 1000cc and 1200cc motorcycles blasting past us was always an eyebrow raiser. I couldn't get over the ease with which some of these bikes seemed to eat miles. They seemed to do so in an effortless way. The Harleys always announced their presence. The BMWs and Goldwings cruised past on a whisper, and the sports bikes howled by.

It felt really strange that Libby and Sir Henry weren't the largest bikes in the picture. But I thought that the Honda Goldwings didn't look much like motorcycles at all. With their giant fairings and mass of lights, they looked as if they would be more at home shuttling between space ships than riding the roads of terra firma. On windy days though, I was envious of their power and the protection their fairings offered the riders. One day I'd been struggling to do 50mph through a really strong head wind as we were riding in the foothills of the Rocky Mountains. Libby's throttle was wide open and I dreaded any upward slopes. But the Goldwings were cruising on past as if it was the calmest day in the spring. And where I was togged up in all my layers, their riders were wearing jeans and leather jackets.

A Goldwing rider had managed to surprise and impress me on a campsite one day. Well, awe actually. He and his partner rolled into the camping area, towing a huge trailer. This thing was twice the width of the bike! The rider parked the bike, having used reverse gear to line up into the spot he wanted. He then climbed off his bike, stretched, reached inside one of his panniers, pulled out a can of beer and popped its top. Just as I was thinking thoughts along the line of, 'he's got it sussed,' the man reached down and pressed a button on the side of the trailer. For a moment, I didn't take much notice.

Then, the top of the trailer split in two and the hinged doors opened out until they were level with the outer edges of the trailer. Four legs then dropped down from the doors, locking themselves into place, feet on the ground. Over the next minutes, while the rider and his partner enjoyed their beers, and the looks they were getting, a trailer tent somehow erected itself from the back of the trailer. Amazing! But Birgit muttered, 'Too many things to break' and walked away to put a cup of tea on.

We were heading for the Dinosaur National Monument. In 1908 Earl Douglas, a palaeontologist from the Carnegie Museum, came to the area to have a serious look around. He'd seen landscapes like this before and knew that those places had yielded some very interesting dinosaur bones. Within a year he'd made his first major find: eight tailbones from a brontosaurus, all in perfect position. This was the first of many thousands of bones to be discovered, including several nearly complete skeletons.

The Monument is a collection of amazing sights. The surrounding area is an arid sandy beige colour, and deep canyons scar the landscape. Down in the depths of the canyons there are rivers whose banks are lined with lush green strips of cottonwood trees and box elders. On the tops, if you are lucky, you'll find a few pines, sagebrush, saltbush and greasewood. It's a bleak setting, but the Monument and all it contains are things that most of us will only ever see in some stuffy old museum or other. To see them here, in this setting, is tremendous. The sight that got to me the most was the wall of the 'quarry'. It's packed with layer upon layer of ancient bones that stick out very recognisably from the rock face.

We procrastinated all the way across Utah, the next State on our route to California. It was a freedom of the road thing. A freedom to roam wherever we wanted, and here the land changed quite dramatically. We meandered through the Manti-La Sal, Unita and Fishlake National Forests and then Highway 132 dropped down onto Highway 6 which led us across a flat-to-the-horizon land that had the bikes cruising easily in deliciously warm air.

In the middle of nowhere we came across a bar and a gas station. The land around was bare, devoid of trees. There was little grass and  no surface water. And no other buildings. There was just the road, exuding heat. The air was so dry and so hot that I could feel the insides of my nostrils cringe as I opened my helmet visor. Outside the wooden building, a tall sign on a post swung back and forth, just enough in the almost insignificant breeze to make its rusting hinges squeal a slow yoyo of sound in the surrounding silence. This silence was broken briefly by the occasional whoosh of a passing car, or the bumping, gravelly sound four wheels made as a car pulled off the highway into the raggedy car park. The glass windows of the gas station were dust-streaked and its broken panes had long since been ignored. An ancient, round-backed car sat rusting to one side in the salty Utah air. Tufts of wiry grass sporadically fringed what remained of the chassis. The car had been stripped to the bones in a way that any customs officer on the border with Mexico would have been proud of. A tall Meccano-style windmill stood on its own. Its sails, which were falling to pieces, were unmoving in air that was just too listless to turn them. Dust devils in the making whirled lazily way back across the plain; they were the only other moving things in sight. The only other sounds to break the silence were our ticking, cooling engines and those from two sleek, tasselled, dusty Harley-Davidsons that were parked in front of the bar.

We filled our tanks. The attendant was a grubby-faced young boy chewing a toothpick, who looked as if he wasn't old enough to be out of school at this time of day. Where would that school be anyway? His sun-bleached, pale blue denim dungarees were dusty on the knees, as if he had been praying for someone, anyone, to come and break the endless monotony. He tucked his shaggy blond head to one side, shot a shy grin at us and took our money. Not a word was spoken. It didn't seem to be required, or appropriate.

We were thirsty. The water in our bottles was at blood temperature; an unappetising thought. The bar's battered red and white sign advertising ice-cold Cokes beckoned. Stuff the expense, the tooth rot potential, and our own scruffy state. We kicked the fine, white dust off our boots on the dried and split wooden steps, and walked inside. We were hit by a welcome blast of air-conditioned, smoke-free, coolness that we knew we'd pay for as soon as we headed back out again. I loved the ban on smoking in bars in the States. After the heavily laden air of the bars and restaurants further south, this was a welcome and continuous delight. It took a moment for our eyes to accustom themselves to the cool, haze-free gloom. We'd stepped into another world.

Inside there was restaurant as well as a bar. Everything sparkled with polish and the barman either had a nervous twitch that had him constantly wiping dust off the wooden top of the bar, or he was on permanent cleaning autopilot. All eyes swung in our direction. Two families sat eating burgers and fries, and the two bikers sat drinking beer so cold that the glasses had dew running down their sides. The temptation was strong. The bikers nodded at us and got back to the serious business of appreciating their drinks.

Beer for us? In this heat, with our thirst, it would have been just too dangerous. I looked at Birgit, mentally muttering to her, 'We could just ask if we could camp here you know.' She shook her head. We behaved ourselves and ordered Cokes. They came in cans so cold that a quick layer of frost had formed on their sides. The first gulp burned deliciously, then the second, and the third. I suppressed a burp, and at that moment the bikers spoke to us.

"We passed you guys a ways back on the road. We wondered if we'd see you again. Come and visit with us." We took that to mean, come and sit with us, so did just that, glad to be sitting on something other than our bike saddles.

The bikers, Bill and Janet, were from Denver. They were about the same age as us and they, like the other Harley riders we'd met, were heading for the bike rally in California. "It's in a place called Bridgeport. You guys should come," they told us. "It's not far now, just a short ride. You continue on this road, which takes you across north-western Nevada. Then, if you follow the Ninety-Five and go south on the Three-Thirty-Eight through the Toiyabe National Forest you'll find it. You won't miss it. You'll see what we mean."

It suddenly struck me that in seven years on the road I'd never been to a bike rally. In fact I'd been such a novice biker when I'd started that I'd never been to a bike rally, ever. We had to go. I looked across at Birgit and she nodded her, 'Why on earth not?' look which I'd come to know so well and like so much. She'd never been to a bike rally either.

The next half hour passed quickly, with us being badgered enthusiastically to tell our story. They were a fun couple and I had to ask, "Do you think Harley riders would be interested in our pendants?" I shot out to the bikes and pulled out a selection. I also grabbed a couple of the six-inch long chopper motorcycle 'sculptures' cleverly made out of wire, that we'd bought in Zimbabwe. (We'd posted them to the States too.) If Bill and Janet liked them then perhaps we'd have our first real chance to sell them at the rally.

"Yeah, you gotta be able to sell some of these. They're great. You'll have to link up with the organisers to ask for permission though, and you'll probably have to pay a vendor's fee. That's probably not more than a couple of hundred dollars though." How much?!! I thought to myself. That would be a big gamble. What if we paid the fee and then no one bought anything from us? Then Janet said, looking across the table at Bill, "We've just got to have one of the bikes for us Bill. How much are they?"

"Um $25," I suggested, having no idea of their worth. We'd paid just a couple of dollars for each of them and then postage had added a $1.50 to each. "Done," said Janet. "Get the money out for the guys Bill." Our first sale, and suddenly the Cokes didn't seem so expensive after all. We followed their advice, but gave them the chance to head off first.

In the next section of our journey side winds suddenly started to batter us, shoving us hard from one side of our lane to the other. Dust filled the air; it misted over my visor and began to creep under the rim of my helmet, slowly clogging my burning nostrils.

In front of us was a warning sign for roadworks. We slowed down, hoping that the wind wouldn't push us off course. Suddenly, an almost ghostly shape appeared out of the dust. A woman stood by the roadside, her face wrapped in a scarf, a construction helmet on her head and a high visibility waistcoat around her body. Not that it was very 'high vis' in this dust. In her hand she held a green and red stop-go lollipop sign. Her job was to stand in this bleak place, in all weather conditions, to direct the traffic past the road works. I just hoped that she was well paid for her work, but I doubted it. I felt almost guilty when, half an hour later, we left the wind and the dry lands behind us.

The two of us felt that lovely tingle of anticipation as we got closer to Bridgeport, and saw more bikes on the road. Each gleamed their shiny paint and chrome in the sunshine. I was conscious of how dirty our bikes were.

We skirted the lake on the last section of road just before the town and then it was obvious why Janet and Bill had said we couldn't miss the rally. There, in the wide central street of Bridgeport, were hundreds upon hundreds of gleaming motorcycles. The centre of the road held two lines of parked bikes, and the sides were lined with so many more that a child could have stepped from one saddle to the next, and made it all the way down the street without ever touching the ground.

We rode through, the sound of our BMW engines turning heads, which then seemed to do a double take at the sight of us. After all, we were wearing the dust of scores of dirt tracks on our patched bike kit, none of which was even remotely black any more. We stood

BIRGIT ON THE FABLED SOUTHERN ALASKAN BORDER

ON THE ROAD IN THE BEAUTIFUL YUKON

YES, THE COLOUR OF PEYTO LAKE IS QUITE NATURAL!

COYOTE BEACH, BAJA CALIFORNIA

ON THE ROAD IN BRITISH COLOMBIA

THE MAGNIFICENT CANADIAN LAKES

FRIENDS OF THE ROAD

NO CAPTION NEEDED!

PLAYTIME IN NEW MEXICO

MONUMENT VALLEY - AN AWESOME PLACE TO RIDE

THE PAINTED
DESERT - ARIZONA

40°C IN THE SHADE AND ONLY WINE TO DRINK

GHOST TOWN OF BODIE - CALIFORNIA

COLORADO SUNSET

CALM AT THE END
OF THE DAY

PETROGLYPH FROM THE FIRST INHABITANTS

A TIME TO THINK...

BIRGIT AT BEAR GLACIER

PEGGY AND PETE

CAMPING AT GRAND CANYON

THE OREGON COAST

THE STUNNING YOSEMITE NATIONAL PARK

CALIFORNIA COASTLINE

IF VEHICLES COULD TELL STORIES...

WATER WINDMILL

A COMMON SIGHT IN OREGON

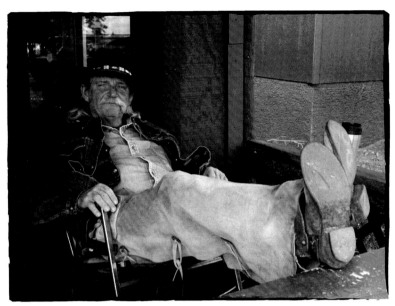

COWBOYS DO EXIST!

THE MAGIC OF MONUMENT VALLEY

INSIDE MONUMENT VALLEY

OUTBACK WASHINGTON

NEED HELP? THIS WAY...

THE BEAUTY OF LAKE TAHOE

BACKCOUNTRY SIERRA NEVADA

out like a couple of mobile sore thumbs. I wasn't sure if I liked this level of attention. I rode praying that neither of us would stall the bikes or worse still, fall off for some reason. I was conscious of how beaten-up and apparently uncared-for our bikes must have looked. Around us sat thousands of dollars-worth of motorcycle kit. And what was that?! Did I really just see a girl with her buttocks fully exposed? I stole a quick look in my mirror. From the front she looked as if she was dressed in black leather trousers and a tiny black bikini top. I must have been mistaken. I shook my head. Perhaps the heat had got to me. I needed another ice-cold Coke.

We made it to the far end of the town, and pulled over at the edge of an enormous car park which fronted a large supermarket. We looked back down the picturesque street with its row of trees along one side, the crisply-painted wooden houses, white picket fences and old-fashioned motel signs. At any other time we would have been thinking that it was a beautiful place and we'd have been keen to press our noses against the glass windows of the shops; they seemed to specialise in things for the outdoors, fishing, hiking and skiing in particular. But now, neither of us was so sure that we wanted to be there, or would be welcome.

Had we anything to lose? No. Had we anything to gain by staying? Yes. It was a bike rally and anyway, we really shouldn't pass up the chance to sell our stuff. A biker rode past us, with his bike sounding completely un-silenced. He was dressed head to toe in black leather, and on the back of his jacket he sported a series of fabric patches. The only time I'd seen that sort of thing was on photos of Hell's Angels. Surely this wasn't some sort of Hell's Angels meet? The only way to find out what was going on was to park up the bikes and go for a stroll. We set off into the streets crowded with black leather, rather timidly at first. Then a biker sitting drinking coffee outside a café called across to us, "Hey you guys. Are you the BeeEm riders? Did I see out-of-state plates on your bikes? Where the hell are they from?"

"Hi. Um, yes that's us. Erm, out of State? Yes, I'm from England and this is my partner Birgit. She's from Germany." "Weell, heell. That's a fine thing. Did you guys ship the bikes over to the US?" So our introduction started and as we explored, I only saw thirty other bikes that weren't Harley-Davidsons.

People stopped us every few yards to talk, right the way down the street, and then we met Chaplain Dave and his buddy Fred, who laughed a lot! Not at us, he just seemed to find a lot to laugh about. Dave quickly drew our story out of us and then asked, "You guys got anywhere to camp yet?" Within moments he'd invited us to camp up by the Baptist church. Dave and Fred were members of the Christian Motorcyclists' Association and they took us under their wings.

Once we'd pitched our tent, and cleaned up a bit, Dave took us down into the Rally to find the organisers. "Fraid not buddy. All the vendors' spots are taken." Around us in the busy centre of the rally we were surrounded by stalls selling every possible accessory a Harley rider could ever wish for. Leather bags, tasselled jackets, shiny exhaust pipes, leather chaps, black 'pudding basin' helmets, jewellery that seemed to be all leather and silver studs, and stalls selling burgers and the like were everywhere. The mood was laid-back and happy. Old friends were greeting each other with laughs, opened out arms and bear hugs. Tattoos and unshaven chins were the name of the game. For once, my hair plait didn't make me stand out and one girl even gave mine a tug as we walked past, and said, "Cool hair." That sort of thing had never happened to me before.

And then I saw 'her' again. I couldn't miss her. I'd been right – she wasn't a heat-induced mirage after all. She did have a bare bum – and a cute one too. She had a thong bikini on under leather chaps which left her backside almost completely exposed. And she wasn't the only scantily-clad girl collecting appreciative looks from the men either.

We felt at a bit of a loss though. No vendors' site was available for us. Then we had an idea. With nothing to lose, we walked back down to the supermarket. We hunted out the manager of the store and asked if it would be OK for us to sell our stuff from the front of his car park. It was quite a long way from the centre of things but we'd seen a steady dribble of bikes coming and going from the car park, so we thought, "If we can make the display look good enough then perhaps we will at least sell something." The manager said yes, for $25 a day. That would do. We collected some empty cardboard boxes from the supermarket and put them upside down by the street with one of our sarongs across the top of them. With the bikes parked behind us we set to laying out the pendants and the wire bikes.

No one stopped. We felt a little foolish. We waited some more. Still no one stopped. We felt even more foolish. People were looking

 but no one was making the effort to pull up by us. What were we doing wrong? Were we in totally the wrong place? Did people think what we had was complete rubbish, so much so that there was no point in stopping for a closer look? A couple wandered over, slurping ice creams as they did so. They looked briefly, ignored us totally, and then wandered on. Oh gosh. This sucked. Birgit muttered, "I'm not sure if I like this selling lark. How long should we keep trying?" Then another guy stopped. "You guys ride them BeEmWubblysdontcha?" "Bad spot huh. Cool gear though. I'll take that one. $20? Sure, no problem and hell, I'll take one of those for my girl. Tell you what, you'd get a lot more people stopping for you if they knew who you were. You should make a sign."

I wrote **'AFRICA TO ALASCA'** hastily, in big black letters on an opened-out cardboard box. Then on a board in front of the pendants, 'Riding round the world.' To our amazement a few people began to stop, but it took nearly an hour before one of our customers pointed out to me that I'd mis-spelt Alaska! Good grief. How daft could I be? No wonder we'd been getting even stranger looks than before. Tsk. Stupid foreigners!

We spent the next couple of days, partly with the stall up, selling pendants far more slowly than we'd hoped but still selling, and partly wandering around seeing the sights and talking to people. Riders continued to flow in and little by little every inch of possible camping space filled up. Huge quantities of beer and Jack Daniels were being

163

knocked back and faces became ever redder, but not for a moment was there even a hint of trouble. Some of the bikes were quite amazing. Real works of art on two wheels. Some were fun, and some had been put together by real characters. My favourite was built by a man who claimed to be a scrap merchant. Every item on his bike had been collected from his scrapyard. The frame of the bike, the engine parts and so on. But then he'd had some real fun. The body parts were made out of things like an old colander, tin cans, a bit of drainpipe, bits of hosepipe and so on. In a very bizarre sort of way, the look of the bike worked. None of it was sane. The collected insanity couldn't have been done better.

We spent the evenings with the people from the CMA. What a fun bunch and not once did they try to push Christianity down our throats. Their way of doing things seemed to be more on the lines of, 'If you like what you see then you'll ask questions'. It worked. I did find myself asking myself questions and watching them even closer. I liked the uncomplicated way that they all got on together. There was an air of open, friendly, trust that seemed to flow through the group without anything being said to encourage it. They all seemed to have a freshness about them which I felt was rare. When they said grace before meals, which we had of course contributed to, and helped prepare, the words were of thanks for the richness of the world around them and the fact that the table was laden with good food. Both seemed wholly appropriate, in part because Bridgeport sits in lush meadows below the magnificent Sierra Nevada mountains.

The next morning was Sunday and on the way to the church meeting that was planned in the centre of town I had my eyes opened yet again. As we walked down into the town I heard the sound of a helicopter. I've never flown in one but I loved the concept and really liked the sound that these things make. I couldn't help but look up. There, slung in a rope net under the helicopter was a motorcycle. We'd seen several people arrive at the rally with their bikes on the back of pick-up trucks. They'd eased them off the back of the trucks to stand by their tents and I'd seen several of them then being ridden around the rally. I wasn't too sure of this idea but thought, well, "Whatever rocks your boat. If doing it this way brings you pleasure, then why not?" I hoped that the helicopter motorcycle was something to do with the Pony Express aim of getting through, come what may. But perhaps the reality was that this was simply a bragging, ostentatious sign of wealth?

The open-air church service amazed me. It was a first. I'd never been somewhere where scores of leather-clad people, who all looked as if they were escapees from the law, would get together and bow their heads in quiet prayer. When they sang hymns they did so with such abandon that they began to draw others to the sides of their group to see what was going on. Many of those stayed for the whole service. The mood was infectious.

The rally drew to an end, after three days of drag racing, slow races, custom competitions and telling of tall tales, Bridgeport was suddenly a little rural town again. The clean-up crews had magicked away the mountains of empty beer cans and recycled the whisky bottles. There hadn't been many of the famous brown paper bags in evidence all weekend! Tyre rubber burn-out and engine oil stains were left to fade away. We packed and said our goodbyes, leaving a couple of ebony fish pendants draped over Chaplain Dave's bike handlebars. With fish being one of the symbols of Christianity, they seemed an appropriate way of saying thank you for the warm welcome and the help we'd been gifted by them.

Quite a few people at the rally had said that there were a couple of sights we just shouldn't miss out on as we headed south, aiming for the Tioga Pass though the Yosemite National Park. The ghost town of Bodie was the first of these and it wasn't far off our route.

The blurb in the tourist office in Bridgeport said that Bodie was a town in 'Arrested Decay'. I loved that description. The blurb went on to say that William Bodey discovered gold in 1859 near what was subsequently called Bodie Bluff, and when a mill was established, a town began to grow. From its beginnings with around twenty miners, Bodie grew to have a population of some 10,000 over the next two decades. By that time, the town bustled with families, miners, storeowners, gunfighters, robbers, prostitutes and undertakers! After a long harsh day digging, blasting and shifting rock up in the claims, the miners would head for one of the 65 bars, the brothels, the gambling halls or the opium dens to spend their earnings. This mixture of gold, sex, and alcohol would often prove fatal and legend has it that a man was killed every day in Bodie. It took two massive fires to kill off the town and it was inhabited until 1932.

This fitted in exactly with the image I had in my mind of how a gold mining town would have been in the Wild West. I wouldn't have liked to live there, but I really wanted to see it now. I also had the feeling that 'Arrested Decay' was going to be wonderfully photogenic, especially if the sun was shining.

I wasn't disappointed. With a rich blue sky above us, the battered wooden houses that are still standing were plentiful enough and in good enough condition to get a real sense of the place as it must have been. The surrounding hills are dotted with rocky crags, punctuated by spoiling slopes where unwanted rock and soil had been cast by the miners. These fanned out down the rolling hillsides. At this time of year the grass between the spoil heaps was green and lush. Some of the buildings are very 'decayed', but several are in excellent condition.

Bodie was really reminiscent of those Wild West movies where you see wide streets edged with hitching posts, storefronts and saloons.

The wooden frontages are tall and wide, some with porches and some with a boardwalk, but behind these expressions of importance, the real buildings are much smaller, though some of them are still two stories high. Yes, there are even old hitching posts still to be found, and horse-drawn wagons sit slowly falling to pieces alongside the buildings. The old Methodist church is in surprisingly good condition and inside you can even see the old wood-burning stoves that must have been vital in those days. Snowfalls are so heavy that nowadays the town is closed off to visitors during the winter.

Thinking about the cold and seeing the wooden buildings made me think about the enormous amount of wood that must have been consumed by the town. The buildings were mostly wooden, the tools wood-handled, the carts wooden, the pit props made of wood and all heating must have been done with wood-burning stoves. The houses we poked our heads into must have been freezing to live in. Many were single-skinned and even those that weren't would have had a hard time retaining any warmth. You had to respect the hardy souls that made their lives in this town. One of the strangest things about the buildings is the amount of equipment left in many of them, particularly the schoolhouse. It's almost as if one day, someone said, "Let's go." And everybody did. What couldn't be carried was left behind, and that is one reason why Bodie is such a delight to visit, though slightly eerie.

The next place we'd been enthusiastically encouraged to visit was Mono Lake. Fans of Pink Floyd will almost certainly know that the inner sleeve cover shot of their Wish You Were Here album is actually a photo of what looks like a man diving into Mono Lake. It's quite a bizarre shot which uses some basic but very effective trick photography.

The colours in and around the lake are stark and crisp and there are strange shapes present. These are tufa towers which would once have been hidden under the lake water. This is quite possibly the oldest lake in America and has recently been the site of a man-made ecological disaster. Los Angeles needed fresh water, so what did the water board do? They channelled off streams that would have run into the lake and sent the water on down to help the growing city. I'd paused for a moment when I'd read this. I'd not forgotten the sight of all the lawn sprayers at work on the gardens of the wealthy and middle class alike in LA. Over the years, this channelling caused the water levels in the lake to drop so drastically that the tufa towers were exposed and what had been islands, and significant nesting sights, had become joined to the mainland. The lake is volcanic and the tufa towers were formed by hot air and water escaping to the surface, carrying minerals with them as they did so. The minerals slowly settled on the tops and sides of the escape vents until they eventually formed the tufa towers.

The towers made me think of sci-fi movies. To the eyes of a Philistine, (me), this turn of events wasn't a sad thing to be seeing, but more something unique and beautiful. But I did feel sadness when I then read that the lake is actually dying. It's an inland lake and as such all the run-off waters from the mountains have carried hundreds of years' worth of minerals and salts down to be deposited in the lake basin. With no run-off from the lake, this means that the saline content of the water is now so great that a person would be extremely foolish to drink it. As the water level dropped from the combined effect of evaporation and the missing regular influx of melt-water, the salinity began to become so strong that creatures unique to the lake's eco system began to die off. Birds that traditionally fed on these creatures began to look for other places to breed. In part this was also caused because their island nesting beds were now accessible to predators such as coyotes.

One of the creatures that didn't seem to be struggling was the alkali fly. These clever insects thrive by the million along the shores of Mono Lake and as we walked, it was as if we were strolling through a seething, living black carpet. More sci-fi stuff. But I'm calling them clever with real respect. These oxygen breathers have developed a system that allows them to get at their food in the lake and to lay their eggs in the water. They feed on algae, which can be so dense in Mono Lake that the water looks like 'pea soup'. To get at the algae the flies walk underwater encased in small bubbles of air. How amazing is that?!

When the air is completely still, the thick saline water is supposed to act like a vast mirror in which the mountains are reflected in perfect detail. Sadly, there was a slight breeze the day we got there, so we weren't lucky enough to see that. However, it was calm enough for the water to be rolling gently rather than rippling. That meant we could imagine the mirror effect quite easily. I'd once seen an oil slick and how that had rolled black across the surface of the sea. The effect here was similar, except that that the water wasn't black. For us, it was like looking at a lake of mercury.

The future of the lake is not lost though. Campaigners managed to get the California State Water Resources Control Board to issue an order to protect it. They did that in 1994. It's estimated that if the full flow of water was allowed back then it would take perhaps twenty years for the lake to fill to an acceptable level again. This does not take climate change and times of drought into account.

If, (and it's a big if), you can ignore the environmental situation, then the views of this enticing lake are stunning, quirky and even perhaps, unique. I was glad that we'd been so strongly recommended to go there. But the flies annoyed the living daylights out of us when we camped nearby!

Chapter Eleven
A Vineyard in a Canyon
'Thought is wonderful but adventure is more wonderful still.'

Oscar Wilde

The next morning's breakfast tasted disgusting! I'd made the unfortunate mistake of packing our sealed plastic bag of muesli in the same pannier as our petrol cooker. Even though they weren't next to each other, and the plastic bag was sealed, the foul tang of petrol had corrupted the cereal. We didn't discover it had done so until we'd taken our first hungry mouthfuls. How strange that even after more than 2,600 days on the road, I'd never done this before. How typical that I'd done it with a brand new bag of muesli! It wasn't a good start to the day. A hungry girlfriend can muster up some very reproachful looks.

Just for the hell of it, because it was there and because we could, we started off the day's ride with a side trip. Just to the south of Mono Lake there's a loop of road off Highway 395 called the 158. Somehow, the bikes encouraged us to explore and to do things just for the hell of it, and riding the 158 was a great example of that. You're never bored when touring on a bike. The rush from overlanding came from the eclectic and unpredictable mix of places, people, disasters, high points, discoveries and the sheer bliss of riding the bike. With perhaps just a year of travelling left to come, this reflection prompted a thought I was constantly trying to ignore: how was I going to cope with a nine to five life when we got home? What would it be like to be in one place, like it or not, and to know that I had to be there for the next significant amount of time? Would I suffer from 'bike withdrawal'?

The pre-trip world that I'd lived in seemed to be a hazy memory of something distant. I resolved to try harder not to think about it until much nearer the end of the trip. For now I'd just concentrate on the ride. I was lucky to be on the road, and I wasn't going to let a 'what if' thought taint the adventure.

Highway 158 took us scooting along the side of Rush Creek and then on past Grant Lake, Silver Lake, Gull Lake and June Lake. It was almost like taking a holiday from the journey. We had Mount Wood and Reversed Peak looming above us as we rode between the aspens and occasional conifers, and we got flashes of pale silvery blue from the calm lake waters. Traffic was almost non-existent, and the only other road users appeared to be men in 4x4s with fishing rods strapped to the roofs. Other than winter skiing it seems that the main annual excitement comes from the Monster Trout Fishing Festival. With hindsight, we should have hired some rods and settled down to a few days' fishing. Mountain brown trout are delicious, especially when they're straight from the water.

The Tioga Pass cuts through the Sierras at 9,941 feet and it's one of the few places where you can motor from one side of the mountains to the other. We were there at exactly the right time. Due to the weather the pass is firmly closed for much of the year, but in late June it was perfect. Highway 120 took us curling and looping along the valley. To the side of the road was a wide expanse of gravelly land that was back-dropped by soaring mountains. A turquoise and grey river rushed below us as the continuous white line that separated the asphalt from the gravel verges kept us on track. The sheer joy of the ride took over, the bikes soaking up the 3,000 foot climb with no effort at all. Fir trees dotted the rocky landscape, their tall slim shapes thrusting skyward in feathery green clusters. The only snow in sight was that on the tops of the mountains, and the small patches that hung on in the shadier recesses under the trees. We snaked on rapidly past the many pull-off points, unwilling to break the mood that had hit us both. This time our shadows were flitting along in front of us, as if they too were eager to get on with the ride. As we climbed, the effects of the harsh winters became more obvious with the broken surface of the asphalt bobbled with patch repairs and occasional ice-wrought cracks. Our bikes soaked up the bumps as if this road was exactly what they had been made to ride. We flashed past tall, red snow depth-marker poles and leaned into the curves, flying along with each bend inviting us to lean first one way, then the other. We rode with symmetry, as if our bikes were joined together with an unbreakable, invisible string.

The air was crisp and clean and had we taken a moment to pull off and stare at the view, we'd have been able to see for miles. I didn't want the ride to end. Everything about us was in tune.

All good things must come to an end though and the road dropped us down into the National Park near the Tamarack campsite. This night we'd pay to camp but we didn't mind at all. This is Ansel Adams territory. We'd both seen his stunning photography and to be surrounded by his inspiration was an awesome feeling.

Ansel Adams was a craggy, restless man who took some of the most stunning photographs of the Sierras ever seen. His work in black and white gives a tremendous sense of majesty and depth, and for once I had no doubt that the camera had neither lied, nor failed to do a scene justice. The clarity of his shots is so good that when looking at his pictures of Yosemite, I felt as if I was there with him. A friend had once told me that Ansel Adams' pictures made him feel as if they had been taken especially for him. Because they were so precise and detailed, he felt totally at one with them. I could now understand exactly what he meant.

The campsite wasn't top of the range as far as facilities were concerned, so we didn't feel too scruffy to be there. The tidy plots were scattered through a meadow and we soon found quite a private spot down by the stream. The plot had a fire ring, a picnic table and a food locker. The wooden table was a bonus. If felt like a touch of luxury to have a table to sit at to eat. Normally we'd each take a pannier off the bikes and use them as seats, while we ate with plates on our knees. It was the first time that we'd come across a food locker too. They were there to protect our food from the bears that still roam the mountains. They see campsites as places to snag a quick feed and were, we were told, real opportunists. A hungry bear that isn't afraid of humans can be a dangerous beast. Our water came from the stream. The toilets were 'long-drops'. They'd do nicely; we were used to the 'al fresco' variety with a 360-degree view of wherever we happened to be.

What was supposed to be a stop for a night became a week of exploring. The bikes were the perfect way to get around and the sensation of riding between the peaks without a roof on was absolutely perfect. We hiked trails, took too many photos, and cooled cans of beer in the icy water of the stream.

The thought of George and Caroline and their vineyard was in our minds before too long though. We dropped out of the mountains through the town of Coulterville and headed west along Highway 132 through La Grange, Waterford and Empire. This ride showed us a side

 of the United States that we'd not been so aware of before. We knew that Americans were fiercely patriotic, but apart from every town having the Stars and Stripes flying in it somewhere, the passion for their nation had not been particularly obvious. It was now. The fourth of July celebrations were looming. This is the day that Americans celebrate the declaration of their independence from Britain, and every town was gearing up for a big party. Almost every house we passed was festooned with red, white and blue banners, streamers and giant rosettes. Every single one flew the stars and stripes, and bunting was hung from one side of the street to the other in the towns. Parade floats were being decorated, always with red white and blue. Huge bonfires were being built in the parks, and celebration posters were on poles that had been hammered into the roadsides. They advertised get-togethers and firework displays.

John Adams, who was the second President of the United States, wrote:

'The second day of July, 1776, will be the most memorable epoch in the history of America. I am apt to believe that it will be celebrated by succeeding generations as the great anniversary festival. It ought to be commemorated as the day of deliverance, by solemn acts of devotion to God Almighty. It ought to be solemnized with pomp and parade, with shows, games, sports, guns, bells, bonfires, and illuminations, from one end of this continent to the other, from this time forward forever more.'

His words had obviously been taken to heart, though two days later than he'd originally envisaged. Usually sleepy country towns were bustling with life. The air of excitement was tangible. Pictures of town mayors were posted in shop widows, each wearing a patriotic rosette.

173

So passionate was the scene that I actually felt a little intimidated, but we had the journey to ride. With a brief stop at the BMW dealership in Modesto to get some more points and condensers for Sir Henry, we cruised on through the warm air and the long expanses of farms and fruit plantations towards the vineyard. Perhaps there'd be a party at the vineyard too and if we were welcome there, then perhaps we could get involved with the celebrations.

The steep but rolling hillsides of the Palomares Canyon were once the home of the Ohlone Indians, and then became cattle and sheep grazing land. George and Caroline discovered the canyon in  1977, and fell in love with it. We could see why as we rolled along the shady, twisting road that in the rainy season has a fast flowing stream alongside it. The shade is provided by tall oaks and bays which hang out over the curves with a sort of ancient majesty. Darting out from under these cool shadows into the clear California sunlight takes you momentarily into warm air that has a friendly, humus-scented mustiness to it. Occasional houses, vineyards, farm buildings and even a monastery are tucked into the sides with long stretches of privacy-giving trees in between. The grassy slopes above were the wonderful golden colour that California is famous for. As we rode I knew that the canyon had to be a favourite ride for local bikers.

To the right of a long run of wooden picket fence, two large stone-pillared gates were 'bookended' with wine barrel bases that had been decorated with the name 'Chouinard Winery' and their logo. The gates were open and above them flew two long mediaeval style flags in gold and wine. The gravel car park in front of the winery was full of cars, which happy-faced people were milling around. To the sides ran neat rows of lush green vines which were growing heavy with fruit. The slopes behind the redwood winery were striped with long orderly rows of vines, and the surrounding gardens were vibrant with flowers in full bloom.

We'd arrived on an open tasting day and the atmosphere was a combination of friendly warmth and professionalism. As we parked up and I pulled my helmet off, a peal of laughter rang out from behind the open doors of the tasting room on the first floor of the winery. A small, slim man wearing glasses stepped smiling out onto the porch of the tasting room. In one hand he had a large glass of red wine, while his other hand was on the shoulder of a customer. The two of them looked as if they had just been sharing the sort of banter that only good friends can appreciate together. When he saw us down in the car park he called "Welcome" to us.

"Hi, I'm Sam and this is Birgit. We are looking for George and Caroline. Joe and Sarah sent us." His face was blank for a moment and

then the penny dropped. He'd known we were coming, but had completely forgotten about it. For a moment we felt as if we'd made a mistake, but when Caroline appeared around the edge of the winery to welcome us, we knew we hadn't. A tall, slim woman with wavy black hair, she greeted us with a laugh and a beaming smile. "You guys made it. That's great. Come on in. You are probably ready for a drink. Come on, I'll show you around." Our planned visit of just a few days soon turned into a stay of several weeks.

The next day started at 6am. In fact almost every day in the vineyard started at 6am, or earlier. Keen to learn about how a vineyard worked, and equally keen that we shouldn't just 'take' from the Chouinard family, we were up and ready to help out. Birgit set straight off up into the slopes to help with binding back the vines. This is a job best done when it's cool. During the previous evening we'd heard that Caroline had recently suffered a heart attack. One of her roles was to look after the flower gardens around the house and the winery, but since she'd been struck she'd not been able to do more than potter. On closer inspection I could see where weeds were beginning to crop up and where some of the plants badly needed water. So, while Birgit headed up into the slopes, I set to work in the gardens. I've always had a passion for plants and growing things, and have to admit that I like the things which give pretty results. It's all well and good growing stuff to eat, but nothing gives me such a buzz as seeing beds full of riotous colour.

That night we settled down with the family to one of those meals that you have a real appetite for when you've been doing manual labour all day. Caroline is a superb cook and with her food, accompanied by award-winning wine, we didn't have to work hard to do it justice.

The two next weeks zipped by as a patchwork of helping with the vines, Birgit learning about making wine, going for hikes in the surrounding canyons and bringing the gardens back into shape. We took trips down into the amazing city of San Francisco, about 80 kilometres away, and rode up into the greater Castro Valley. We met the family's friends and partied with them all several times – the 4th of July being the first occasion. They were a fun bunch who made us feel as if we had discovered a special place and had every right to be there with them. George and Caroline's eldest son Damian was off hiking in the Sierras but their other son Rick and his wife Julie and their very cute daughter Amanda also began to treat us as part of the family rather than two vagabonds who were just passing through. Rick and his family were as charming and as multi talented as George and Caroline. Rick, a master electrician was also a marathon runner. He moved with a relaxed rangy simplicity that spoke of the ability to run all day. Julie ran a small bakery and we knew that if we weren't careful, we'd both be piling on weight. Julie had a skill for making mouth-watering goodies that would come in a never-ending flow if we'd have let them. And Amanda? This obviously intelligent lass who was not yet into her teens, had a smile that could melt anyone's heart, and a talent for playing soccer. The other member of George and Caroline's family was a loopy, lovable, overgrown, tan-coloured Boxer dog called Heidi. She thought that overflying aeroplanes were invading her airspace and therefore should be barked at with every ounce of energy she could muster.

I was delighted to find that I could have access to the vineyard's computer, so could at last settle down to writing a series of articles about Central America for the UK's Motorcycle Sport and Leisure magazine. We barely thought about Alaska for those first two weeks.

Being on the vineyard was just too special to hurry. The semi-alcoholic haze with which the evenings passed also helped our thoughts to remain firmly in the canyon.

Birgit was badly bitten by Californian nature, but not in a good way. She discovered poison oak. The hillsides of the canyon were dotted with this very attractive plant. It's more of a bush than a tree and at certain times of the year it has flaming red, orange and yellow leaves which make it look as if it would be the perfect addition to a flower arrangement. Birgit wasn't much interested in arranging flowers but she came into contact with the stuff while up on the slopes. Caroline had warned us both about poison oak but the sides of the canyon are infested with it and it's very hard to avoid.

The plant contains oil called urushiol and when this poisonous substance comes into contact with your skin you can be in trouble. Some people are very badly affected by it and their bodies react against the poison by producing red wheals on the skin that then turn yellow and weep an oily substance. The wheals itch like mad. I only copped a mild dose of it and it nearly drove me dotty. Legend has it that the local Indians were never affected by the stuff, but I wondered if it was more that they were smart enough to avoid it. It's also said that they used poison oak as the first known version of chemical warfare. When at war with another tribe, they'd wait until they were upwind of their enemies and would set fire to it, causing toxic smoke to drift down on them.

You can pick up the poison from any part of the plant and even from someone else's clothes or from a dog that has been walking through the stuff. Birgit copped it big time. At first she didn't know what was going on and thought she'd just picked up some sort of rash that would go away. But over the following days this rash seemed to spread to other parts of her body. Not wanting to complain, she didn't say anything to anyone about it.

The only remedy for contact with poison oak seems to be to wash in icy cold water, within ten minutes of contact. After that you are in trouble. Birgit's spreading rash probably came from the fact that she had the oil on her hands and so passed it onto other parts of her body. The other parts weren't so bad because as she touched other surfaces the oil became diluted. She may well also have had the oil on her clothes and touching those, she just made the problem worse. She didn't know better.

After a few days her rashes had become so nasty that she had to talk to Caroline about them, who was horrified about how bad they had become. Caroline brooked no argument and took Birgit straight to the doctor. He gave her a shot of corticosteroids and slowly the itch began to lessen and the pussy wheals began to disappear. It took nearly two weeks for the itch to stop and for her skin to heal. The severity of the episode shocked Birgit. She's normally pretty much bullet-proof – she needed to be to travel with me!

Caroline encouraged us to get out and to do some exploring. We scooted off to visit a country fair. This was packed with gleaming farm machinery on show, and there were competitions for everything from best fruit and vegetables to the finest pigs and sheep. The show was a window into American country life and we were fascinated by it.

We decided to ride down the coast a little to the city of San José and to Big Sur. San José was an attraction because just a short distance away in a town called Watsonville, we had friends of friends who ran a second hand motorcycle parts business.

Chris and Rebecca were friends of Mike and Sally, whom I'd first met in the early days of my trip. In fact I'd only been on the road for a couple of weeks when I found their bike nestled in the depths of the massive ferry that ran between Greece and Egypt. Out of the 50 bikes already on board, theirs was the only one destined to go any further south than the border between Egypt and Sudan. Mike was a highly skilled motocross rider and they were on their way around the world. Sally was not so experienced and was not so sure that what they were doing was a good idea. The deal she had with Mike was that if they went round the world on their BMW R80GS, they would have babies on their return. She seemed relieved when she realised that I was heading their way, and that Mike was vastly more experienced than me.

The three of us rode together through the rugged hot lands of Egypt, Sudan and Ethiopia before we went in different directions in Kenya. They'd found work in Nairobi and I'd just got to the stage where at last I was beginning to feel in control of my bike and that dirt roads were fun rather than something that had to be treated with pure white-eyed fear. I was on a roll.

Though we heard of each other from other travellers as we both slowly made our ways down the continent, it wasn't until Namibia that our paths crossed again. We met on the main street in Namibia's capital city Windhoek. I'd just stepped away from being mugged. I was actually in a bit of a state. Only the day before, I'd been released from hospital following my major accident while crossing the desert in northern Namibia. I'd just stepped out of the bank with replenished funds when the mugger had struck. Fortunately, in spite of my arm being in a cast, and my legs being wobbly from being in a hospital bed for so long, the mugger hadn't got away with anything. But if there was ever a moment in my life when I really needed to see two good friends, that was it. And there they were.

I'd missed them again by just a few days in Singapore and again in northern Thailand. They had shipped across from the USA, having ridden up through South America. Knowing that I was on the way to the USA, they had given me the contact details for Chris and Rebecca. This is one of the things that I really like about being an overlander. There's a huge grapevine of information that gets passed along and each titbit of information goes a long way to adding to the quality of the journey. Sometimes the info might be about border crossings, places to stay or things to see, but sometimes it was about people who enjoyed the company of travellers. Nowadays the best place to get this sort of information is from the overlanders' website Horizons Unlimited. This site has opened up a whole new world of information that previously would only have been passed by word of mouth.

As the owner of EuroTech, Chris knew his way around BMWs expertly and Mike had said that if we ever had problems with the bikes then we should try to get to him. Birgit's bike was now becoming very

179

expensive to ride. Some weeks it felt as if she was keeping the points and condenser manufacturing industry alive. No one seemed to be able to work out what was causing the problem. We had run out of options and knew that Chris was going to be able to make or break the situation for us. It really wasn't fun for Birgit to have to ride never knowing when she was going to lose power.

Chris listened to the problem, listened to the bike, rode it round the block and then started to work on it. "Your backing plate is bent," he said. "If that isn't flat then you'll keep on burning points out. I think I have one in reasonable condition somewhere." It did the trick and in payment for the part, and a replacement mirror for one of Sir Henry's which had lost its ability to reflect, we helped Chris and Rebecca by tiling their bathroom. While I finished that off, Birgit painted the walls in their separate loo. A good trade all round, except I wasn't as sure as Birgit was about the deep purple colour chosen for the loo walls…

Being in this area also gave me the chance to get the rear shock on my bike serviced. Slowly but surely as we'd travelled across the USA I'd become aware that it wasn't as it should be. The thing had had a hard life anyway and I worried that the tope incident in Mexico had done lasting damage. I knew that I'd been lucky to make it this far without a real problem. I simply hadn't realised, because the damage had been worsening imperceptibly on a daily basis, just how bad it had become. Within the last 50 miles the damping had finally given up on me. The service engineers at Lindeman Racing told me that I was riding on little more than the spring. With the shock rebuilt, the ride was wonderfully firm and so responsive that I might have been riding another bike! I kicked myself for not getting it looked at earlier. The cruising I thought I'd been doing through the Tioga Pass had probably been more of a waddle!

Big Sur is a stretch of coast where the Santa Lucia Mountains drop down into the Pacific. We'd heard from a couple of bikers who'd stopped off at the vineyard that the riding was excellent down there and that the views along the coastal cliffs and bays were magnificent. They'd also said those magic words, "There are plenty of spots to free camp too."

Highway 1 follows a winding route between the coast and the mountains and one of the things I really liked about it was the complete absence of roadside advertising billboards. Another thing I liked was that local bylaws forbade any building within sight of the road. You do see a few older buildings but that's it. In any event the terrain is so rugged that scratching a living here isn't easy. That was a bonus for us. A few sand and rock tracks headed off into the mountains and we rode them, finding out of the way spots to pitch our tent with ease. One pitch was so far off the beaten track that it took on a rather spooky air. We sat outside our tent that night, listening to the noises of the forested valley we were in. Strange groans floated towards us on the wind, and every so often a loud 'Crack!' would come from the shadows. It took both of us a long time to go to sleep that night, our imaginations running free with wild thoughts of bears, ghosts of crazy gold miners who'd got lost and never left the mountains, and of growers of illicit marijuana.

At the end of the next day's ride we camped in the dusk on a stretch of hillside that looked down onto the darkening coastline. In the morning we were treated to the crisp view of jagged cliffs, a deep blue sea and rolling white breakers that were hitting the rocks below with a force that sent plumes of spray up into the pale blue morning sky.

On the way back to the vineyard we popped in to take a look at the town of Carmel. This small town came into being largely as a result of the great earthquake and fire of 1906 which wiped out much of San Francisco. The people who headed there from the city were in the main, those from the arts community. It remains a quirky and attractive town, whose inhabitants include a lot famous names. It has no streetlights or parking meters, Clint Eastwood was its mayor for while and there's a law which forbids the wearing of high-heeled shoes on its pavements. In the past there was a law that said no one could eat ice cream on its streets!

We arrived back at the vineyard to find preparations for a musical occasion in full swing. These were regular events to which customers were invited to bring a picnic to enjoy in and around the shady vine-covered pergolas. Local musicians played for them and each event had a theme; sometimes Spanish, sometimes Country and Western, sometimes Cajun and so on. Roger Cardinal was a real favourite. Wine of course was the drink of the day.

The vineyard was buzzing with all hands on deck. Paths needed sweeping, flowerbeds tickling, cases of white wine put into chillers, glasses washed and laid out with a hand-polished gleam on each, and the lights needed to be strung over the stage and through the trees. Extra chairs and tables needed to be put out and anything that was out of place was firmly put back in the right location.

A noticeable chill to the late evenings told us that it was time to get on the move again. If we didn't get a scoot on we'd never make it up into Alaska before the snows came. Time-wise, we were skating on the edge and we had a long way to travel but as August started, we felt quite optimistic; naively so.

Chapter Twelve

Go North

'Travel and change of place impart new vigour to the mind.'

Seneca

A thick heavy fog lay over the city of San Francisco and we rode across the famous Golden Gate Bridge, unable to see over the sides. I

 was glad that we'd been able to see the city, Alcatraz and the bridge in the sunshine, on earlier visits. The thick, white air hung densely around us and though Birgit had wanted to see the lighthouse at Point Reyes, we decided to try to ride on out of the fog.

Highway 101 tempted us as we rode myopically off the north end of the bridge. It's a fast road that cuts inland and then runs parallel with the coast but in spite of the fog, we'd set our minds on riding the fabled Highway 1. This road hugs the coast where the geography lets it.

We stopped off for the night at Fort Ross. There's a quirk of North American history here that couldn't be ridden past. The land had once belonged to the Russians! I'd no idea that the Russians had owned any land south of Alaska. The fort itself was built in 1812 and was active until 1841. Only one of the original buildings still stands, but volunteers have reconstructed the other buildings from what is known about how the fort had once been. It was built by the Russians to act as a base for growing produce to send up the coast into their lands in the north. I really rather liked the idea that the Russians had once owned part of the continent, and as we walked through the fort I wondered how many subsequent Russian leaders had regretted ever giving up this toe-hold. The quirky thing is that it had operated very successfully as a multi-cultural arrangement for its lifetime. How times then changed.

Alaska was bought by the United States from Russia in 1867 for the grand sum of $7.2million, or just two cents an acre. I wondered how many multiples of that price had been dragged out of the land since then in the form of gold and oil alone.

The first Russian colony was founded in Alaska in 1784 with the aim of hunting sea otters for their pelts. At the time these furry skins were highly prized. Grigory Shelikhov kicked things off on Kodiak Island, where, according to the history books, he subdued the indigenous Aleutian people with some horribly brutal methods. He killed hundreds, and took hostages to enforce obedience from the others. When I'd read this I'd thought, "Time doesn't change much then." It seems that the stronger still do this sort of thing to the weaker all over the world.

At one time the colony's population grew to 40,000 people, though most of those were actually local Aleuts. From Alaska, the Russians explored right down into what is now British Colombia. The colony was never really profitable though, mainly due to the distances involved, and when the US offered to buy the territory the Russians agreed. There are still some in Russia who say that the land was never sold but was leased until 2017. Now that would be a turn up for the books! I suspect it was just wishful thinking and anyway, would the mighty US ever let Russia, with whom there has been so much antagonism, take over such a huge expanse of land right on their doorstep? I don't think so.

We always found it harder to find a free or budget price camping spot when we were near tourist attractions, and this was no exception. The Fort Ross State Historic Park has a small campsite, but it's run on a 'first come, first served' basis. We arrived at 1pm to find that everyone else who'd got there first had been served. There wasn't a plot left for us. The only alternatives seemed to be large commercial RV sites further inland. They didn't appeal at all.

When the park ranger saw our crestfallen expressions she made a suggestion. "Honeys, you have two choices. You could try to find someone else to share their pitch with you. As you guys have got bikes that might not be a problem."

We understood what she meant. Most pitches on organised campsites were massive. Land is so much more freely available in this vast continent than back home in Europe. Many pitches were big enough to cater for RVs, and certainly big enough for whole families to set up a group of tents, so this might well not be a problem. In comparison, in the tiny UK, most sites seem to have been set up for nationals who are used to living in each others' pockets, and not for a night in the wilds.

Then the ranger said, "You might be better off taking a spot I have in mind." She took us down into the camping area and there, by the side of the road, was a spot just big enough to park two bikes and pitch a tent. "If you don't mind and are only going to be here for one night, I can let you camp here for $5." Perfect. The only slight worry was the large sign over the grassy corner spot that read 'NO CAMPING'. We collected funny looks from passers-by as we pitched the tent. We felt like naughty schoolchildren doing something we knew we shouldn't. With hindsight the simple solution would have been to put a couple of carrier bags over the sign. Wish we'd thought of that at the time! But Fort Ross was well worth our slightly red faces.

That night we ate 'Chilli a la Damian' for dinner. When he can escape from the vineyard, Damian Chouinard is an avid hiker. But he's a lightweight, literally. Damian's way of camping is completely minimalist. He carries virtually nothing. Often he won't even have a tent. He has an ultra lightweight sleeping bag and sleeps directly on the ground. He carries no spare clothes in his thin-skinned parachute material type of daypack. So, when the clothes he is wearing need washing, he'll find a launderette in a small town somewhere, will pull on a black plastic bin bag and wait for his clothes to wash and dry before setting off again. I really admired his ability to think so light and cringed at the amount of stuff that we carried in comparison. Some of the things he did carry were plastic freezer bags full of meals he'd made and then dehydrated in a machine he had for the purpose. These highly nutritious meals, with all the proteins and carbohydrates etc needed to keep an active go-for-it merchant on the move, were spot on. His mother Caroline had kindly given us some of these ready-made meals to take with us when we left the vineyard. But she'd warned, "He likes to make them hot, guys." Not a problem, we'd thought.

185

We should have listened! The chilli was so hot that it instantly had tears rolling down our cheeks. My tongue felt as if I'd just bitten into a burning ember. We glugged every drop of water we had to try to put the fire out, to no avail, and then ran for the standpipe. The other campers watched us, bemused, as we drank litres of water and washed the outside of our mouths – even our lips burned. And the heat went all the way down! The fiery sensation stayed with us right through the night and my stomach gurgled in constant angry complaint. The burps subsequently emitted made me think I'd be better off taking up a career as a fire breather! Damian must have long since burned every tastebud out of his mouth. How on earth could he possibly make so many award-winning wines?

As far as we were concerned, Highway 1 earned its right to be fabled. We loved every minute of the ride as it took us ever northwards through small towns, alongside bays and beaches and through clusters of forest. Eventually it led us back onto the 101 where the Smithe Redwood State Reserve straddles the road.

One of the high points for me in the USA was to get to what's left of the coastal redwood forest. Once this forest stretched across 8,100 square kilometres of western USA but over the years, logging and development had cleared much of it. Now, enthusiasts work hard to ensure that this area, that must have been like a northern Amazon Rain Forest, isn't allowed to get any smaller.

The coastal redwood is from the Sequoia family and these magnificent giants can live for 2,200 years, and can grow over 115 metres tall. That's 379 feet, or 62 times taller than me. They are evergreen and can grow to a diameter of 8 metres and weigh 500 tons! They like mountainous country, but the oldest trees grow down in the gullies and valley bottoms where they can get the most water. The coastal forests of California and southern Oregon are in a rocky mountainous land where not much will grow because of the poor soil quality, so the trees have developed to the stage that when a tree dies, the surrounding trees will absorb all the nutrients from the dying tree – the ultimate in recycling. They love the fog that this coast is famous for. The fog provides cool moist air which stops the trees drying out in what would otherwise be an arid area. But fog isn't an essential aspect of redwood life. It just allows the trees to grow over a far greater area. The trees' thick bark, and the fact that they have no resin, makes them highly fire resistant. They recover quite quickly when a bush fire has blasted through them. It's said that in the Great San Francisco Fire which followed the 1906 earthquake, it was the fact that an area of buildings had been made out of redwood that stopped it spreading. The Smithe Redwood State Reserve is a relatively small section but as we eased along the 101, which was surprisingly quiet, I knew that I was seeing something special. I also knew that a little further along the highway was the much bigger Humboldt Redwood State Park and then the main Redwood National Forest itself. For once, on the road, we were going to be able to get several bites at the redwood 'cherry'.

When travelling, you often have to make a choice. To see or not to see? And if you do go and see something spectacular, then you may never see the like of it again. Each bite is inevitably a bittersweet mouthful because it leaves you wanting more when you are about to ride away. But hey, I wasn't complaining. At least I'd been lucky enough to see some cherries, let alone taste so many of them. Seeing the redwoods was a real bonus and the Humboldt gave me the sensation of riding though some sort of dream.

The trees stand proud and vertical. They grow closely together in groves. Their lower trunks are covered with a dark reddish bark that is thick, sinuous and almost papery in texture. Deep, irregular, angular grooves line the bark as if nature has thoroughly enjoyed fooling the observer into believing that he is seeing something quite random. When you ride through the trees they are dangerous. They draw your eyes ever upwards, towards their spiky-leaved tops, but for so long, that you risk taking a tumble. When you walk between them, you find yourself arching your head back, and then your back as well, as you strain to see all the way up to the small clusters of sky that are still visible. Shafts of sunlight plummet earthwards into the cool darkness around you, in spotlights of golden warmth. We parked the bikes, feeling that we had to do some walking through this lot. The risk of having something pinched off the bikes was more than worth it. And as ever in the USA, there didn't seem to be any real risk of someone walking off with any of our kit. When you lie on the ground in one of these groves, and look upwards, it's almost as if the trees are clustering their heads to look down at you, perhaps in concern, but always with a feeling of friendly welcome.

The next town we stopped in was like stepping back in time. Ferndale is a small wooden Victorian dairy town down on the coast. Elegant shuttered houses and shops line the narrow, (for the USA), streets. Each seemed to be painted in gentle pastel blues, creams, greys and greens and many were finished off with stark white window and door frames. Ferndale is the location for the Humboldt County Fair and as such it has a permanent fairground. We could camp there for $5 a night, and it had blissfully hot showers.

We'd only managed to camp on a town's fairground once before. That was on the way from the Rocky Mountains to California. We'd  enjoyed that experience too, but particularly because the showground was often used for rodeos. Not that we were lucky enough to be passing through when one was due, but we could get a taste for the place. The earthy, dusty ring was surrounded by tough wooden walls and tall, galvanised metal gates. The air smelt of old horse and cattle manure, diesel, leather and sweat. We were allowed to see the showrooms, the stables and of course the showers for competitors. The county kept the facility open year-round and were happy for the likes of us to pay a small fee and then use those showers and toilets. Perfect.

This particular town had also had some excellent 'thrift shops', so we'd gone shopping big style. By that time most of our clothes were almost falling to pieces. T-shirts had holes, jeans had patches. We'd also learnt from experience that it wasn't worth patching the crotch area because it felt like wearing a nappy (or 'diaper' as Americans would say). We also managed to replace the thermos that had got broken months before in Baja California. We'd missed being able to wake up to a cup of coffee and also stop along the way for a hot drink. But new thermos flasks were just too expensive on our meagre budget. We were mooching around one of the thrift shops when the assistant, an elderly white-haired lady called Muriel, came across and asked, "Anything ah can help you people with?" This was said with such a kindly voice that we said, "Well, yes, you don't happen to have any thermos flasks do you?" and explained why. "No dear, ah don't, but leave it with me, I can look through the stock. Where are y'all staying?" To our surprise, about three hours later Muriel turned up at the showground with a choice of three flasks for us to look at. We chose the 2-pint builder's flask that was made out of aluminium and had thick protective rubber rings around its skin. That would do nicely. From that moment on, each coffee was started with a toast to Muriel. I've always wondered if she went home and pulled the selection of thermos flasks out of her own cupboard. It wouldn't have surprised me. Thanks to her thoughtful effort on our behalf she'd improved the quality of our travelling life and in the months to come that thermos would be a lifesaver.

Birgit and I wandered around Ferndale, slowing our pace as suited the mood of the town. Most of the shops, that weren't dealing with goods for the surrounding farms, looked after visitors. Small shops stocked all sorts of locally made handicrafts. Bakeries stocked a huge selection of homemade cakes and cookies – Birgit's diary has an entry that gleefully says 'Giant Chocolate Chip cookies'. There were plenty of antique shops too. We found the quirky things the most amusing; my favourite was a poster left over from the last fair which advertised 'Pig Racing'. What an excellent image that conjured up. We also got talking to a couple of bikers. Barbara and Gary knew Leedy, one of the guys who'd befriended us back at the Harley Rally in Bridgeport. Leedy had mentioned us to them and they'd been on the lookout for us.

My centre stand was mangled by the air cargo company that flew our bikes from Colombia to Panama and I'd been having problems with it ever since. They'd welded it back together at the airport but it wasn't a great repair and it had always been a chore to get the bike up onto it. On rough ground it wasn't too hard to do, but any firm surface meant that Birgit always had to give me a hand. I really liked having the centre stand as any maintenance was far easier to do when the bike was on it. Fixing punctures was as easy as that chore is ever going to be when I could get Libby balanced on her centre stand. But its generally weakened state was also now a worry. Large rusty holes had started to appear in it and I was sure that one day soon the thing would collapse under the weight of the bike and my gear. Inevitably that was going to end up with me having a red face and even, perhaps, some expensive damage to the bike or kit. Being a farming town, it didn't take us long to track down a bloke who welded farm machinery. Birgit bought chocolate chip cookies as her souvenir of Ferndale, and mine was a refurbished centre stand.

We carried on meandering up the Redwood Highway. We couldn't help feeling inspired. When the tree-friendly fog is around, it does something rather magical to the light. The spotlights of sunshine between the giants become diffused and gentle. The resulting light seems to fill the air with an ever-changing single colour. That sounds really weird, but the air between the trees is filled with a hundred shades of soft, golden-green light, as if every molecule in the fog is bouncing mini light rays out into the world of green, and then absorbing what colour is reflected back again. This beautiful but mysterious foggy sunshine sent my imagination running wild. These trees haven't changed much since the time of the dinosaurs. It wasn't hard to imagine that a brontosaurus might suddenly come crashing through the undergrowth.

As usual, we explored the areas we were travelling through, taking full advantage of having the bikes. The ability they gave us to go virtually anywhere was wonderful, and though we knew the Alaskan weather clock was ticking, it felt as if it would be a complete waste to ride too far each day and to ignore the sidetracks. We found tucked away, flower-filled meadows and streams, craggy valleys and we rode steep dirt tracks through the ridges. We hardly saw a soul and yet again I was happy that our bikes were so quiet. It would have felt completely wrong to have been riding noisy bikes in such a beautiful place. Even Sir Henry had stopped firing off 'shotgun blasts'. Chris's solution of a new points backplate had worked.

My favourite campsite from this part of America, was only just inside California. Our Free Camping book described how to get to a spot a few miles off the Redwood Highway, about thirty miles inland from the Jedediah Smith Redwoods State Park. The instructions went something like this: 'Remain on the 199 for approximately 20 miles past the South Fork Road turning. On your left you will see three tall redwoods standing on their own together. 20 yards later you will see a trail leading off to the left. Go over the bridge and take the first fork left on the trail. This will follow the creek for 5 miles. Not advised for motorhomes and trailers. The site is on a bend in the creek. There are no facilities other than a fire pit. Beware of bears.'

It sounded idyllic and the directions worked perfectly. We left the coastal cool behind us and followed the Smith River inland. The three trees were exactly where we'd expected them to be and the stone and wooden bridge was as described. The trail was definitely not suitable for RVs; you would never have got one up the track. It quickly deteriorated into a rough path which threw little challenges at us with every metre until we came to a section that looked more like a dried up streambed than a trail. Three large, rounded boulders stood in our way. We began to wonder if we'd taken a wrong turning somehow, but when we stopped to look for a way round the rock, we both agreed that we'd not seen any turnings. We looked for a way to pick a path. I wasn't sure how my GS was going to cope so how was Birgit's ancient R60 going to manage, with its lower ground clearance? There appeared to be a small earth-filled gully between the rocks. This had to be the way. With a narrow, lightweight trailbike, it would have been fun, but on our bikes…

The bikes' engines idled as we sat looking at the obstacle. The only thing to do was to 'go for it'. We'd make it or we wouldn't. Neither of us considered that going up would be far easier than going down again. As always, Birgit went first. She gunned her engine a little, as if to make sure it hadn't gone to sleep and was ready for what was to

191

come. Standing on her foot pegs, she eased forward, and then went for it, her eyes fixed on the smoother trail beyond. We'd both learnt by this time that often this is the only way to get through a situation like this.

Pick your route, plan what you are going to try to do, and then focus on the other side leaving the power of the bike and instinct to deal with the problems. With a roar, Sir Henry hit the gully, his back end jiggled furiously and then, bucking, he took Birgit up and through the rocks. Not once did she look as if she was going to fall off. I was impressed, but now it was my turn.

My front wheel hit the side of the first rock. I'd just misjudged it. The wheel twisted, jerking the handlebars hard to the right. I kept my eyes focused on the other side and opened the throttle. My instincts were saying, 'Stop! Take another run at it' but it was too late. If I stopped I'd be off. Committed, Libby leapt forward, her front wheel hitting the next rock and her back wheel jamming momentarily because of the angle and then, with the back wheel spinning, I was through. I thought I'd really stuffed that one up. Birgit didn't look very impressed with my effort!

When we got to the bend in the creek, it was a beautiful spot. The site had been left completely clean by previous occupants. All that remained were the tracks of their knobbly motorcycle tyres. There were no camping pitch markers laid out – it was entirely up to you to pick your spot. We chose one on a small bluff right next to the river but a couple of metres above it. That would keep us safe from flooding. We pitched the tent in the shade of a small stand of pine trees, collected firewood from the boulder-strewn riverbanks and then hunted for a taller tree. We'd been rather blasé about the bear problems when we'd been in the far south but the further north we travelled, the more warnings we were seeing about the risks. Now we followed the rules. We always loaded our food, shampoo and soap into one of our rucksacks and then hoisted that up into a tree.

Our most likely unwanted guests were going to be black bears. The more I understood about these intelligent and powerful beasts, the more I respected them. A male can weigh around 165 kilos and I'd read that they can run at 36 kilometres an hour if they feel the need. I knew I couldn't run that fast, even if something had scared the living daylights out of me. These bears have poor eyesight but have highly developed senses of hearing and smell and we knew from all the warnings that they could scent food from great distances. If whatever it was smelt sweet, then as far as a bear was concerned that was a big bonus. The fool in me conjured up a nice image of a bear sitting on its rump sucking toothpaste from its tube like some sort of popsicle. But the sane side of me had taken good note of the photos we'd seen of the damage a hungry bear can do to a car to get at food locked away inside.

One such photo showed a completely mangled front door of a 4x4. The bear had managed to hook its claws in over the top of the door and had bent that down with such force that the upper section of the door was at ninety degrees. The bear, now with a much better grip, had ripped open the rest of the door. It must have climbed inside the 4x4 in its search for food as the inside of the car looked as if drug-crazed yobs had vandalised it. I'd even heard that bears would drink such things as chainsaw oil – it apparently tastes sweet.

Part of me was really conscious that I was a visitor in this land and as such I had no right to disturb nature. Yes, we free camped, perhaps in places that we shouldn't have, but we were always careful to respect nature and to leave nothing behind. I knew that bears which had discovered how easy human food is to get hold of around campsites often had to be put down because of how dangerous they became with this discovery. We didn't want to be the cause of the death of such magnificent creatures. Female bears that have discovered tasty human-created delights even have the intelligence to teach their cubs about campsites and so on.

If you have a vehicle of a suitable size you can buy bear-proof containers for your food to be stored in when out in the wilds. They are like small oil drums, though not completely airtight, but are so smoothly surfaced that bears can't get a grip on them, so can't open them. On bikes, they weren't an option.

We'd learnt to cook our food well away from the tent. When we weren't cooking then we'd find a tall tree that had a branch a good three metres off the ground. The branch had to be strong enough to take the weight of our bag, at least a couple of metres away from the trunk. Bears are expert climbers. Finding suitable trees wasn't always easy though, especially when we were camping amongst pine trees and other evergreens. We either couldn't reach suitable branches or they just weren't strong enough for the weight of the bag. Rather than carry an extra rope, we stripped off our luggage ratchet straps and clipped them together. We'd tie a weight to the end of them and use that to help us throw the strap over the chosen branch. Birgit had a better eye for this than I did.

By now you've probably noticed that I often skip between talking about miles and kilometres, yards and metres, pounds and kilos. For most of the past few years we'd been riding in countries which used kilometres and metres. Being in the US, where miles were used confused me because I now thought in kilometres. Birgit's speedometer was marked in kilometres, but mine, and everything else in the USA, was marked in miles. Sometimes, thinking in kilometres worked because as they are shorter, we seemed to be covering more ground, but at other times, the longer miles made it feel as if we were cramming more into a day. It was a mind tease, but once I'd got over the feeling that I really ought to be thinking in the units used in the land I was in, I enjoyed not caring what measurements I thought in. The freedom of our lives actually meant that it didn't matter...except when we were judging fuel stops.

The bend in the creek was idyllic and the temptation was to stay there longer. We bathed nude in the rushing chilly water, the sun warming our upper bodies as the parts below the water wrinkled and froze. We washed our clothes and lay them out on rocks to dry in the sunshine. We cooked and ate, we sat by our fire and swopped stories about the riding done over the past days, and we pored over our maps of Oregon. We were suddenly keen to move on into another State. It felt as if we'd been in California for a very long time.

There was only one place that I really wanted to see in Oregon: Crater Lake. The rest of the time I felt that we were going to be able to sit back and enjoy the ride. Oregon sounded lush and beautiful. It sounded like perfect biking country. We'd been moving quite slowly but the call of the north was now really strong and we had some connections to make in Washington State, north of Oregon.

Highway 199 took us hurtling inland until we got to the town of Grant River, where we set off north-eastwards along the 234 and the 62. The surrounding mountains and peaks awed us and the valleys were full of forests and meadows. Oregon didn't disappoint us and somehow, once again, everything seemed to be in tune. Each mile had something interesting to look at, and the towns and villages showed a way of life that seemed to be in a sort of time-lag zone. There was hardly any other traffic and we let the bikes have their heads. For a change, they dictated to us how fast to go and where to ride.

I let my hands loosen on the handlebar grips and let the front wheel guide me. I listened to the ticking of the engine's valves beneath me and the drumming of the tyre treads. I could feel the gentle warm air that was slipstreaming over the cylinders onto my boots and ankles. I could smell the familiar tang of hot oil, hot rubber and petrol. I gazed at the humming grey asphalt that whizzed in an ever-faster blur beneath me. I watched the suspension working my front mudguard up and down over the undulations in the road surface. I imagined all the moving parts beneath me, parts that were working rhythmically together with a familiar well-oiled slickness. My shadow stretched out across the road beside me, as if trying to race the real me. I rode soaking up the views, and loving the pure, balanced co-ordination that the bike and I seemed to have, but thinking about our neighbour's comments on the campsite back in Las Vegas. I knew for sure why he had little interest in what went on in the outside world. I was beginning to feel that the USA is a world all of its own. I knew better, but there was just so much to see. At the end of the adventure, the UK was going to feel tiny. I revelled in the freedom of the ride and the open road. I wouldn't have swopped my motorcycle for a car for any amount of money anyone could offer me.

Up in front, Sir Henry seemed to hesitate, his smooth flowing ride abruptly interrupted. He jerked and then all became smooth again. I wondered if I'd imagined it. A few miles later, he did the same thing. I got closer. He sounded really rough, and then I realised that something was very wrong. Birgit eased her bike over to the side of the road and jumped off to look down at the engine. "He's only firing on one cylinder," she called to me. "I've no idea what's wrong."

I always get a bit of a sinking feeling when something like this happens. I'm not an expert mechanic and as far as I am concerned, anything to do with the electrics might as well be black magic. But when something happens on my bike, I'm not so bothered. It will either get fixed, or it won't. Birgit's bike was a different matter. It was a purely, and very much mistaken, macho thing. I couldn't help feeling that, as the bloke, I was supposed to be able to fix things. Not that Birgit ever expected me to do anything other than help her when requested. It was her bike so she was going to fix it. For her I suspected that this thought stemmed from two things. She's a very determined character who likes to know how things work and doesn't like to be beaten. But it also came from the days before we started to travel together on two bikes. Back then, I'd said to her that if she was going to have her own bike then she would have to maintain it. She'd be a safer rider if she understood what was going on beneath her and she'd spend less time worrying about the unknown, if she knew how to sort basic things at least. She'd taken this to heart of course.

This time it appeared that my slim skills were not going to be needed. Calmly and logically, she worked her way around the bike, ticking off possible causes on a mental list until she came to the carburettors. She didn't even have to open them up to see if dirt was clogging a jet or some such thing. There was a fuel pipe loose, but some sort of air lock appeared to be stopping the fuel from flowing out of the pipe – she was lucky! She pushed it back on, noted that the rubber had stretched with age and should be replaced in due course, started the bike, and Sir Henry ran with his usual smoothness once more. Good stuff.

A few metres into the Crater Lake National Park, he did the same thing but this time fuel spewed all over the asphalt right in front of the ranger's office. Birgit's face was red with embarrassment. So much for looking after nature! She quickly turned the fuel taps off and with a final dribble, the flow from the leaking carb stopped. But strangely, the fuel pipe was still firmly fixed in its place. The rubbish bin provided some sheets of newspaper, which Birgit placed under the offending carburettor. The cause of the problem was immediately obvious.

The lower section of the carb, the float bowl, houses the float mechanism. This helps to regulate the amount of fuel to be mixed with the air, before the mix is exploded with a spark from the sparkplugs in the cylinder heads. The float had jammed fully open and this was causing the carb to overflow. A couple of firm jiggles loosened it up and with the float bowl back on, the problem was solved. The rangers hadn't seemed to notice.

Crater Lake is so stunningly beautiful that it had me wondering how much more beauty the USA could possibly hold. There's a road that skirts the top of the lake walls and we couldn't wait to ride it. The steep sides drop down into the caldera of what was once a taller volcano. At the bottom lies a lake of a colour I'd never seen before. The water is 1,932 feet deep.

When light is in the air it's full of colour, most of which we aren't aware of seeing. When light hits clear water, the various colours are slowly absorbed. First to go are the reds, then orange, the yellows and penultimately, the greens. That leaves blue. This blue, aided by the colour of the sky above, is what we see as the colour of the water. If the sky overhead is a grey blue, then so will the water be.

The day we arrived, the sky was an unwavering, almost electric, blue. So too, rather eerily, was the water. On this windless day, it reflected the sides of the caldera so precisely that it was hard to tell where the water stopped and the land began. We could have turned the scene upside down and almost no one would have been any the wiser. We stood gobsmacked by the serene but bizarre beauty.

197

The park's roads are often closed due to snow from September onwards and some of the campsites close at that time too. Winter  sports are encouraged though, and that night, as the temperatures dropped, we could see and feel why this was the case. The still air had a raw bite to it that encouraged us to keep all our bike kit on as we put up the tent and set to cooking pasta carbonara for dinner. The scents of bacon, onions, mushrooms, the creamy sauce and pasta eased into the air around us. Later, as the coffee water in our billy can came to the boil, it shot out a plume of steam which seemed to hang in the air for a moment, and then to dissipate. I thought to myself, "It's turning to ice drops!" But of course it wasn't.

We'd free camped in a quiet corner and then realised that we'd made a mistake by doing so. The only spot we'd been able to find didn't have any trees tall enough with strong enough branches to hang our food and toiletries from. The question then was whether to do the best we could and hang the bag on the best option, or whether to take it out into the trees, a good distance from the tent and then leave it on the ground. The debate was all about whether hanging the food up would make it easier to smell. We didn't know any better, so hung it up as best we could, and then climbed into our sleeping bags with fingers crossed. And hot water bottles.

Its funny how the simplest ideas can take the longest to percolate through the grey cells, and how often, they are the best ideas. Before going to bed that night we filled both of our metal drinking water bottles with hot water, wrapped them in spare socks, and tucked them down into our sleeping bags. Bliss, and a cheap option too. We'd boiled our water as always, so we could drink it the next day when it had cooled.

As I gently slipped to sleep in the cosy warmth of my sleeping bag that night, a happy thought came into my mind. How easy it was to travel in the States. Even on a tight budget and sleeping in some odd, out of the way places, life was very good. In Africa, the way days went had often been dictated by keeping safe and surviving. In South America, enjoying the Andes or the jungles had been complicated by bad roads, having to deal with everything in a foreign language, by the constant challenge of dealing with the fear of the unknown, of corruption and the effort of finding places to stay. In Mexico it had been heat, strange customs and the tingling uncertainty about the future.

Here we were basically free. Free, within reason, to do what we wanted, when we wanted. One of the things that Birgit had commented on within days of crossing the border was how wonderful it was to be able to drink water straight from the tap without worrying about catching lurgies. But safe, warm and dry in my sleeping bag I also pondered the fact that some things were not so easy. We'd been cleaner in Africa, Asia and South America. Because cheap accommodation abounds, getting a wash each day wasn't a problem. The wash may have been standing in a large, garishly-coloured plastic washing up bowl scooping mugs of water over us in an African fleapit, or under the dodgy electrics of a Peruvian shower, but the opportunities were there. With all the free camping we were doing in the US, most of our washes seemed to come from the waters of chilly creeks, when we'd been able to find a creek to camp next to.

But how easy it was to get to the magnificent sights that abound in the USA. And because it was so easy, I found myself with the time to learn so much more. My mind seemed freer to take in so many more of the things around us. Yet this was a different culture, and the land was so varied and so dramatic, that there were enough daily challenges to have the combination of awe and adrenaline buzz I loved so much about travel.

I wasn't complacent. There were so many things to learn from the States and their people. I admired the way that lives had been carved out of this rugged land and I wanted to learn more. It was all there for me to learn. I just had to keep living my dream with my eyes wide open. Grubby-faced, I snuggled closer to my hot water bottle and drifted off.

Chapter Thirteen

Pure Dumb Luck – or Not

'Believe you can and you're halfway there.'

Theodore Roosevelt

In the morning, under a clear blue sky, the cold didn't seem to matter so much. Perhaps it was because I was becoming more accustomed to constant changes in temperature or perhaps because I now felt completely at home with where we were and what we were doing. I didn't know, but the sun was shining and there was a ride to do.

Even after just a couple of days away from the sea, we missed it. Birgit and I dropped down from the hills and reached the coast again at the town of Reedsport. Our target here was the Oregon Dunes National Park. We'd read that these dunes were spectacular, and they didn't disappoint. We cruised on up Highway 101, passing through the small tourist towns that dot this very pretty coastline. Free camping was harder to find but we succeeded and once again let the bikes take us where they wanted to.

We rode on instinct, with no plan except to head north. We cut across Saddle Mountain and headed up into Washington State via the town of Kelso. Just as we rolled across the state border, Birgit pulled over. I could tell she was agitated. She jumped off her bike and frantically searched her pockets. She looked up at me, her face a picture of complete dismay. "I've lost my keys!" she said with a dumbfounded tone. Both of us carried our ignition keys on one key ring and the keys for the panniers and padlocks on another ring. We had clip-on clasps for them and normally we'd use a key and then clip the bunch straight back onto our belts. It's a routine that after a few weeks on the road had become a habit that neither of us was aware of doing any more. This time she'd obviously been distracted by something when we'd done the final bike loading and she'd not clipped them back on. Or perhaps she had, but not fully.

What a pain. The locks would have to be cut off and replaced. Or we'd have to break into her panniers to get at her spares. As I stood looking at her dejection I couldn't help thinking how stupid we'd been. Why, after all this time on the road, had we never arranged that each of us would carry spares of each other's keys? I walked over to her, not sure what to say. Then I looked down at her bike.

There, on the top of her pannier, was the bunch of keys. We'd just ridden 150 miles of curves and bumps and the keys had been sitting there all the time. We looked down at them with disbelief. Talk about lucky. The only things I could think of that had enabled them to stay there were the construction of her bike panniers, and her smooth riding style.

When we were preparing her bike for the trip, we had not been prepared to pay the price for the rather poor quality aluminium panniers that were available at the time, so we'd made a set for her. We knew exactly what we wanted. They had to be strong enough to cope with crashes without disintegrating, and to stop those with sticky fingers from getting inside them easily. They also had to be strong enough to sit on at the end of a day's riding yet light enough to carry away from the bike fully loaded. Last, but not least, they had to be easy to unlock and remove – that allowed us to get the bikes through doorways in hotels in dodgy countries. We made them a little wider than the other widest point on her bike – her handlebars. With her R60 being basically a road bike, her bars weren't as wide as those fitted to trail bikes, including my own GS80. We wanted the boxes to be narrow enough for her to be able to jiggle her way through manic traffic easily, but wide enough to fit her kit inside. Their depth was limited by the two silencers the R60/5 had running parallel beside the back wheel, and to keep the centre of gravity low we couldn't make them too tall. A low centre of gravity is a tremendous aid to staying upright on dirt tracks.

We got hold of some 2 millimetre-thick sheet aluminium and made it into a box shape with the aid of lengths of 20mm aluminium angle brackets. It was all held together with pop rivets and sealed with silicone to keep all the seams water and dust tight. The lid of her pannier was a single sheet of the aluminium, with the alu angle forming a frame which gave both rigidity and the lip to close down onto the main box. The panniers had worked very well and had dealt with everything the road had demanded, except the time I ran into her from behind in Colombia. This 'frame' was 2mm thick and must have provided just enough resistance to stop the keys from going over the edge. Thank goodness for luck, a great suspension system and for a relaxed riding style. Even so, we'd learnt a rather good lesson.

The only reason for heading inland at this stage was to get to Mount St Helens. We'd been following the American continent's line of volcanoes all the way from Chile and they had become old friends. They fascinated us both. The shapes they make are a majestic addition to the landscape and many of the volcanoes that we'd been lucky enough to get close to had given us great adventures. With Crater Lake so fresh in our minds we itched to see this one. It has a special story.

The last time I'd been close to an active volcano had been way back in Indonesia where I'd escaped an eruption by just a few days. I'd actually stood right on the rim without realising that things were about to blow. And we'd been in the Ecuadorian capital of Quito when one of the nearby volcanoes started to scare people. Newspapers, the radio and the TV were all full of the impending eruption. People were leaving the city for the countryside and those with nowhere else to go were battening down the hatches. Fortunately it didn't happen and we were able to ride on, very happy for all those people whose lives would have been devastated by an eruption.

People around Mount St Helens hadn't been so lucky. On Sunday May 18th 1980, Mount St Helens erupted with an earthquake - equivalent of 5 on the Richter scale that triggered one of the world's largest recorded landslides. The top and 1,300 feet of the mountain cascaded down into the valley below. When the landslide exposed the molten rock that had been hidden deep within the volcano, a huge blast of steam, gas and rock levelled the trees and buildings over a vast area – 150,000 acres in total. The blast also killed 57 people. It was pure luck that the eruption hadn't happened a day later, when the loss of life would have been far greater. Then the forests would have been full of lumberjacks.

We'd both seen some absolutely bizarre photos of the landscape after the blast. The trees had mostly been flattened and stripped of their leaves, and they all lay pointing outwards from the centre of the eruption. Ground cover had completely disappeared, leaving the ash-covered land looking as if it belonged to a grotesque planet in outer space. President Jimmy Carter is reputed to have commented, "Someone said this area looked like a moonscape. But the moon looks more like a golf course compared to what's up there." As a geographer, Birgit had been fascinated by the event and Mount St Helens was firmly on her list of 'must see' places.

Even twenty years after the eruption, the after-effects were still plain to see. Amazingly, the fallen trees had been harvested rapidly enough to avoid decay setting in and damaging the timber. At one stage there were more than a thousand people harvesting the fallen trees, and then the work started to re-plant the land. Over the next seven years, more than 18 million trees were re-planted. Birgit reckoned that with the new planting, the land looked as if it had been given a military crew cut. The landscape had changed forever though. Not only did Mount St Helens look completely different with its top and side blown off, but in many places the blast had removed the soil right down to the bedrock. Trees would never grow there again.

Suddenly conscious of the changing weather, we dropped down to ride a major highway for once. On our way to Canada, we wanted to stop off to meet up with a friend of George and Caroline's at Gig Harbour called Sandi. We also wanted to link up with our friends from the Grand Canyon, Peter and Peggy, who lived just outside the strangely-named town of Concrete.

Interstate 5 took us towards the city of Tacoma at a pace which made us feel as if we were hurtling across the land. We hung a left onto the 16 and within what felt like the blink of an eye we were in Gig Harbour. Sandi's home was close to the shore of Puget Sound and it looked out towards the snow-topped Olympic Mountains.

Our attempt to get a move on stalled at Sandi's. We instantly saw why Caroline had encouraged us to link up with her. She greeted us at her door with a wide grin and a quizzical look. Caroline had told her that we were travelling by BMW but hadn't mentioned bikes. The following morning one of Sandi's friends who'd heard we'd turned up on bikes, actually phoned her to make sure she was still alive. Ahh, the reputation we bikers have in some people's minds. But good to have friends that care...

Sandi was a very warm and enthusiastic woman who was also the northern queen of bargain shopping. She's thrift shop royalty, a bloodhound for garage sales and knows exactly where to get the best of everything at a bargain price. We'd thought we were good, but in comparison to Sandi we were rank amateurs. When browsing she had the ability to be both friendly and anonymous, but when she latched onto a bargain, she slipped into a determined, no-nonsense mode of operating. She opened our eyes to the possibilities and as she took us from one source of bargains to another, we explored the area. It's stunning and it fast became a place that I could see us living, and it would have been great to have Sandi as one of our neighbours. The only doubt I had in mind came from the sound of the winters she described, and she was at sea level!

While in the area, we also stopped at the town of Edmonds to see a guy called Larry Hoppe. Larry ran the business for Avon Tyres in the United States and when we'd been passing through Colorado he'd kindly organised sets of tyres for us. It would have been rude not to drop in; we wanted to thank him in person. New rubber on the bikes made an enormous difference to the quality of our lives. But doing so showed us another side of life in the USA. Larry lived in a condominium right down by the pretty marina at Edmonds and there was something very pleasant about chatting to him, while cable-clanking sounds emanated from the rigging of moored yachts. As an enthusiastic sailor, Birgit feels right at home in such an environment and for me, well, it brought back memories of one of my first ever trips to Australia. I'd ended up working in one of Sydney Harbour's yacht marinas. It had been a great job. Well paid, for a traveller, and the work cleaning and painting boats, was outside in the sunshine. It also provided me with plenty of chances to learn a little about sailing when boats were being delivered.

We island-hopped our way north from Gig Harbour – this area of Washington State has almost as much water as land. The ferry took us across to the 100km-long Whidbey Island, which forms the northern rim of the Puget Sound. The island is famous for its wildlife, particularly for those at sea. Whale-watching seemed to be a particular draw and we were told that dolphins often come into the sounds. Yachting and kayaking opportunities were advertised all over the place. We could see why. With a rich, clear blue, sun-filled sky, this was our kind of country. The winding roads take you through a tree-lined paradise. Douglas fir, red alder, maple and red cedar line the two-lane asphalt as it wanders northwards. More than half the population of the island live in rural areas and many of them are artists, writers, sculptors, photographers and musicians.

Splitting Whidbey from the next island along, Fidalgo, is a thin streak of blue sea called Deception Pass – so called because the first explorers hadn't realised that it was anything more than a narrow bay. Nowadays the pass has a steel bridge over it and we had arrived at just the right time to see something special. It was low tide and at this time the currents through the channel do something spectacular. Far below us, the ripping current was forming steep-sided waves, eddies that made the water look as if it was boiling and some big whirlpools which looked like the plughole in a basin through which the sea was draining away. The noise was an experience in itself. Riding out these challenges, brightly coloured kayakers where whooping with the buzz that came from battling with the waves and the roiling water.

Almost everywhere we went in the States there was some interesting local history. Much of it involved skulduggery and some of the stories were quite gruesome. This one caught my attention. In the waters of Deception Pass lies a chunk of rock called Ben Ure Island. In the 1880s Ben Ure and his partner in crime, Lawrence 'Pirate' Kelly, ran a smuggling operation from the island. They were smuggling illegal Chinese immigrants into the States. Ure, fearful of being caught and not concerned about loss of life, would tie the immigrants up in burlap sacks. If he was approached by US Customs on a run in, he'd toss the sacks overboard, leaving their occupants to drown. This happened so often that a bay on San Juan Island to the north is actually called Dead Man's Bay.

How on earth does a town get a name like Concrete? We'd been enjoying seeing Indian names on our maps. Snohomish, Mulkilteo, Taholah and Tahuya, but Concrete? Was the town going to be made of the stuff? Were all the buildings going to look like wartime bunkers? I just couldn't form an image in my mind of people such as Peter and Peggy living in a place called Concrete. I tried not to let preconceived ideas into my mind. The reality could only be better, couldn't it?

Concrete lies at the base of the Northern Cascade Mountains, which sounded a little more enticing. And the reality was far better. The

town had taken its name from the giant Portland Cement factory that had once provided much of the local employment, and the buildings, like so many others in the region, were mostly wood-framed structures and some were really rather pretty. Peter and Peggy lived in a house in the forest to the south of Concrete. They had built the house themselves – though Peggy said she'd hardly known one end of a hammer from the other when they started. The two-storey building glowed from the golden-red of the wood they had used. As an engineer and a practical man, Peter had designed a large workshop as the focus of their house. The barn-like structure stood in a clearing surrounded by fir trees, and in the ramshackle garden stood the small caravan he and Peggy had lived in while the house was going up. The caravan was to be our sleeping quarters while we were with them as the living area above the workshop was an open-plan living room-cum-kitchen, with just the one bedroom tucked on the side. Almost everything was made out of wood, which gave a warm, comfortable feeling to the living area. The walls were covered in motorcycling memorabilia, pictures of friends and of Peter's yacht Bluegrass. When we made admiring comments, Peter complained that he'd still not finished the house. As a home it was wonderful but as is the way with such projects, there must always be a hundred small things left to do. Peter pointed out where, for example, he still had skirting boards, or 'kick boards' as he called them, to fix on. We'd easily made admiring comments, not only because of the meticulous way they had built the house, but because both he and Peggy had full time jobs, and they had lived through winters in the caravan while the building was in progress.

The workshop was kitted out with workbenches and rows of tools. It housed their pickup truck, the Harley-Davidson and gleaming in the corner, a delightful 1946 Indian Chief. The classic V-twin motorcycle shone its vivid red at us and Peter watched to see our reactions. He kicked it into life and the bike burbled with a slightly raucous note. Wonderful. Any other man would have smiled with pride at the attention we were giving it, but not Peter. He just stood and glowered at the world in his usual fashion. We'd already worked out that he was very hard to read.

We took some days out to enjoy Peter and Peggy's company, to explore some of the rides through the Cascade Mountains and to meet two friends of theirs, Dave and Sue, who lived in the coastal town of Anacortes on Fidalgo Island. Dave ran a business making concrete floors for new houses and garages – back-breaking work.

The two of them were bikers, and Dave was a BMW fanatic. He just loved them and when he'd heard that we were both on BMWs he was determined to meet us. Dave was a tall guy who walked in the way that I expected a mountain man would walk – long rangy strides that he took in an almost effortless way, except when his back was troubling him. When he was riled about something his voice took on a slightly higher pitch which seemed incongruous with his craggy face, wavy and slightly-too-long brown hair and his shaggy beard. His eyes were surprisingly deep – not sunk into his sockets but you could look into them and have the feeling that you were never going to find where the pool bottomed out. To top all this off, Dave had a wry and very ready smile, which he used often. He and I chimed as fellow back-sufferers!

Sue ran a leather workshop making all sorts of kit for motorcyclists. She may not like me for describing her as motherly but there was something about her that instantly made you feel safe. This made her smoky, infectious, slightly naughty laugh even more unexpected and very attractive. They had a young and very pretty daughter called Jessica who was just beginning to discover what a pretty smile can achieve. She was a likeable minx. We didn't know it at the time but they were to become very good friends.

We were now in the last days of August and a small voice told me that we'd stuffed up. We were too late to get to Alaska but Birgit, more positive than me, scoffed at my worried comments. All we could hope for was an Indian summer. As leaving presents, Peter and Peggy presented us with two Maglite torches, two Leatherman Wave penknives and even more thoughtfully, sets of silk long johns and long-sleeved silk shirts. We were quite taken aback by their generosity.

I'd not even known what a Leatherman was until a short time before. When I explored the tool, I could see what a fine piece of equipment it was and knew with certainty that they were going to be very useful. When Peggy handed over the 'Leathermen' she said, "They'll be really handy for helping to sort out broken down Harleys!" She said it with a giggle and a smile in Peter's direction – he liked his bike to be running just right, all the time. The Maglites were far better than the rather unreliable cheapo torches we'd been using, and the silks made an amazing difference. Not only were they very warm, but travelling the way we were, it was a real help that they dried so fast when we washed them.

Time to get north if we were to have any chance at all of seeing any of Alaska. We stopped off for a night at the home of Tommy. He and his wife lived just before the border with Canada and they were friends of Chris Canterbury's down in San José. This fitted in very nicely with our usual strategy for border crossings: hit them in the early morning if at all possible. It felt weird after all our time in the USA to be contemplating a border crossing. They popped up every few days as we'd ridden up Central America, but in the US, crossing state lines was the closest we'd come to it and they were only marked with signs saying 'Welcome to' whichever state it was.

Tommy was planning to ride down through South America with James, a friend of his, and that gave us the chance to give a little back for a change. That night we settled down over beer and pizza, and had a mostly one-way brain-picking session. I think it did Tommy's wife Allie some good. She'd been quite nervous at the thought of him riding down south. To celebrate where we were heading, Tommy had bought in bottles of Alaskan Amber. It was from one of the microbreweries that were just beginning to pop up as more and more people in North America appreciated that beer could be more than merely refreshing and alcoholic. It could and should taste good too. The Alaskan Amber was delicious and I took that as a good omen.

The border town of Blaine is a place with a quirky history. I liked border towns because there always seemed to be a rawness about them, of a type you'd never find anywhere else. At one time Blaine was a major logging town with sawmills that produced much of the timber used to rebuild San Francisco after the 1906 earthquake, but as the forest stock dwindled, fishing had taken over as the main source of employment. A vast fleet is still harboured nearby. But Blaine has a seedier and more dangerous side to it too. Smuggling.

Many of the town's buildings were founded on the proceeds of smuggling. It reached epidemic proportions after the advent of prohibition in the US in 1919. At that time one of Canada's largest whisky stills was in business just a short way up the Strait of Georgia on Texada Island. The strait runs between Vancouver Island and the mainland. But even when whisky smuggling was no longer profitable, other forms of smuggling went on. In part this has been encouraged by laws and currency exchange rate fluctuations between the two countries. If something is far cheaper in Canada then it gets smuggled over to be sold at a profit, but still cheaply, in the US. At one time British Colombia, the Canadian province just over the border, had strict laws regarding the sale of alcohol on a Sunday. During that time Blaine had a thriving bar trade, with prostitution as a subsidiary business. In more recent times, the most popular smuggled items have been people and marijuana. More punitive drug laws in the US meant that growers would set up in BC and 'BC Bud' was their popular product. Apparently tons of the stuff was smuggled over.

On a happier note, Blaine is the home to one side of the Peace Arch. This symbol of peace and friendship stretches from one side of the border to the other. As we rode the last stretch of Interstate 5, I found myself with the usual pre-crossing jitters. I sometimes wondered how I got through; I must have looked so guilty. I blame my mother for my inherited border crossing genes; I don't know what it is about her but she is always the one who gets pulled out of a queue to be searched.

The US side of the border was a doddle. Our documents and those for the bikes were handed over, stamped, handed back and that was that. The crossing had opened up at 6am so, as usual, we were there to take advantage of what we hoped was going to be early morning quiet. It was blissfully so, with just a couple of cars in front of us. They both had BC number plates so I guessed that they weren't going to get held up for long.

On the Canadian side they asked us some very pointy questions. Third degree at the border! Because of the much-publicised hunt for illegal immigrants, we'd expected some questioning, but the intensity really surprised us. The grilling ground on with a series of suspicious stares being flung in our direction. We actually had nothing to hide, except perhaps the patches on our clothes and a bit of US real estate that was plastered onto the bikes.

One of the rules for crossing any border is to answer all questions honestly, but never to give more in your answer than you've been asked for. You don't know all the rules for the new country, so chatty informative answers run the risk of opening up cans of worms. If you aren't asked about something, don't mention it. Equally, if you really don't need the answer to a question at that very moment, don't ask it. Wait and hunt out the answer somewhere else when you are safely ensconced in the country.

We'd heard all sorts of scary stories from people about our bikes not conforming to Canadian requirements and that therefore, we'd not be allowed in with them. They were from people who'd not tried to temporarily import a non-US bike though, so we'd decided to wing it.

With British and German passports we needed no visas, no application forms and supposedly no forms for anything else. This was a really nice change from most of the borders we'd crossed in our years of travelling around the world. Thinking about it, we were probably a bit blasé and though we were clean, we must have looked decidedly road-worn. But, this was a crossing between two first world countries; it just had to be easy, didn't it? For once language wasn't going to be a problem, though the down side of that was that we couldn't plead ignorance when put on the spot. Shoulder shrugs and blank innocent looks probably wouldn't work.

The customs officer was a thin man who looked as if the uniform suppliers hadn't been able to find one small enough for him. In a quiet and rather bored voice, he asked: "Got any of the following? Eggs? Poultry? Fruit or vegetables?" We hadn't, but we might have had. Those items were usually amongst the things we carried. He then said dryly, "I suppose you are going to tell me that you've not got any pet food either." His face then cracked up as if he had just made the funniest joke ever. He must have been really bored! Then much more seriously, he asked if we were carrying any guns.

He then checked the bikes' papers and our driving licences; we signed off on temporary importation papers and that was it. His part of the job was done. Not a word about emissions, size of the headlights on the bikes, the position of the indicators, or any of the other things we'd been warned about.

The immigration officer was a different ball game. She, I reckoned, hadn't had her first cup of coffee. She had her brown hair scraped back severely from her face and tied in a tight bun on the back of her head. It was so tight that it looked to me as if it was giving her eyes a slightly oriental slant. No wonder she was having a grump. Her uniform was pristine. I was sure she'd not sat down in it since she'd put it on as there wasn't a crease to be seen anywhere. Perhaps her feet hurt too. I tried not to let any hint of my cynical thoughts cross my face. Normally I try to respect other people until they demonstrate that they don't deserve to be respected, but this woman's behaviour squashed the respect with which I'd entered her office. In the background, other busy Immigration officers scuttled around a very tidy office, and the sound of clattering keyboards formed a gentle background noise.

Intimidation came to her quite naturally. I swear her fingers almost clicked as she held her hand out for our passports. None too gently, she opened mine, flicked over the pages and then looked at me. Mine was one of the big old British dark blue and gold passports and there were ninety pages in it, of which 87 had been stamped. It took her a while to work her way through it. She handed it back to me without a word. I said my best and most friendly "Thank you", and hoped that there hadn't been a trace of sarcasm in it.

She pulled open Birgit's German passport and flicked through it, taking note of Birgit's own 'stamp collection' as she did so. "How long are you staying and where are you going?" she asked. "A couple of months we think," replied Birgit. We are heading up to Alaska and then back into the USA. The woman raised an eyebrow at this comment. After all, September was about to start. The next question caught Birgit by surprise. "Where do you live?"

In a spur-of-the-moment attempt to explain why we were travelling together, Birgit replied, "I live in England." She then had  to explain in great detail to the very suspicious officer, why she could live in England. The officer didn't seem to understand that in Europe you can basically live in any other EU country without too much hassle. Eventually the woman became either bored with us or convinced that we weren't going to get up to any skulduggery. She handed Birgit's passport back with a sweet smile that absolutely transformed her face, and said, "I hope you both really enjoy your visit to Canada. Just watch out for the elks when you get up north. Bye." With that, she turned to the next person in the queue, with the tight-eyed expression back on her face.

There was no sense of anticlimax as we stared up the BC 99 highway. A vast new country's roads awaited us. I quietly hoped to myself that snow wasn't waiting for us as well. That really would be our dumb luck.

As always, the dividing line on the map meant different sets of rules, habits and customs. Canada also gave us new fuel prices. They were much higher than in the States. This was bad news. Our bikes were both a bit thirsty when driven quickly. I tried to get my brain to think in kilometres again. We'd just left miles behind. On a very good day at 90 kilometres per hour (55mph), with a very gentle use of the throttle, coasting downhill's, and more than a hint of a tail wind, the bikes gave us around fifteen and a half kilometres to a litre or 70 miles to an Imperial gallon. But on a normal day and above 90ks they had the ability to guzzle fuel. In most countries riding around 90ks had been absolutely fine. There were too many potholes, stray dogs, goats with no road sense or just too many views to be looked at to make us want to ride fast. But now, we were rolling into a big country with open roads in excellent condition, and we needed to get a scoot on. In front of us was some of the most fabulous scenery in the world and those open roads were supposed to be some of the emptiest in the world. Canada has nearly 900,000 kilometres of road — enough to circle the globe 22 times.

In the overall scheme of things, petrol prices and fuel consumption didn't really matter. We'd arrived, we were on two wheels and we were free. We'd made it to Canada. Sure, it was almost the end of August, late in the season to be heading north, but we were riding in sunshine and that had to be a good omen. Didn't it?

Chapter Fourteen

Invitation to a Bear Fest

*'You come to a point in your life when you really don't care what people
think about you, you just care what you think about yourself.'*

Evel Knievel

The plan was to change our riding style. We weren't going to
take side roads any more. We were going to ride north on the big boys.
We were going to ride hard and hope to make it all the way to Alaska
before the start of the winter snows. Winter comes early at this latitude
but we knew that if we were very lucky, we might still beat the
weather. We weren't going to stop off to visit people. We weren't going
to explore sidetracks, and we weren't going to stay in beautiful spots
for days at a time. Any sightseeing would be done when we'd finished
the day's ride and had found somewhere to stay.

The bikes were ready for this. They were serviced and still
had plenty of rubber on the tyres. We'd stocked up with emergency
rations, bought more warm clothes and were mentally set to 'go for
it'. Our riding styles took on an urgency that changed the view in
front of me. Birgit rode with a sharp precision that was very
different from her usual elegant, almost gentle way of making her
machine almost float across the asphalt. She rode the line, making
use of the tightest angles, as if each yard saved would get us up to
Alaska faster.

Canadian road signs were as clear as the ones in the US (in
contrast to the ones in Latin America) and the traffic that swirled
around us as we skirted the sprawling city of Vancouver was well-
mannered. In Argentina the road signs had been sporadic and bullet-
holed. And the traffic in all South American cities had been fuelled
by machismo and fate to the stage that it was manically
unpredictable. Soon, Route 99 was rolling under our wheels again.
We eased on round one looping bend after another. It was one of
those great roads that inspires a kind of frustrated love-hate

214

relationship. A perfect biking road which also provided great views; but which to concentrate on? Carving perfect fast lines on the tarmac or enjoying the views?

The '99' is rightly famous among bikers. When you are out of the comparatively crowded school holiday season, the road is two  wheel fun time. The 300-odd kilometres of bends start with a run along the coast and there are views out over the blues and greens of the island-dotted Strait of Georgia. Then it curls inland past log-strewn bays, dense forests, mirror-like lakes and the craggy mountains of the Garibaldi Provincial Park. In winter the area is a skier's paradise. In an August like this one, a biker knows he's alive. We zipped on past babbling brooks and pine trees strung with beard moss, and watched birds of prey circling on the thermal currents. I felt like a tiny dot surrounded by all this magnificence. I felt as if all my senses were singing with pure exhilaration from the ride.

I couldn't remember the last time we'd ridden with such a sense of urgency, but we only made it as far as the ski resort of Whistler. It was enough for the day. The border crossing and Vancouver's traffic had eaten too much time to do more. We pitched the tent and walked into the town. We had a plan B to investigate. If things went pear-shaped weather-wise, and we weren't able to make it to Alaska, perhaps we could wait out the worst of the winter in this area. To do that we'd need somewhere warm and dry to live, and we'd need to earn some money. With Whistler being a ski resort there just had to be an opportunity to find work, even though we didn't have work permits.

Colin, the reporter from Whistler's local newspaper, caught us at a moment when we were feeling really dejected. After two hours of knocking on doors it had become clear that no one would take the risk of employing us. And the weather forecast was terrible. Snow was forecast in Alaska and in the far north it was already on the ground. Being interviewed gave us a burst of energy. After all, we were supposed to be the hardened travellers. We'd make our own

215

luck. With those thoughts in mind, the interview seemed to go quite well. To our delight, Colin said that he'd send the article on to us when it was printed. So he did, and thankfully neither Birgit nor I came across as complete idiots!

We fell exhausted into our tent as the last of the sun disappeared. But I was flying on adrenaline and it took me an age to go to sleep. All sorts of 'what if' thoughts were buzzing through my mind. What if we weren't going to make it? What then? What if we'd put ourselves in the position of having an unachievable dream? What would Birgit feel? What if we just tried to get as far north as we could? What if my back couldn't deal with the cold and the hard riding that would be involved? What if we just accepted the idea as a bad job and made another plan? But what other plan could we make? We were in the north of North America and winter was about to hit. I was horribly conscious that the ride northwards was going to take us through autumn in a blink of an eye.

There was no way we could escape. I sweated in my sleeping bag all night. The ground was hard. The noise from the river nearby was too loud. I felt quite lost. I slept for just four uncomfortable hours. Birgit didn't fare much better.

Sleep is an amazing thing though, even when you haven't had enough. In the morning, over steaming bowls of porridge, we thought, "What the hell, let's just go as far as we can. If the dream isn't to be, then we'll make another one. And hey, what a beautiful place this is!"

With the sun shining we set off through the forested valley, running north through crisp air that invigorated rather than chilled. The appropriately named Sea to Sky Highway, and then the 97 took us

 weaving through the towns of 100 Mile House and Williams Lake. A little over a year and a half ago we'd been all the way down at the southernmost tip of South America. In the Tierra del Fuego town of Ushuia or 'Fin del Mundo' (End of the World) as they call it, cities with names like Prince George and

Prince Rupert could have been from a different planet. Now I had to pinch myself that we were actually there, on the road to Prince George.

The 396 miles took us nine hours to ride. This was the longest day's ride we'd done for a very long time and my body knew it. It was a wakeup call. Push hard like this and there was going to be trouble. My slipped discs weren't happy and by the time we'd put the tent up and cooked a meal, I realised that I'd ridden the last couple of hours on autopilot. What a waste that had been. It had been too fast, and too long.

That night, over endless cups of steaming hot coffee and hot chocolate, we discussed what we were up to. We had some serious thinking to do. If we carried on riding like this, well, what was the point? We'd be putting ourselves in danger and we'd be zipping past the very things that we ought to be looking at. After all, we might never, ever, come this way again.

We tipped some of the last of our brandy into our plastic mugs and looked at each other over the rims. "Do we really want to keep going like this?" I asked Birgit. "I know we said we'd go to Fort St John and join the Alcan Highway next but is there any point?" Birgit had obviously been having the same thoughts.

"Why don't we go a different way?" she said. "How about going west from here? Why don't we go to Stewart? You remember Jean and Pierre in Panama? Didn't they say something about the salmon run over in Hyder? That was this time of year wasn't it? And Hyder is in Alaska."

We'd bumped into Jean and his buddy Pierre at Panama City's airport. Both were on BMW 1100GSs. We'd just arrived with our bikes from Colombia, heading north, and they were arranging to fly their wheels south. After a lot of research we'd all decided that flying the bikes over the infamous and road-less, bandit-ridden jungle of the Darien Gap was by far the easiest, quickest way across. When potential harbour baksheesh payments were figured into the alternative seaborne option, flying was actually cheaper too. We'd also taken into account the Panamanian port of Colon's reputation for being the most dangerous port city in the world.

An info-swapping session had followed that night over far too many ice-cold and very excellent Balboa beers. The first floor balcony of the once elegant Hotel Central was the perfect venue for tall tales of the road. There's a great view over the plaza that fronts the now rather decrepit building which had once been Central America's finest hotel. Now, it's cheap and cheerful but still has a big bonus: secure parking. Our three generations of boxer BMWs were down below in the Central's former Palm Garden – the perfect parking spot for the three GSs and Birgit's R60/5. Inevitably, the conversation had turned to bikes.

The guys had made it down to Panama with wings on their heels. They had little time, and a long way to go. In his French-Canadian twang, Jean said, "The bikes 'ave been superb, zey were fast, smooth and very comfortable." Their reliability was also good to hear about. Once, the new 'oilhead' GSs had been considered to be too 'high tech' for a long third world tour. But as we'd ridden up through South America, we'd met, or heard about, several overlanders using them. Our veteran 'airhead' boxers had long since proved their reliability and in fact, the ancient R60/5 had had seven owners before Birgit got her hands on it. We'd no idea how many kilometres it had munched in its lifetime, but we did know the full history from new of my R80GS. By the time we got to Panama she'd already covered nearly 170,000 miles of sand, dirt, gravel and asphalt. She'd done really well. But I was amazed by how much better the new GSs were on fuel consumption. Their fuel injection systems also made easy work of low octane fuel and constant altitude changes.

The conversation turned to Canada. "You can see bears fishing" Jean had told us. "If you make it to British Colombia by August, get over to Hyder in Southern Alaska. Salmon are heading upstream to spawn at that time of year and that brings ze bears out for a pre-winter pig out. It's an amazing sight."

Bears fishing? In the chill of our tent, the what-to-do-next decision had just been made for us. Right place, right time, and Birgit's a bear freak. We had a little laugh at the thought of bears in waders and fly-strung fishing hats though. A costume for a bear fest perhaps? This was a party we had to get to.

We dug out our map of British Colombia and using our new Maglites we traced the route across. It looked to be about 450 miles.

That was a two-day ride at our normal pace. It would be nice to get into a little of Alaska, even if it was the far south of the state. And if the salmon were running, that ought to be a spectacle well worth seeing.

Route 16, or the Yellow Head Highway, carried us west. It's called the 'Yellow Head' after the blond trapper and carrier who pioneered this rugged route from the interior. The further we travelled in Canada, the more we learned about these tough early explorers. They travelled in most weathers, but I'm not as tough as they were and as the sun eased behind a purple-grey cloud, I was glad that I could pull on yet another layer. It was my fourth. Birgit by this time was well layered up too. She had on silk long johns and a silk long-sleeved vest, a long-sleeved T-shirt, two fleeces, her bike jeans, her leather bike jacket and over all of that she wore her wet weather trousers and jacket.

The rolling countryside continued to roll for hour after hour. The bikes' engines ticked and purred as they should and I sat enjoying the ever-changing scents and sights of Canada. Evergreens were more and more frequent and the lakes became darker and more tea-like with tannin oozing in from the forests. Rivers began to appear more opaque as rocky silt became increasingly concentrated. Then, around just another swooping bend, we found the reason why. The Bear Glacier sat squat and brooding on the mountainside above us, dangerously beautiful. We stopped to take a closer look at its menacing grey bulk but after a moment a cold wind wrapped itself around us and suddenly we were happy to ride on. Ten minutes later, quite aptly, a black furry blob shambled across the road in front of us. It had just jumped up an embankment with a sleek agility and gracefulness that was completely unexpected, and it appeared to have not a care in the world. Once on the other side, it paused to watch us go by and then with a drunken sailor roll, it pushed its way into the undergrowth. Brilliant. Our first wild bear.

The little fishing town of Stewart hangs onto life on the Canadian side of the border with Alaska (whose narrow southern tip dangles down the Pacific Coastline to the west of Canada). The roads are tarred and the well-maintained houses are wooden. Fuel there was even more expensive and so was the food, except for salmon. Snow-topped mountains loomed

 high over the town and I rather liked the atmosphere. When we crossed into Alaska, we found that Hyder, just across the border, was a town from the history books. Ramshackle and often paint-less houses, a potholed gravel road, a few shops and hotels for tourists, and not much else. At that time of year, it also had a bear problem. With so many bears up for the fishing, hassles were inevitable. The problem was made worse by the influx of humans and the resulting rubbish. The campsites warned us that bears would visit and wouldn't take 'no' for an answer.

We'd really liked the look of the campsite back in Stewart so set up in a spot tucked away in a quiet corner. It made a change to be using an official campsite and that night we had the treat of a piping hot shower. We had some repairs to do to the tent; heavy rain and high winds had bent one of the poles and as we put the tent up, the pole snapped. We hopped over to the campsite shop and bought a can of coke. Using a tent peg as a splint we curled the cut-open can around the pole and duct taped it together. This repair lasted us for another 20,000 miles. It's what I call 'African engineering'. We'd found Africans to be incredibly adept at using whatever materials were to hand to repair things. Often the repairs weren't pretty, but who cared when they worked?

Leaving Birgit's R60 in Canada, we made a two-up hop over to Hyder on my bike. Hopping back and forth across this border was really easy. The crossing at the time appeared to be completely unmanned and why not? Who would want to sneak across illegally? And if they did, where were they going to go? To the north through Southern Alaska all they'd find were more glaciers, forests, mountains and a few rough dirt tracks that seemed to peter out in the wilderness.

The rangers had told us that early evening was a good time to find bears 'at it'. Down in the surprisingly shallow river, fat salmon were swimming lazily upstream. On the riverbanks, sleek-coated black bears shambled along seemingly unaware of the fifty-odd camera lenses that were pointing in their direction. One furry fellow sat on the bank staring at the lazily wriggling shapes in the icy clear waters.

I swear he flexed his claws. I thought his next action would be to dip a paw in the water and flick out a fish. I'd seen them do that on TV documentaries, but not this guy. One, two, three, jump! Right on top of the fish. I'm not sure if his idea was to stun the fish, or scare the living daylights out of them. Whichever, it worked and the bear sat down to munch on his still wriggling prize.

More than 130 species of vertebrates dine on salmon at some stage or other of the fishes' lives. They provide dinner for everything from eagles to mink, otters, seals and seagulls. And humans, of course. As we stood watching the waters seething with the fish heading upstream, I wondered how many forms of life might become extinct if we ever made the mistake of over-fishing the salmon. Bears rely so much on them that I suspect the loss would be devastating.

As it happens, the waters around Alaska are the most intelligently managed in the world. There are strict regulations regarding quotas and times of year for fishing, and just as importantly, these regulations are actively policed. As the waters around the rest of the world are rapidly being overfished, the waters around Alaska are still teeming with all the species that ought to be there. I'd seen a shocking report which said that it would only take a couple more decades for the world's seas to become so overfished that permanent damage would occur. This damage was going to reach this stage so fast and so devastatingly that the oceans would never recover. Alarmist? I had a nasty feeling that they were realist, and being here seeing how much life depended on just the salmon, made me think hard on the subject.

All the black bears disappeared when a grizzly came on the scene. Just a young fellow but you could tell the difference straight away. No shambling from him, every movement had pure menace. No wonder the other partygoers disappeared so quickly. Most of the tourists were far too dumb to take note. We stared amazed as one old chap climbed down to the river to get a better shot with his camera. The rangers scurried to haul him back up the bank. Meantime, the grizzly flicked a long stare over his shoulder, gave a series of 'don't bug me' grunts and then set to ripping a salmon to pieces. A very fleshy sound.

We could have stayed and watched the fishing for days. Each bear was a character and the people were almost an equal source of entertainment; we never knew what they'd do next. But the sun was out again and the northbound Cassiar Highway was just around the corner. We'd heard fine tales about it. It sounded like our kind of road.

From Stewart, the Cassiar is the only route north towards the Yukon Territory and northern Alaska (apart from meandering dirt tracks that we'd not found maps for). The highway is part asphalt, part gravel and part mud. It was supposed to wind through some of the most beautiful land in British Colombia and I hoped we'd be lucky with our wildlife spotting on the way. Moose were top of my list and we'd also heard of wild bison up this way. I wanted to see elk and we'd been told of stags with antlers over a metre and a half long. That, I had to see. Then of course, with luck, there'd be more bears. They were always going to be on our list, but from a distance.

We watched 4x4s, trucks and an occasional giant RV come off the highway from up north. They were all covered in mud. It looked as if it might be hard going, but we'd ridden on mud plenty of times before. Just when we were making wry comments about waddling RVs on dirt roads, a truck driver told us about a mate of his. He'd just heard over his CB radio, that his friend had 'lost it' on a slick corner and had ended up at the bottom of a steep-sided gully. Accidents were apparently a common event on the Cassiar.

The unknown always adds an edge to the start of a new adventure and these sorts of stories just honed that edge. However, sometimes I think that perhaps it's a good idea not to listen too hard to warning tales. It's better to just get on with it. Then a sports bike coming the other way put the unknown into perspective. It belted past as if the asphalt behind us was magnetized. I think it was a Yamaha FZR 1000 but its new 'mud' job made it hard to tell for sure. As it passed, the sun came out, our concerns melted away and with our trail tyres humming a happy tune we ran for the north.

Hardly a house, rarely a village, seldom any traffic; what a beautiful road. We were on one of the fabled bikers' highways of Canada. Within minutes of rolling onto it, it had started to live up to its reputation. Just road, forest, flowers, lakes, rivers, bears and a few road repair crews for added diversity. In the distance, craggy peaks, lightly dusted with snow, formed one of nature's perfect backdrops. The curving, dipping surface of the Cassiar Highway eased from asphalt to gravel to short sections of thick glutinous mud. Fun time. Above us, clear blue sky and a sun that warmed our backs as we headed north. Alaska here we come. Maybe…

I liked the air here. It smelt clean and mostly unadulterated by humanity. Just occasionally, as we headed north, we'd get the faint drift  of wood smoke from a homestead tucked out of sight in the forest, but other than that, the air tasted so clean that it was rather like gulping down draughts of crystal clear spring water. Aficionados say that you can get the tang of peat in a good whisky. I don't know about that, but faint tangs of pine lightly flavoured the air here. With my visor open it was rather like being force-fed a sumptuous meal.

Then the sky suddenly opened and it rained. It rained as if a long drought needed to be broken. The mud and gravel quickly turned into oil slick and swamp. I dreaded falling off. Every so often a truck hammered past us, with their trailers sliding viciously from one side of the road to the other. As they did so, they splattered us with mud. Wiping my visor clean was quickly impossible. I was just scratching the thing and even the rain wasn't strong enough to wash the mud away quickly enough for me to be able to see the next hazard in the road. I rode feeling that I was in some sort of nightmare. I wished I could wake up. I had to ride with my visor up, which meant trying to peer through rain-streaked glasses and maintain enough control to flip it back down again at just the right moment for a passing truck. As the rain hit my face, I could feel it working its way down my neck, past my scarf, and then I could feel its icy trickle as it eased down my chest and back. I began to shiver badly. My hands were numb now, my leather gloves soaked through. My boots were sodden and the plastic bags I'd covered them with had long since worn through from the constant gear changing

223

and the occasional dab of my feet onto the gravel in a desperate, last-ditch attempt to stay upright. My reactions were slowing. We were riding on autopilot, our brains numbed. At stops, we climbed painfully off the bikes, not really wishing to relinquish the small oasis of warmth we'd created on our saddles, because everything else was cold.

We stood and looked miserably at each other, shivering uncontrollably as we did so. It felt as if we were standing in a huge fridge. Having a pee was bad enough for me. Just the slit in my bike gear open to the elements let a blast of cold and rain into my trousers. After the third pee, it felt as if I'd wet myself. I was horribly conscious of how bad this must have been for Birgit. She had to battle to strip layers off and then expose far more of herself to pee. She looked utterly miserable. I wondered how I looked, but I didn't really care. We just had to survive. I think that hypothermia was beginning to creep in and I knew how dangerous that could be, but my slow-thinking brain was telling me that we had to keep going. We needed to find somewhere safe and warm and dry to sleep this night. I didn't think I'd ever been this cold before. We'd had a thick frost on our tent over the last few days, and the inner tent had gone stiff with frozen condensation. Our drinking water froze solid every night and the bikes had become reluctant to start in the mornings. This cold made the snowy conditions at the Grand Canyon feel like early summer.

As we reached the Yukon border the sun suddenly came out and started to warm our backs, but in front of us grey cloud stretched as far as we could see. Rolling over the provincial border was like walking through the open door of a freezer. Overhead, great V-shaped flocks of geese were raucously heading south. At Watson Lake the decision had to be faced, and urgently. To the north, the 'Top of the World' Highway and the famous road to Prudhoe Bay awaited. To the south and east, the wonders of Canada. It was a hard decision as we'd dreamed of Alaska for over a year and a half in South, Central and North America. A solitary pure white goose feather drifted down in front of me like a flake of snow. It was as if nature was sending us a tiny but obvious warning sign. "Respect me or else!" the feather seemed to say.

Knowing that we were making a sensible 'adult' decision, we turned south. I watched a dream fade in my mirrors. In front, Birgit was riding hunched over her handlebars with a posture that showed just how disappointed she was. But would we have had any fun in the worsening conditions? We didn't think so. We weren't doing the trip for a pain gain, and neither of us were doing the ride just so we could say we had. The travel package for us had to be a combination that allowed plenty of time to stop and look at things, to explore the sidetracks and to take advantage of the unexpected opportunities that always seem to pop up.

We would come back another year. Putting Northern Alaska away for future dreaming, I grinned and started to think about what lay in front of us.

If you ever dream of the open road, dream in the direction of the Alcan Highway. There's mile after mile of it. You can travel for a full day with hardly a change in the height, shape or colour of the trees. A glimpse of a river is a much-prized sight but thankfully great sections of the road meander enough to challenge you, and keep you awake. I filled my time by listening to the GS's engine ticking and purring, by watching for wild life and by thinking about the amazing feat of engineering that this road is.

The museum in Watson Lake made the miles come alive. Each hill on the highway had been a mountain for the engineers to overcome and the valleys had fast become swamps as they worked. Men's faces grew swollen almost out of recognition by insect bites and a bath, what was that? The whole task had been completed under a cloud of political wrangling and with the pressure of a deadline that very few thought could be met. The Second World War was in full swing and the dreaded winter was approaching. With the Japanese knocking at the door, the US knew that Alaska was going to be crucial to the safety of North America. A supply road had to be built, and fast. It had to include curves so that life for enemy fighter-bombers was not made too easy.

We rode over Suicide Hill, once so slippery and steep that travellers had been warned 'Prepare to meet thy maker'. And, we found a touch of paradise. The Liard Springs were once the location for a major highway construction camp. The springs are sauna-hot at source and a blissful temperature a few yards downstream. The construction men, according to legend, allowed the ladies of the camp exclusive use of the springs at the weekends for their soaks.

We stripped off our layers and jumped in and for the first time in days were totally warm, and clean. This was a modern times unisex Wednesday. It's a really odd sensation to go within minutes from ice cold to sweating hot, and all surrounded by people dressed for a Caribbean beach. The heat generated by the springs also does weird things to the surrounding vegetation. Plants with a distinctly tropical flavour form an island of humid forest that's completely encircled by hundreds of miles of birch and evergreens. We rode on, full of admiration for the workers who'd dealt with such a hard life in this harsh environment.

Our decision to head south was working out well. We seemed to be constantly in the right place at the right time. Bears shambled across the road in front of us, we found the rare White Mountain goats feeding next to a lay-by, deer ducked nimbly into the bushes and elk screamed their call from the bush around our wild camping spots at night. To our delight, we  were even treated to the sight of wild bison grazing serenely by the roadside. We sat on our bikes, engines off, for a good half hour just watching these amazing, chunky beasts. Each day gave us a new wildlife sighting, but still no moose.

Every so often we'd catch a glimpse of a flash of orange out in the woods. Even at our gentle pace we were going too fast to see what it was and I began to wonder if the flashes were a figment of my imagination. Not so. They were elk hunters, and were wearing bright orange jackets and hats so they wouldn't shoot each other. Apparently orange is a colour that elk can't see. We camped the night in a small clearing by a stream. There was an RV, some 4x4s with bull bars and lots of lights, a couple of large tents and a large green canvas awning spread at head height between four trees. The male occupants wore the orange jackets, got around on ATVs and all of them carried big guns, some of which had telescopic sights. The atmosphere was family outing, with both children and wives on the hunt, but not actually hunting. The children were running around whooping and yelling at each other as they darted through the scrub around the clearing. The women were hard at work preparing food and keeping camp. Later, as we watched the barbecue the women had set up, we couldn't help but notice the vast quantities of beer that were being sunk. A friendly bunch though, and we were soon being invited across to party with them. There was something rather surreal about partying in a chilly environment such as this, with such happy, enthusiastic unshaven men who'd drunk enough to laugh at the smallest things. Their laughter always sent plumes of beery white breath out into the evening sky. The women seemed to be just as hyped as the men and were really quick to take the mickey out of the guys. The men hadn't managed to shoot anything this day, so they were the butt of many good-natured wisecracks from the women. We felt privileged to have been welcomed into this experience.

Gunnar, a Danish motorcycle overlander had once written to us, 'If you make it to Canada, you must go to the Jasper and Banff National Parks. They are wonderful for the biker's soul.' We valued his opinion but as we neared Jasper, the skies opened and we rode into three days of torrential downpour. At times we had just five metres of visibility and before long everything we owned was wet. On days like these I really 'love' biking (not!) but at least the BMs were now cleaner than they'd been for weeks. As usual, there was an 'up' side.

Birgit's bike really needed a wash after a bizarre incident at the petrol station in the Banff National Park where we'd stopped to fill up before setting off to explore the mountains and lakes within the park. She put the gas pump nozzle into her tank, as you do, and pulled the lever. All well and good until the tank was full and the lever jammed open. Within seconds fuel was shooting out over the sides of the bike, soaking her hot engine and splashing her enthusiastically as it did so. The attendant came rushing out, grabbed the nozzle from her and banged it, still shooting fuel, onto the ground. The flow stopped immediately. The attendant looked at Birgit and said in a very matter of fact voice, "Does that all the time darn it." and left her standing there in the middle of a lake of petrol. Fortunately, no one was smoking!

The sights in the parks more than made up for the fuel-spraying episode. The scenery was stunning, even at this time of year and with this

 weather. Mid-morning, the rain suddenly disappeared and we realised for the first time that we were surrounded by the magnificence of the Canadian Rocky Mountains. They were freshly layered with snow and there in the bushes was a proud-looking stag with the largest set of antlers

I'd ever seen. Silver birch trees and the snow-covered hills and mountains formed the perfect backdrop. The trees, with their bare branches lightly dusted with frosty snow, gave the world a feathery, gentle feeling, while the hillsides had been turned into smoothed-off ripples by heavy rolling banks of snow. The mountains had been changed into soaring white silhouettes against the azure sky. Within moments all was well with the world of overlanding and then, with perfect timing, we had a bonus. It was a moose, and this fellow was concentrating so hard on grazing a lakebed that he seemed totally unconcerned by our presence. After all the road signs warning that they were around, I'd have been pretty disappointed not to see any of these comically ugly, but reputedly dangerous beasts.

The clear blue sky stayed with us for the climb into the hills for a look down at Lake Peyton. It was filled with water the most beautiful shade of turquoise we'd ever seen, and the contrast with the surrounding snow-topped mountains and green, tree-clad slopes in the valley was awesome.

Gunnar was right. Jasper and Banff left us feeling inspired. Mountain peaks, fabulously coloured lakes, waterfalls, glaciers, evergreen forests and the explosion of colour that the last days of autumn were bringing to the deciduous trees in the valleys couldn't fail to inspire. Through squinty eyes, and with a healthy dollop of imagination, the valleys looked as if they were alight with the yellows, oranges and reds of the leaves dancing in the breeze.

Rather cheekily, we camped that night under the roof of the barbecue hut of a park in one of the small towns. This wooden building  had no walls but the roof was a real bonus. Now back down at a slightly lower altitude, the heavy rain had been plaguing us again. It had been so heavy that we were soaked through, again! Just to be able to walk around out of the rain felt like complete luxury, and when we'd found that the previous people to use the shelter had left a stack of logs and kindling, we knew we'd got it made for the night. We soon had a fire blazing happily in the stove and we used the rafters to hang our gear up to dry – it must have looked like the aftermath of an explosion in a clothes shop! If we stayed close enough to the fire we were warm enough and the thought of being able to climb into dry, though smoky, clothes in the morning was wonderful. But I made a stupid mistake in my attempts to dry everything out. This fool put his boots too close to the fire and within half an hour the rubber soles had shrunk and bent so badly that the only way I could get my feet in was to curl my toes. Walking was uncomfortable, to put it mildly. As I took dainty little hopping steps to the toilets, I must have looked a comical sight. Birgit was only just holding herself under control. But, she was also feeling worried and concerned. How was I going to ride the bike? I couldn't

229

very well cut the end off my boots. My toes would have frozen within minutes. I'd also shrunk a couple of fingers on my bike gloves! Bloody daft really. I really should have known better.

Well, you do what you have to do, don't you? And for once, the chilly temperature helped. My feet soon numbed from the cold so I could no longer feel my curled up toes, but I made a series of terrible gear changes. A camping shop sorted me out with some walking boots that had blissfully efficient waterproof linings. I'd always steered clear of such things before because the linings make your feet very hot, and we'd been in too many hot countries for that to be bearable. If I'd been sensible I'd have splashed out some pendant money and invested in a pair much earlier.

Our wild camp that night was in the shelter of a suspension bridge. At least under the bridge we could put up and take down our tent in the dry. We slept uneasily with the sounds of heavy trucks pounding overhead and that made us decide that we'd stay wet next time!

The roads continued to be biking perfection and we looped and curved to our hearts' content. Our gear dried out and our trusty steeds ticked and purred us down into Canada's fruit bowl.

The Okanagan is a large area in the south of British Colombia which follows the Okanagan River down to the border with Washington state. At times it's almost desert-like. At others it's lush and fertile with one of the most gently constant climates in North America. By now it was late September and even down this far there was a crisp snap to the air. We cruised past mile after mile of orchard and vineyard. Long rows of fruit stretching out as far as the eye could see. We pigged out on fruits and vegetables straight from the farms for ridiculously low prices. Oh for a sidecar for a few days! Vineyards? Canadian wine? As unlikely as it may sound, it's actually pretty good stuff. Of course we felt obliged to test a few bottles, just to make sure.

Chapter Fifteen

Indian Summer

'A person should only travel if he is willing to be surprised completely.'
Oscar Maria Graff

"It's an Indian Summer, some years we are lucky," the locals told us. June weather in September! To the north, Alaska was wintery, but here in the Okanagan Valley we were the warmest we'd been since Mexico. It seemed as if we were being rewarded for having the sense to say no to going on northwards.

The temptation was to slow down a little and really explore, but we had a bee in our helmets. Just a few hundred kilometres to the west lay the normally grey and wet Vancouver Island. This rare gift of perfect biking weather had to be a good time to explore the largest island on the west coast of North America. As we pushed on to the coast, two options faced us. Either the busy Route 5 and then the '1' to the city of Vancouver (which is on the mainland) along with everyone else who had to be there yesterday; or, we could slip down towards the border with the USA and twist and turn our way along Route 3 with its provincial parks. No contest, and there were stacks more opportunities to camp along the '3'.

A 'BC' ferry took us across the Strait of Georgia from Powell River to Vancouver Island, which is huge – 460 kilometres from one end to the other and over 30,000 square kilometres in area. It's roughly the same size as Taiwan. The sun stayed with us for the 80 minute crossing, the sea was flat calm and the horizon a misty blue against blue. Sleek cormorants fished from the rocks of small, vividly green islands and the ferry's wake gently rocked passing fishing boats as we cruised across the water. In Alaska, the weather had taken a severe turn for the worse, snow storms were a daily event.

The ferry landed at Comox. This small town calls itself 'The Village by the Sea' and it does have a village-like atmosphere. People said hello to each other when they passed on the street and shopkeepers seemed to know many of their customers by name.

One of the things that had really impressed me with our brief stay in the city of Vancouver, (which I'd liked as far as cities go) was the collection of totem poles down in the waterfront Stanley Park. I'd heard about totem poles and of course I'd seen them in the movies, but I'd never seen one in real life. These ones impressed me and they seemed to fill a blank in our journey through Canada. We'd not seen or heard much about the original occupants of the land. That was almost certainly due to our desire to keep riding, but doing that had left a gap. I'd read that Vancouver Island was home to many more totems and I was keen to see them. I really liked the way that they stood so tall and proud. Some of the carvings are almost arrogant as they stare down directly at you or even straight over the top of your head as if you don't exist at all.

The town of Campbell River sits on the coast just to the north of Comox. It's on the side of a vast bay that's back-dropped by snow-topped mountains and edged by fjords. With the sun out, the greens and blues of the land and sea were in perfect harmony. With these colours around us, the colours and angular shapes on the totem poles in and around the town stood out with a sharp vibrancy that reminded me of the colours and designs the Aztecs used. That thought made me think about just how far we'd come over the months in Mexico, the US and Canada. It was a happy feeling and even now, whenever I see a picture of a totem, I still have a little buzz from the happiness of that moment.

Totem poles are usually carved out of Western Red Cedar, and the tallest totem is claimed to be 52.7 metres high. It's thought that in the past, totems were not objects of worship, as the first Christian settlers had believed, but used more to proclaim the status of a powerful member of a tribe, or clan. Even now, it takes around six to twelve months for a skilled carver to make one. The eagles, people, frogs and other creatures that are depicted on totem poles are thought to recount legends, and remarkable events, and can also describe a clan's lineage. At

232

one time the people represented on a totem were thought to be placed in order of rank. The more powerful you were, the higher up the pole you were placed. The reality, however, is different. It doesn't matter where the most powerful person is on the totem. Each culture has its own, sometimes complex, rules regarding the carved designs. They are always stylised and some were carved with the aim of publicly ridiculing a person or clan that had done wrong and deserved some 'stick'. That concept tickled me. I could think of a border official or two that I'd like to carve on a totem pole! The more totems I saw, the more I liked them.

The Port Alberni road to the west coast of the island is a gem. It's another of Canada's 'Where do I look?' roads. But this was the best yet. It felt like riding a dream. This time I concentrated on riding the road; the view of the snow-capped mountains could wait for the return journey.

Windswept, fog-bound and wet. That was the west coast's grim reputation, but for us, the sun shone. The moss on the trees in the rain forest ceased to drip and the lakes looked like mirrors. Birgit and I cruised on, catching glimpses of sandy, log-strewn coves and rolling

 'white horses' in the surf until we hit the end of the road. The town of Tofino proudly proclaims that it's the furthest west that you can drive in Canada. Of course we had to stop and pose under that sign. In the background, small floatplanes lifted off from the flat calm of the bay. The planes are a common sight in these parts. For many people they are the only alternative to several days of overland or sea travel just to get to the nearest town.

Just to the north of Tofino is one of the most extraordinary phenomena in the world: a coastal, temperate, rain forest. Such forests exist only in a handful of other places including the South Island of New Zealand, Southern Chile (Birgit and I had ridden through the forest on our way up the gravel tracks of the Carreterra Austral), the Olympic Peninsular in Washington State and here on the west coast of

233

Vancouver Island. This type of forest is much rarer than tropical rain forest, covering only a fraction of one percent of the earth's land surface. Amazingly, they hold twice as much organic material per acre as tropical rain forests.

We'd been lucky enough to do a little hiking on the Olympic Peninsular on the way north and there, we'd been astounded by the forest. It was as if we had stepped in to an ancient, fairytale world. Lush green mosses carpeted the ground in rolling soft green waves. Mist filled the air, competing with and enhancing the musty scents of age. Feathery ferns collected in clumps in the shadier, damper recesses of gently decaying fallen logs. Giant trees drooped with dripping, straggly, grey tree moss. The moss reflected the pale yellow sunlight through each drop of moisture so that the world looked as if we were seeing it through a section of a kaleidoscope. All the sounds around us were deadened by the moisture-filled air: the breeze in the treetops, the calls of birds, and the tumbling water in a nearby stream. The majestic calm, and the fluttering, magical beams of light that worked their ways through the treetops, made me want to hold my breath, as if just the sound of my breathing would break a spell. We'd stood absolutely stock still, until I could hold my breath no longer. But I'd not broken the spell at all. Around us, the fairytale world had continued to work its magic and we'd hiked on, enthralled by the majestic trees and the lush, rumpled green land.

Now though, I was really happy not to be actually in the rain forest and I was equally happy that it wasn't raining. That night we didn't have to hunt hard to find a spot to camp. We just rode until we'd had enough, and then picked one of the many wooded riverbanks to put the tent up on. The bikes were brilliant for this. In an ordinary car you didn't have a chance, but 4x4s and bikes could always get to deserted and beautiful spots. This spot was right on the snowline. Just a few metres to one side of the tent, the ground was covered in a light dusting of snow, which deepened into snow drifts as the hillside climbed. In spite of the sunshine, the river was icy cold from the snow run-off. I couldn't believe it when Birgit said she was going to take a bath! But bathe she did, and then made pointed remarks about the state of feet that had sat under hot cylinders all day. Shamed into it, I dunked too. I'll try most things once and I have to admit, the air inside the tent was sweeter that night.

The morning sunshine allowed us a treat. We'd camped up in the mountainous backbone that runs along much of the length of Vancouver Island. These mountains are veined with a series of streams and logging tracks. There's a sad but typical story about them. Over the last two centuries over three-quarters of Vancouver Island's very  ancient forest has been cut down. Now, in an attempt to save some of the old growth, a biosphere reserve has been set up but many of the other forests are still fair game. In fact, an enormous part of the island has now been replanted with a mix of faster growing timber for controlled logging, but also some of the original red cedars. Most of these gravel tracks are privately owned and at weekends they are open to the public. During the week, some of the tracks can still be used, but with extreme caution. The forests are still actively logged and the giant, thundering logging trucks stop for no-one. Their drivers are paid by the load so they really shift. We weren't worried though. The bikes were easy to get out of the way and even with helmets on, we could hear the trucks well before they got to us. We listened hard and rode hard. It's playtime out there. Loose gravel, sand, steep hills, single lane wooden bridges and the ever-present threat of a darting wild animal made the tracks an even more challenging ride.

Covered in dust, we sped on through the forests, stopping only for photos and food. There are hardly any road signs and lots of tracks, so we managed to get lost quite a few times. No worries. We had no time limits, plenty to eat, water wasn't a problem and the bikes were running well. We pretty much grinned our way back down to the coast. There was just one tumble which caused only a bent pannier and a broken mirror. There was a red face too though.

The tumble had been one of those situations when everything happens to work against you at just the wrong moment. The gravelly roads often narrowed down to single track when there was a bridge over a river or a creek. The rule of the road is simple: if it's bigger than you, let it go first. That's fine, but this time everything about the bridge was a problem. The road on our side swooped down steeply to it and the surface was loosely scattered with pea and walnut-sized gravel. The bikes skipped down the gravel slope quite comfortably but we both braked cautiously as we got close to the bridge – the loose stuff on its wooden boards would be the next challenge. Immediately after the bridge was a steep climb for about 30 metres, followed by a sharp turn to the left. This meant that as we were lining up to take the bridge we didn't see the pickup truck that came hurtling around the corner, until the last minute.

The driver obviously hadn't expected to see anyone there and he almost broadsided his truck in his attempt to stop before hitting us. Birgit already had her throttle wide open with the aim of rushing up the gravelly hill on the other side. Her momentum carried her half way up the other side to within a few metres of the pickup, before she managed to stop. That was one of the worst situations for her. The back brake on her bike wasn't good enough to hold the bike on a steep slope. She needed to use the front brake too, but the bike still slid backwards on the gravel, the sheer weight of the bike conspired with gravity and the loose surface to overcome the brakes. She'd stalled the bike and it was in third gear. She couldn't get the bike back into first, and start it again before the slow slide changed into a sickeningly fast rush back down towards the bridge, and the deep gully it spanned. She had no choice. Much to the bemusement of the guys in the pickup truck, she jumped off and let the bike fall on its side.

I suddenly found myself battling with the slide too. I hung on tightly, trying to keep upright while trying to change down from third to first. The bike would have stalled if I'd tried to pull to safety in third. I got into the lowest gear at the last possible moment and with a spray of gravel, I belted past Birgit and the pickup to the top of the slope. Parking up hurriedly, I ran back down to Birgit. The men were still sitting inside the pickup; with a flash of worried anger I rather cynically wondered if they thought we'd just put on a show for their entertainment. They had front row seats after all. I shouted to them to give a hand as I ran past them to Birgit, who was already trying to pick the bike up. A hopeless task, as every time she almost got the bike onto its wheels, the thing slipped over on the loose gravel. To give the guys credit, they both jumped out and within seconds we had Sir Henry upright again. With not a word, Birgit climbed on board, fired him up, clicked into first gear and with much spraying of gravel, made it to the top.

The guys were looking at me with question marks all over their faces. As Birgit walked back down to thank them for their help, I explained what had gone wrong. They were full of apologies. "We were going too fast I guess." the driver said. "Where are you heading for?" We explained that we were looking for a place to camp and they gave us directions to a 'great spot by the river', just ten kilometres further along. A little shaken by our narrow escape, we took their advice and called it an early day. About three hours later, when we'd already curled up inside the tent, we heard the sound of a vehicle crunching up the gravel to our spot. The powerful engine was switched off, and then there was a rather sinister silence. It could have been anyone. Through the fabric of the tent we could feel eyes on us. It stayed silent outside. No footsteps, no banging doors, nothing. I had to look. If this was trouble then we'd be better off dealing with it face on.

No worries. It was just the guys with the truck. They'd been wondering if we were in the tent or had gone for a walk. When they'd not been able to see us, they'd settled down to wait. They'd been fishing and had brought us a large salmon as a sort of apology, not that one was needed of course. A nice gesture.

For once, the weather forecast was right and the Indian summer finished as predicted, but it ended with a vengeance. Unwilling to pay the campsite prices in Victoria (Vancouver Island's capital), we wild camped again. That night, the delayed winter fought back and we realised we should have spent the money on the campsite. We set up camp in the last rays of the sun. A gentle breeze was floating in from the sea. The view from our west-facing ridge was well worth the steep rocky climb that even the bikes had made hard work of. As usual we slipped into our sleeping bags when the sun finally disappeared. That was one of the things I really liked about being on the road. Mostly we lived by the sun: early to bed and early to rise. If there was a sunset, we saw it, and the peace and light of early mornings always made a gentle start to a day. But this time, if only we'd known what was going to happen next we'd have really made the most of the sunset.

The threatened weather change didn't just roll in gently, it arrived like an avenging banshee! A windstorm belted in from the Pacific with enough force to rip branches from the trees. Fortunately our tent had loads of guy lines. The months of putting them all out, just in case, paid off. Even so, the force 8 gales pushed and shoved us around so much that by morning we felt we might almost have flown off the island by three-berth tent-turned-hang glider rather than by ferry.

Indian summer? That last stormy night brought our time in Canada to an emphatic close, like an exclamation mark from the weather gods. We'd lost the dream of getting right up into Alaska, but we'd lived another. We'd ridden wonderfully on borrowed time and the bikes had done everything we'd asked of them. Now it was time to move on. We would soon be exchanging kilometres for miles in the USA but first, Canada had one little going-away present to surprise us with.

While in Victoria we hunted out Island BMW; it was a long time since we'd been to a BMW dealership. The staff treated us with friendly warmth and we nattered with them as we wandered around fingering top quality gear of the like we'd probably never be able to afford. I asked one of the salesmen, what the Alaska attempt would have been like if we'd had really good gear instead of our rag-tag collection of worn-out kit and thrift shop purchases. The salesman pointed to a bit of clothing and said, "You guys should have a couple of these. The difference they make is significant." I looked at what seemed to be a thin fabric waistcoat and wondered what on earth he was talking about. My kit was better than this. He saw the confusion on my face and said, "It's a heated waistcoat. You plug it in to the battery on your bike. They're great." We'd never heard of such a thing, but the more I thought about it the more they seemed like a wonderful idea. Wow, if we'd only had these on the run up the Cassier Highway…

The heated waistcoats were over a hundred dollars each and that put them right out of our price range, however much we drooled over them. A hundred dollars was a week's living for us, and we were running out of living money. We still had to make it all the way across the USA, and then still have enough money to pay for getting ourselves and the bikes to the UK. And I'd promised myself that I wasn't going to arrive back in the UK skint. I couldn't think of anything worse than arriving back from a trip like ours with no money left at all. We had family and friends to see, and we'd have new lives to build. Those lives would have to be built as if we had just come out of college. We'd be starting from scratch. But the temptation to break into the money we'd set aside and to splash out on a couple of the waistcoats, was really strong. I resisted, and Birgit agreed. We'd done OK so far, so we'd keep going as we were.

But a little voice in my mind said that perhaps this was the wrong decision. Inside the waistcoat was the manufacturer's label and to my surprise, it was a Vancouver Island address. We explained our predicament to the salesman who very kindly let us take a look at his phone book. The company was listed. I'd have a talk with them; see if we could do something on the price.

Back in the city, we made the call. To our amazement the owners of the New Age Motorcycle Accessories Company said, "No, we can't give you a discount, even in exchange for a mention in one of your magazine articles, but we do have seconds. We could probably let you guys have some for around $20 each. You'll have to come here for them though." The waistcoats did cost just $20; their only blemish was a bit of dodgy stitching. That didn't matter at all to us and we rode away in heated bliss.

The ferry from Victoria dropped us off in the town of Anacortes on Fidalgo Island. We were just twenty minutes' ride away from the home of Dave and Sue, the biker friends of Pete and Peggy that we'd met on our way north. They'd invited us to stay with them if we came back their way, so we took them up on that offer. They had an old camper van in their back yard that was parked between Dave's motorcycle workshop and Sue's leather workshop. "You guys can stay as long as you like. Hey, Christmas isn't far off, why don't you at least stay until then?" This was too good an opportunity to miss and it would give us a chance to think about what to do next.

Winter was here. We had a couple of choices. We could carry on with the ride and try to make it across the northern States to New York. We could do that fairly easily in a month, but it would be a hard cold month and we'd be spending most of our time concentrating on putting miles under our wheels, and surviving. Neither of us fancied that idea much. Or, we could hole up for a while, do odd jobs in exchange for food and places to stay, and wait out the worst of the winter. In the spring we could set off again. If we headed south we'd ride out of the bad weather and would be able to ride across the States in the warm. That idea appealed.

We sat down to talk things through with Dave, Sue, Peter and Peggy. Dave and Sue reiterated their invitation for us to stay as long as we liked, and if we wanted to do odd jobs to 'pay' our way that was fine with them. There was plenty to do. Peter and Peggy said that they had a few jobs that they could think of straight away and that in any event, if we wanted to hole up with them for a while then we'd be very welcome to do so. The decision was made. We'd stay in Anacortes for a couple of months. As for the odd jobs, well, they would stop us feeling as if we were taking advantage of these very hospitable new friends.

I'd once hitchhiked around Europe for a year and I'd kept myself fed and on the move by doing odd jobs for people. There's always a lawn that needs mowing, a hedge that needs cutting, windows to wash, a vegetable patch to dig over, or a car to wash. It'd worked then and I'd managed to get under the skin of each country I'd travelled through by spending real time with people. I'd met some amazing characters too. One of the guys I'd worked with was a professional sewer digger in Greece. He had a tremendous pride and everything had to be done just right. The ditches for the pipes had to be exactly the right depth, with the correct gradient, whatever the terrain. The walls of the ditches had to be straight and the earth had to be cleared of rocks before it was put back into the ditches after the pipes had been laid. All the work was done by hand, with shovels, under a blazing Greek sun. But he was a man who was happy with life; he laughed a lot and that meant the work was never a chore.

Birgit wanted to find out about pouring concrete floors and she was intrigued by what Sue managed to conjure out of leather. The bonus for me was that with the camper van to live in I could get on with writing articles and that would bring some money in. If we were going to get another six months in the States then we'd have to earn some hard cash.

The weeks passed rapidly and preparations for Christmas were well under way locally. We'd not seen anything like it before. Most of the houses in and around the town are wood-framed and wood-clad. We liked this style and when you have so much timber on your doorstep it seemed like the right material to be building with, so long as its harvesting was properly managed and sustainably done. But soon, most of the houses were almost unrecognisable, because they were festooned with Christmas lights. The electricity grid must have been working overtime to cope with them all.

At night, Anacortes was like something out of a Christmas fairy tale. Reds, blues, yellows and greens shone out into the dark. Ice lights tumbled in electronic twinkling white and blue waterfalls from people's gables. Santa and his reindeer walked across many lawns and Santa was often to be found climbing the sides of houses like some sort of illuminated burglar. Glowing plastic snowmen sat on lawns, and shining green elves clustered around walkways, their cartoon character faces flushed with rosy-cheeked Christmas cheer. A happy, anticipatory mood settled over the town and shop windows displayed a vast array of goodies. The local motorcycle club did their Christmas charity run through the town, and I suspect that just about every resident was there, muffled up in thick coats, to watch them cruise through. It was a time of unity and if there had ever been any bad feeling between the town's residents, it didn't show. The mood was one of 'Love thy neighbour'.

241

A guy walked over to us and said, "You two are the travellers aren't you?" He was a short man with a bulging waist. Between the open front of his jacket we could see that he had a shirt with two buttons missing and at some time he'd collected a food stain down it. His shoes were battered and his trousers didn't look as if they'd seen an iron since they were bought. I was a little suspicious of him but had thought to myself, "Well, he's not going to be too much trouble if he looks like this." Then he said, "I like to get the chance to talk with unusual people."

As we talked we had no idea who he was, but Dave put us right at the end of the day. The guy was a local millionaire. He ran a large construction company and had an unusual hobby. He collected military vehicles. "Bill has a warehouse full of tanks, jeeps, a half-track and he's just bought A MiG fighter jet. He's taking lessons so he can learn to fly the thing." Books and covers?

One of the jobs that Peter and Peggy had for us was to put up a plasterboard, or 'sheet rock' (as they call it) lining inside Peter's workshop. Before we started, it was so cold you could see your breath in there. The first thing to do was to slot into place thick sheets of pink polystyrene insulation. That was the easy bit and it instantly made a difference. The next job was easy too. We lined the walls with sheetrock, and that gave a nice neat finish and some additional warmth as well. But, because the flat was above the workshop, all the insulation had to be covered with a double layer of much thicker sheet rock. This wasn't so easy. Normally a small scaffold tower would have been the thing to use but Peter didn't have one so Birgit and I wobbled around on top of stepladders. Soon our arms and necks began to ache from the effort of holding the sheets while we fixed them in place with nails. We must have looked quite amateurish but at least we were getting the job done. Peter wasn't too impressed by my wimpy attempts to get the four-inch nails through the two layers of sheetrock and into the timber beams above. He commented dryly, "In America a builder isn't a builder unless he can get nails like that knocked in with two hits. A good guy will do it in one! I know a guy who can do it in one with his fist!" It was taking me four or five, with a hammer! That was also the

242

day that Peter told us that he could kick-start his Harley by hand. That was impressive. It took both Birgit and me two or three jumps on Sir Henry's kick-start to get him going.

Peter gave me his orange waterproof heavy-duty Alaskan fisherman's trousers. At one time he'd worked the fishing boats up north. Though he wouldn't talk about it much, we understood the work to be harsh, dangerous and gruelling, but when the catches were good it was well paid. He didn't give me the trousers to wear on the bike though. He had no further need of them and we needed to make some other protective gear. One of the things we'd seen at the Christmas motorcycle run was a couple of bikes with muffs over the handgrips on the handlebars. These had seemed to be a great idea. Not only would they help to keep our hands dry, but they'd keep most of the wind off them too. We had to have some. I also thought that the bright orange colour would help to keep me noticed in bad weather. Birgit used the equipment in Sue's leather workshop to stitch a set together for me. She made a set for herself out of some redundant bright yellow waterproofs which we'd found in a thrift shop. At this time we didn't even know about the existence of heated handlebar grips (despite the fact that they'd been around for many years, as I discovered later).

Sue kindly stitched me a replacement saddle cover out of thick black cowhide. The old one had disintegrated from the years of hard use and where the vinyl had split, the foam underneath was a sponge for all the rain we'd been having. Once the vinyl had split, my sheepskin saddle pad also became saturated with water, and this meant that I was always riding on a cold soggy surface, which wasn't exactly an aid to keeping warm.

The first month of the new year came and went, and we decided that we should move on before we outstayed our welcome. We'd also given Dave a few surprises. I still had to do an hour of physio exercises for my back every morning and some of them were quite active. One morning, Dave came out into the backyard with Jessica. He was taking her off to school. I'd been making the camper van rock suspiciously, and as I was doing so we heard Jessica say to Dave, "Why is the camper van rocking like that Dad?" Dave, thinking that Birgit and I were getting close inside, muttered something we couldn't quite hear, but when he got back he couldn't resist a bit of leg-pulling. Embarrassed, I tried to explain. Dave's expression was one of 'Methinks he doth protest too much', which he combined with a broad, man-to-man grin.

We left Anacortes with a plan. We'd head south to the Chouinard vineyard again, trying to take as different a route as possible. It would be a real bonus to see everyone there again and Birgit was bubbling with the anticipation of being there during a different stage of the wine making process. She'd become absolutely enthralled with wine making and I of course was quite happy to try some more of the vineyard's produce. It would also give me the chance to get some spring planting done in the gardens.

The weather the day we left Anacortes wasn't too bad, but it started raining again as soon as we hit the highway south. Thanks to our new heated waistcoats the chilly rain was unpleasant but not unbearable. In fact, it was far warmer to keep riding with the waistcoats plugged in than to walk around on leg stretches or sightseeing. I did wonder whether all the water that was sneaking down my neck was going to blow a fuse or frazzle me. Happily, it didn't.

We carried on with our 'odd job' hunting and as always were happily surprised when someone gave us work. Then I had an offer I couldn't refuse. It was an irresistible combination of the chance to help someone out of a hole, and to learn something new. We'd stopped off at a café where a bike club had pulled up for a break on a ride out, and were wandering around looking at the bikes and nattering to people. Whenever we found someone who looked and sounded sympathetic, we asked the question. "We are looking for any odd jobs you might have for us to do. We are happy with a meal and somewhere to stay in payment, though a bit of pocket money if we do a good enough job would be very welcome. Got anything for us to do?" We weren't being very successful at it, but perseverance was the name of the game.

Then, a man from the crowd stopped us and the next thing I knew he was saying, "I have a small business and a job that needs doing but I can't find anyone to do it. It's three weeks' work. Can you drive?" "Too right I can," I replied. "What's the work?" At this stage I didn't like to tell him that I'd not driven anything with four wheels for about ten years.

"You come and see me tomorrow morning, we start at 7am. Here's the address." With that, he turned and disappeared into the crowd.

The next morning, I arrived at the address to find that it was the yard for a construction company. It was bustling with life. Pick-up trucks were coming and going, a digger was moving hardcore in one of the corners and another was loading sand onto the back of a big green Mack dumper truck. There were seven of these enormous trucks in the yard and behind where they were neatly parked in a row, were a steamroller and a battered yellow bulldozer. On one side of the potholed yard was a set of Portakabin offices. I parked the bike in the most out of the way corner I could find and walked past all the muddy 4x4s and cars outside the office. The ice-edged potholes were filled with muddy water. Around the yard, the leafless trees dripped with freezing rain that had set in for the day.

Before I could knock, a large man in work clothes came bustling out of the office. He saw me, nodded his yellow hard hat in my direction and said, "I'm the foreman. You must be the new guy. This is your truck over here." Thankfully, he pointed at one of the pickups and not at one of the Macks, most of which were now sending black smoke into the sky from their roof-mounted exhaust pipes.

"You take this truck full of gear and follow that pickup over there. The driver's name is Bobby." With that he spun on his heel and headed out of the yard shouting, "You goddam fool! Mind those bricks. They'll come out of your paypacket if you hit 'em." I couldn't see who he was shouting at but decided that I'd try my best not to get on the wrong side of the foreman.

My problems started at the pickup. Bobby was sitting inside the cab of his truck and looking at me expectantly and impatiently. The keys were in the truck but oh gloom. It was an automatic. I had no idea how to drive one. I'd only ever driven a car or van with a manual gear change. I sat inside looking at it, trying to work out how to make the truck work. Bobby meantime was getting edgy, but when I went over to explain what the problem was, he cracked up laughing. I knew that this was a story he'd be telling in the bar that night.

Driving an automatic was a doddle and I drove hard, trying to keep up with Bobby who must have been a rally driver in his free time. At this stage I had no idea what I was supposed to be doing and I had no idea how much I was going to be paid.

Bobby shot off up a side turn onto a dirt road. He splashed his truck through the muddy potholes as if his one aim in life was to trash the suspension on it, or at least to change its colour from green to brown. Suddenly we arrived on a building site. The guys were building the roads and making a drainage reservoir for an estate of houses. The back of my truck was full of iron rods and shovels. I still had no idea what I was supposed to do. "You park up over there," Bobby yelled. "I'll get the keys for your truck. Don't worry, it's not an automatic!" He grinned as he said that! Um, keys to my truck? Wonder what he's talking about?

I climbed out of my cab to watch what was going on. On the edge of a large hole, perhaps 200 yards across, was a bright yellow digger. It was scooping out buckets-full of earth from the bottom of the hole, swinging the bucket round and dumping the earth in the back of one of the big Mack trucks. This truck, when full, hurtled off to the other side of the plot and dumped its load to join the fast growing pile. This pile was about three quarters of a mile away from the hole. While he was doing that, another truck had taken its place and two more trucks were working within the load and dump loop. The pace was frantic, but very efficiently done. The digger operator judged every scoop perfectly and every turn he did was done with such fluidity I could see instantly that he was highly skilled. The trucks were bouncing back and forth across the rutted field, their giant tyres hitting the ruts and making the trucks leap as they went, especially when they were empty.

Suddenly Bobby was back with me. "That's your truck." He pointed across at a Mack that was sitting idle by the edge of the field. "Fire her up and get in the loop. Driven one before? You haven't! Oh shoot. Come with me." With that he strode briskly off towards the truck, which had by this time taken on an air of evil malevolence.

"You got lotsa gears. But you only need first through third for this job. You change 'em like this." He operated a hand paddle and shifted a gear. "You pull this lever to dump your load." And with that, he was gone.

I sat looking at the scene before me, thinking "I can't do this! I'll hit something. And reverse, where's the gear for that? How do you reverse a monster like this anyway?" I hadn't been confronted with anything as scary as this to do for years. Give me a South American border crossing any day!

I hit the ignition button and gently pressed the accelerator pedal. The giant dumper truck roared at me and I swear I'd already turned some heads on the site. Then it lurched forward in a series of kangaroo hops. Very embarrassing! Bloody scary too. I set off with the truck heaving itself over the ruts and bumps; I didn't feel in control at all. Somehow I got it to join the queue. I drove forward, trying to line it up so that I could reverse back under the digger's bucket. My turn.

I put the truck into reverse. The only thing I could see was the digger, bucket in the air, waiting for me to get in there. "Blast. I've lined it up wrong." The digger driver took pity on me and swung his digger towards me with such skill he might have been spinning a coin. With an angry blast on his horn he started to load my truck. With a double toot on his horn I was full, and the tone was, "Get the hell out of here!" I plonked the truck into first gear, praying that I wasn't going to stall. I was being too slow. Two other trucks were waiting. That hadn't happened while I'd been watching. I got the truck into second gear and we bounced across the ruts, and then into third just in time to get to the dumpsite. I swung the truck around as best I could, backed it up a little and pulled the lever. The truck instantly felt lighter. First gear, off round the loop. There was no-one under the digger's bucket. I was being too slow. I was causing a jam. I hurriedly lined up again, and backed up, praying that I was better lined up this time, and not, heaven forbid, going to drive the truck into the hole.

I'd stuffed it up again. The digger driver gave me three head turning angry blasts this time. Then the load was full and off I went across the field, driving crazily fast in second gear, almost flattening the humps as I went. I swung the truck around, angry now. I dumped my load and made it back to the digger. This went on for hours, but even with practice I was still holding everything up and my reversing skills didn't improve much, but I was beginning to enjoy myself. The key was to ignore everyone else and to concentrate on what I was doing. But I started to have a new problem.

The driver's seat in the Mack was well sprung but in spite of that, the jolting across the rutted field when the truck was empty was miserable and before too long my slipped discs began to complain. By the middle of the afternoon I was in trouble, but I stuck at it. It was a pride thing. Stupid really, but I also didn't want to let anyone down. And of course I'd been living out that childhood dream of driving a truck like this. But the dream hadn't included this sort of driving.

I almost fell out of the truck at the end of the day, but honour was kept. Even so, I'd made a decision. I wouldn't be able to cope with another day like that. I'd have to explain. I hunted out the boss back at the Portakabin offices. "I'm really sorry," I started. "I've got to tell you that I can't do this work. I'll only be letting you and the other guys down." I went on to explain the situation to the boss who, to his credit, listened hard. "Don't worry. I've got other stuff for you to do. How did you get on with the pickup?" He'd obviously already heard the automatic story. "Can you drive a steam roller?"

"I've never tried before but I'm quick to learn," I replied, with fingers crossed that he was sensible enough not to give me a job that my bones couldn't deal with. I spent the next three weeks driving the steamroller, delivering equipment to the company's various sites and driving round to other companies with drawings and settling invoices. I was also tasked with hand-finishing ditches for laying drainage and utility pipes. My back didn't mind this work at all, and of course I had

248

some experience of the job from my time in Greece, though this time gradients were worked out with lasers and not just by eye.

The three weeks with the crew gave me the chance to learn all sorts of things about work and American life which I was certain I'd never have come across at home. Drive a truck, or a steam roller? It also gave me the chance to learn about this way of life. It's hard to make a living in the winter doing this sort of work. You never stop for the weather and even snow didn't hold things up for very long. Time was money and everything was done at top speed.

I couldn't help but be impressed by the work ethic of the crew. I didn't see one single person turn up late. All the guys arrived, got their orders (which always seemed to be well thought out) headed for the site and got stuck straight into the work. I was really surprised that there wasn't a guy who played the part of the fool. I'd never worked within a team of people where there wasn't a full set of characters, with apparently preordained roles to play. There always seemed to be a serious one, a muscle man, and a slightly thick guy who was unceasingly willing and would turn his hand to everything and anything that was asked of him. I'd worked in a couple of crews where this guy was often the butt of jokes, but not on this team. He was accepted for his enthusiasm and not criticised for the fact that he was a little slow on the uptake. There would always be a scholar and there'd be the guy who was a slacker. The final stand-out character was the grump. This team had its scholar. The guy was vastly knowledgeable about the building industry but seemed to back away from any form of responsibility. He liked what he was doing and he seemed to like being one of the boys. No one slacked, and no one stood out as the grump. Interesting.

Most of the crews also had a 'wide boy' or 'spiv'. This guy would always be looking for a way to make a fast buck and if the rules had to be bent to achieve that, well, so long as no one was looking... And one of the other key members I always seemed to find was the joker in the pack. There'd always be something funny going on around the guy who played the fool. Sometimes the jokes would be a bit close to the mark but whenever stress relief was needed, this guy would always pop up with something that would crack everyone up. But such a character was strangely missing from this crew. In spite of that, the work atmosphere was good humoured. The team as a whole got on really well together and actually, everyone wisecracked. The respect between them was obvious and I couldn't help but be impressed at how focused they were, and how they always wanted to finish 'the job' before going home. I wondered if the way this team was, was down to good management, luck, or the way that Americans were when they were in an environment such as this. Those three weeks gave me a perspective on a part of American life that I would not have got any other way.

Chapter Sixteen

Deserts, Discoveries and Doglegs

'Knowledge is awareness, and to it are many paths,
not all of them paved with logic.
But sometimes one is guided through the maze by intuition.
One is led by something felt on the wind, something
seen in the stars, something that calls from
the wastelands to the spirit.'

Louis L'Amour

The Chouinard vineyard was cool and the surrounding canyons were covered in fresh green grass. California poppies were dotted along the roadsides and in clusters up on the slopes. I'd never seen bright orange poppies before and their colour gave a look that was slightly unreal. It was almost as if this time nature had got it wrong; the vivid orange clashed madly with the fresh bright green of the grass. The skies over the Castro Valley were a light grey, tinted with silver and pale blue. This far south, summer was already on the way.

The next weeks shot by in a jumble of helping on the slopes, assisting with wine tasting days, helping with the music events and with  planting and weeding in the gardens. We also had the chance to see how cess pits work. There isn't any mains drainage for sewage this far off the track so every home has a cesspit. This deals with both grey water and with sewage. The cesspit at the vineyard had somehow blocked up. It's not a pleasant job, unblocking a cesspit, but a useful life-skill to have acquired none the less. The music events gave us a chance to hear more live music from around North America and to meet many more of George and Caroline's customers and friends. Birgit and I really enjoyed being able to help out, and there was always something new to be learned. By this time the vineyard regulars knew who we were and seemed happy to rub shoulders with us, but we had just two months left on our US visas and I had a slight sinking feeling.

Two travellers couldn't have wished for better or more challenging adventures, but the days on the calendar had clicked by far too fast. The vineyard had become a home for us and we'd both been wondering if there was any way we could wangle the paperwork to allow us to live there for another year or so. Birgit itched to learn more about wine making and Damian said that she had a nose for the work. I just knew that I liked the area, the Chouinard family and the wine they made and felt completely privileged to have been able to taste so much of it.

One of my favourites was a clear white wine which they made from Californian Granny Smith apples. At first glance I'd thought it would probably taste like a weird sort of cider, but not so. It had a clean, crisp taste with a light apple tang that was slightly effervescent. This wine proved to be the perfect thing to complement cheeses and pork dishes.

Damian had tried a test run on making some port. I love port, so when he brought a sample bottle in to try after dinner one night, we certainly won't going to refuse a tasting. We all sat in the den and the bottle was slowly passed round. He'd done a great job for a first attempt and yet again I could see why Damian had such an excellent reputation as a wine maker. But Damian and Birgit got a bit carried away and by the time they finished off the second bottle, the two of them were sitting on the floor with silly dreamy expressions on their faces. Sore heads would surely follow! And so they did…

Sadly our additional year was not to be. Once we realised how long the application process was going to take, we knew we'd be overstaying our visas. We also had the feeling that we weren't going to be able to tick enough of the qualifications boxes we'd need. This didn't make us down though. We still had an achievable adventure in front of us.

Time to go. The family generously loaded us up with bottles of wine. Stashing them was a bit of a problem and we set off with overloaded bikes and huge grins. We'd drink toasts to the Chouinards all the way across America.

With the April and May in hand we worked out a winding route to New York that would take us across the southwest and then up through the centre of the country. We knew that most people don't do this ride across the middle, and that seemed to be a very good reason to do it. Besides, Birgit had seen a lot of the south eastern States on her last visit and it seemed only fair that she should have the chance to see places she'd not got to before. The bonus was that we'd be able to drop in on Sarah, Joe and the girls in Evergreen again. We'd take a loop through eastern California, on through Arizona and then cut across New Mexico before heading north up to Denver and Evergreen.

The combination of desert terrain and our heavy cargo of wine got us into trouble on our second night out from the vineyard. As always, we

 wanted to wild camp as much as possible but we couldn't find anywhere near the road where we could be enough out of sight to camp comfortably. We had plenty of water, so an excursion off into the desert wasn't going to be a problem. However, the lack of trees meant that we'd have to get right off the beaten track to be out of sight from the highway. Even though there'd never been a problem camping, we always felt a little vulnerable when pitched close to a highway. It was sensible to be cautious.

We found a track that looked promising; it headed out of sight over a bluff. If there was anywhere over the hill to camp then we were set. There weren't any trees other than an occasional Joshua tree and the cactus stands weren't big enough to hide behind. The track started off as gravel, which was fine. Then, around a bend, it started to get softer. The bikes struggled. The sand got softer still and where 4x4s had been there were deep soft ruts. We could only follow in the tracks. All well and good until, for no apparent reason, they suddenly swung off out into the desert. At 3pm, the sun was high overhead and we were both sweating madly – such a contrast to the riding of just a couple of months before. I didn't mind though. Give me a good old sweat any day.

Then we were in trouble. Just before the bluff, the sand turned so deep and so soft that it was impossible to ride the bikes through. It was also impossible to turn them around to get out again without completely unloading them first, and now we were worn out from the effort of getting this far. How stupid we'd been. The additional weight of the wine had sunk us, literally, into the sand. There was nothing to do but lighten our load. We could still make out the distant shapes of trucks on the highway but decided we were far enough away not to worry about going any further. Birgit and I sat semi-naked, using our bikes as backrests, and settled down to our own private wine tasting session. Memories flooded back with each bottle we opened.

The peace and tranquillity of the desert was completely enhanced by the wine. When we'd arrived we'd had the sounds of pumping blood and bike engines in our ears, but that soon changed to an appreciation of the sounds in the air around us: a lizard scuttling in one of the scrubby bushes, the breeze floating through the stems of the brush. A bird was calling out from somewhere nearby, and as if beating in time with nature, our bikes ticked and clicked as they cooled. The only other sound came from the gentle flapping of our clothes on the bikes and bushes where we'd hung them to let the sweat dry out.

When night fell, the desert air was still more than warm enough for us to remain in our underwear just sitting out under the vast starry night. With our senses now comfortably dulled, we drifted off into a peaceful deep sleep. It felt as if we had the desert to ourselves.

I love waking up to the excited chatter from the birds as dawn begins to ease over the land. It's as if the thin layer of protection that a tent gives you is insignificant and no real barrier to the world. You may not see what is happening beyond the sloping walls but you are very much a part of it. I always feel as if though my sight is dulled, my other senses are enhanced in compensation.

I loved this feeling as I lay inside our tent the next morning in the early cool of the desert. My head was throbbing gently, but hints of sun made it through the flysheet to make the yellow inner gleam with a promise for the day to come. Outside, I could hear the sounds of the waking world. The breeze rustled dried leaves as it flowed through the scrubby brush. The sandy swish as a lizard scuttled past on its hunt for a sunny spot to warm its cold blood. In the beyond, the sound of a cock crowing, staking his claim to his territory, his shrill bragging call vibrant and enthusiastic.

To me it's an exotic mix that hints of a day's adventures. It's the set of moments when the beginning of the day's heat acts as a reminder that life is in no way ordinary. Outside the tent, the sun was easing its way into the sky in a soft mix of orange, peach and apricot. These colours back dropped by an ever-growing electric blue in a surreal mix that could only have been conjured by nature.

As with our first few months in the States, every day's ride held a surprise or two. Sometimes it was a petroglyph carved by some ancient hand into the rock, or a field of petrified tree stumps, or a range of hills that nature had painted in creams, pinks and reds and of course we couldn't miss out on riding some of the famous Route 66. It has been described as 'The Mother of American Roads'. Route 66 originally ran south west from Chicago, through  Illiinois, Missouri, Kansas and Oklahoma and then ran more or less due west on through the top of Texas, New Mexico and Arizona and on into Southern California before ending in Los Angeles. It was 2,448 miles long and had been a major route for immigrants heading to the west. Its peak was during the massive migration at the time of the 'Dust Bowl' in the Great Depression of the 1930s. That period had seen a natural disaster: a devastating drought that combined with high winds to ruin much of the farming land in the central states, Oklahoma in particular. Faced with starvation, thousands of 'Okies' were forced to migrate through the immense dust storms, with the hope of making a tolerable life further west. The soil-turned-to-dust from these storms was carried east by the prevailing winds all the way to New York and the eastern seaboard and much of it ended up in the Atlantic Ocean.

Many of the migrants headed for California. John Steinbeck's book 'The Grapes of Wrath' famously tells the story with graphic precision. For anyone planning to travel Route 66, this book is a 'must read' beforehand. It gives you a real sense of the times and part of the reason for the fame of this road. The song 'Route 66' written in 1946 by Bobby Troup and recorded by Nat King Cole, Perry Como, Chuck Berry and The Rolling Stones (amongst many others), plus films and TV shows have kept the story alive and I knew that many motorcycling visitors to the USA came with riding the route as the main focus of their trip.

Although Route 66 was once 2,448 miles long, over the years it has been adapted and some sections have almost disappeared. It was finally removed from the official US highway system in 1985 when new, faster roads replaced it. Many maps no longer even show it, which seemed to us to be a national sacrilege. But there are special maps still made and with these you can still follow the original route pretty closely, though some sections have now degenerated into rough gravel tracks. Oh dear, just what we like!

I didn't want to ride the whole route but there was one section that sounded particularly interesting. It had actually been one of the toughest sections of the 66. At the town of Topoc we cut north from the

40 onto the 66 and followed it towards and through the old gold mining town of Oatman. This section is full of hairpin bends and claims to contain the steepest sections of the route. Originally, some travellers had even hired locals to help navigate the road through this section. Now, the road hopscotches between beaten up asphalt and gravel, and we loved it. Many of the road signs proudly stated that we were on the 'Historic Route 66', and some of the other signs warned of wild burros. These creatures are the descendants of the beasts of burden originally used by the gold miners. Set free, they have prospered in the hot rocky landscape. 'Mom and Pop' type businesses still survive on the route but only thanks to tourists now. When route 66 was bypassed, many such businesses went bust as the flow of traffic dried up. However, many of the original signs and buildings still survive and they are a step back in time for travellers like us.

One of the roads in Oatman was called 'Andy D' and seeing it made me smile with a happy memory of Australia. I had no idea who the American Andy D was, but I knew one in the land of Oz. When I worked in the yacht marina in Sydney harbour I shared an apartment with this Andy, who was a really eccentric character. The apartment we shared was in an idyllic location on the edge of the park that backs onto one of Sydney's beaches. Mornings often started with a hop over the garden fence, a sprint across the grass of the park and a swim in the rolling breakers. It couldn't have been much better, but a separate, full sized fridge on the veranda just to store the beer in made life idyllic. But Andy, a completely lovable rogue, always had stories to tell and I never knew if they were complete bullshit or were based in truth. A short man with slightly bowed legs and a wavy, completely unruly thatch of reddish blond hair, he was most at home in beaten-up old jeans and holey T-shirt. He loved to drink Navy Rum – the darker and stronger the better, and I don't think I ever saw him completely sober. Life was a gamble for him, lived on the edge, and every moment of it had to be grasped firmly with both hands. He blasted through life with a flamboyancy that always had him almost in trouble, but somehow miraculously avoiding it. His guardian angel must have been permanently knackered. He drove around in a beaten up old blue Mini-Moke, with a non-functioning handbrake. For those who don't remember, these vehicles used the old British Leyland Mini engine and running gear in an angular and minimalist jeep-like chassis, with no real bodywork at all, just a windscreen and foldaway canvas for a roof. (They also memorably starred in Patrick McGoohan's cult TV programme, The Prisoner). The Moke was fun, but you could always tell where Andy had parked up because he left his mark as dents on the base of lampposts and road signs all over the city: his handbrake replacement was an anchor on a rope tied to the Mini-Moke. I'd loved his energy and life had never been remotely boring around him, but I've often wondered if his guardian angel finally went on strike.

The gravel on Route 66 was fun to ride, rather than a battle, and around us the land allowed us to look out over deep, dry, beige-coloured valleys, bluffs, small gorges and craggy outcrops of rock. Heat waves danced up from the rocks and in the distance, the outcrop of rock had turned mauve and purple in the shimmering heat haze. Not a lot was growing there other than spiky grass, small clumps of sage, cactus and sporadically placed yuccas. They were beautiful at that time of year as they were in full waxy white flower which contrasted wonderfully with the blue sky and the vivid crimson and cerise colours of the cactus flowers on the ground. We also had a run-in with our first rattlesnake. I'd stopped for a pee and had just climbed out over some rocks, my mind on two things – the view and a bursting need. I'd just undone my fly and was happily contemplating the scenery when immediately in front of me I heard that distinctive and very scary rattle. There at my feet was a disturbed and rather unhappy three-footer. He'd been sunbathing and was decidedly defensive once he'd worked out that I was too big to be a meal. I stood stock-still, my hand still reaching inside my fly. I was sure that if I moved even an inch, he'd strike. He weaved at me menacingly, for what seemed like an eternity. I hardly dared breathe. He watched me, still weaving slightly. Then, with a flick of his body and a final shake of his tail, he shot off into the scrub and I could finally take a breath, and have my by now very urgent pee!

We were also treated to another night at the Grand Canyon – this time on the opposite rim, and yes, it snowed on us again. It was almost a year since we'd been there last so what else should we have expected?

Our stay in Evergreen, Colorado with Sarah and Joe turned into a time of organising. We knew next to nothing about how to organise a ship to the UK, and had no idea of the costs of flights. We'd nowhere to stay in New York and if the bikes had to be crated then we'd have to organise tools and timber when we got there. We also wanted to try to link up with Paul, a friend of Birgit's. Paul lived in St Louis and they had become friends when he had stayed in her family home in Germany as a school exchange student. Birgit also had her friends Joe and Nancy in Chicago, and I was happy to meet them if they were going to be around and in any event, Chicago sounded fascinating. It certainly had a riveting history. Motorcycle Sport & Leisure magazine had emailed to say that one of their adventure writers was going to be in New York at the same sort of time and could we link up with him? Chris Bright was due to ride down through the Americas and Peter Henshaw, the magazine editor, thought that we might be able to pass on some useful information to Chris.

Sarah and the girls also gave us the chance to spark an idea or two in some young minds. We were invited to go to Emily and Hannah's school to do a talk on the trip. Neither of us had done anything like it before, but this felt like a good opportunity to provide some knowledge of the wider world outside the USA. If we could get the message across that travel in foreign lands is a fascinating thing to do, and that most people of other cultures and creeds are fun and genuine...

It was also a small way to say thank you to the family for all their friendship and hospitality. The talk went really well and we were delighted by the sharpness of the youngsters' wits. The questions they asked were top notch and not what I'd expected from junior school age children. We loved being able to share some of the wonders of the journey but I was a little disconcerted by the hero worship looks that some of the kids gave us. That wasn't something that either of us had expected. When we rode away, I think that more than a few of the youngsters were already dreaming of the road. I hoped that not too many of the parents were going to think that we were leading their children astray!

Highway 70 took us on a dogleg out of Denver, east out of Colorado and then on what seemed to be an almost straight line across the state of Kansas. This was a long, windy ride over the rolling plains. We rode through towns with names such as Goodland and Grainfield, which underlined the pre-eminence of agriculture. Wheat and corn stretched away from us in absolutely huge fields. This was another ride that was almost devoid of trees and the tallest structures were usually the giant grain silos that just about every town seemed to have. These towns were far more likely to have sales yards for gleaming green farm machinery and pickup trucks, than car showrooms.

I was struggling though, or rather, Libby was. We'd serviced the bikes before leaving the vineyard and thought they were in tip-top condition, but as we hit the plains I seemed to have lost some power and Libby was handling strangely. It felt as if she was trying to tell me something, but I was too stupid to work out what the problem was. Birgit, because she created less wind resistance, often found it easier to ride in windy conditions than I did. Now she was blasting away from me all the time and then having to slow down to see where I'd got to. I rode on, worrying about the bike. She'd had a hard life; maybe she was finally giving up on me. It felt like a bit of a kick in the teeth to be so close to journey's end and for that to be happening. The bike farted far too often for my liking and each time she did I seemed to lose more power. We had to stop to find out what was wrong; this was getting pretty desperate and I'd soon be a hazard to other drivers. At the same time, my fuel consumption seemed to have shot up, but that I'd put down to riding into the wind. With my throttle wide open I was often managing no more than 40mph.

By the time we reached the town of Lebanon, I'd had enough. We found a spot to camp and then started to take the bike to bits. I worried about the wind which was strong enough that we ran the risk of getting dust and dirt in the engine. Taking all the panniers and our roll bags off the bikes we did our best to make a wind shelter. We began to tick things off the list. The electrical connections were all clean and sitting properly and the electronics were replaced with spares that I'd been carrying but had never used. Then we stripped the carburettors. The jets were clean, there wasn't any water in the float bowls, and I knew the diaphragms were OK; I'd checked them again in Denver. One of the spark plugs was a bit blackened so I replaced it, but still we couldn't find the problem. I had the nasty thought that a big bill might be looming. We rode on after having visited the stone marker that states it's the geographical centre of the USA, but the problem continued. The bike and I were suffering, but Birgit was ever patient. She confessed later she was thinking "I'm glad this isn't happening to my bike." After all, she'd had more than enough problems with all her points and condenser hassles.

I went to sleep that night with a slightly sick feeling of impotence. This was only the second time the bike had done something like this to me. The last time had been in the sweaty heat of northern Colombia when for some reason the bike's revs kept shooting up even though I'd closed the throttle. Our friendly dealer back in London, Bob Porecha, had diagnosed that problem over the phone for me. He's a very experienced mechanic on 'airhead' BMWs. Then the problem turned out to be worn threads on one of the idle screws on a carb. A dash of Loctite had sorted that problem out and so long as I always remembered to repeat the treatment when I serviced the bike, it gave me no more problems.

We finally worked out what the problem was and thankfully, it was easy to solve. When I'd checked the bike over, and had looked at the carb diaphragms in Denver I must have missed a pinhole in the flexible rubber disc; this had now become a split which rendered one of the two carbs next to useless so I'd been running on little more than one cylinder. Why hadn't I checked the diaphragm again sooner? Another lesson learned, and with the damaged diaphragm replaced, Libby flew along.

St Louis, Missouri was a total contrast to the open plains of Kansas. I'll never forget standing in the middle of the city, looking up at all the skyscrapers. Most of them seemed to have reflective glass windows that were only separated by thin strips of metal framing. As each pane of glass has very different properties, so the view that each reflected was different. Each pane held a section of the view before it, which when sitting next to its neighbour was so at odds that it looked as if someone with the jitters or a pictorial dyslexic had built a glass wall jigsaw puzzle that didn't quite fit. Seeing this sort of thing for the first time captured my imagination and I rattled through almost a whole roll of film in an attempt to do the effect justice.

Dotted around and in amongst the skyscrapers the names of the older buildings read like a history lesson. The French had once owned the land, until Napoleon flogged it to the United States in 1803 – the city flag still bears the fleur-de-lis, the centuries-old symbol of France. This land sale was called the Louisiana Purchase and strangely, the US didn't really know exactly what it was buying. Equally, the French had little idea of what they were selling. It must have seemed like a good idea to them at the time. Napoleon Bonaparte is said to have commented, "This accession of territory affirms forever the power of the United States, and I have given England a maritime rival who sooner or later will humble her pride." Ironically that was just two years before Nelson's emphatic victory at the battle of Trafalgar and seven years after that, the British navy shelled the White House in the war of 1812.

What the US had actually bought was a vast territory stretching from Canada to the Gulf of Mexico, without which the USA as we know it today could never have been created. It actually doubled the size of the US at that time and was equal in size to the vast tract of south western Spanish-conquered territory which the USA later acquired from Mexico. The Louisiana Purchase stated that the land sold included all tributary land of the Missouri River. How much land that involved just wasn't known at the time, and the States had really only been after the rights to use the seaport of New Orleans! It turned out that the US had paid just $15 million for no less than 828,000 square miles of land – less than 3 cents an acre!

Since then, migrants from all over Europe, but particularly Italy, have influenced St Louis with their grand designs and memories of home. It makes for a pretty eclectic mix, but I was glad that so many of the older buildings had been saved for posterity rather than flattened in the name of progress.

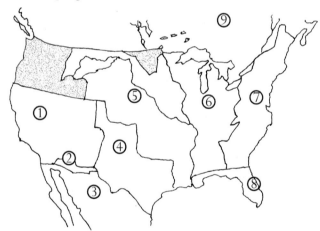

① California - ceded 1848
② Purchased from Mexico 1853
③ Mexico
④ Texas - Annexed 1845
⑤ Purchased from Napoleon 1803
⑥ Acquired in Paris treaty 1783
⑦ The original 13 States
⑧ Florida - purchased 1819
⑨ Canada

St Louis stands at the confluence of the Missouri and Mississippi rivers, and on the west bank of the Mississippi stands the Gateway Arch, symbol of the city's role as the 'Gateway to the West'. At 630 feet high, it's the tallest monument in the USA. The arch had lodged itself in my memory banks as one of the pre-visit images I had of the USA. The shining stainless steel arch dwarfed us. I suspect that the reason the image of the arch had stuck with me was because a legendary American expedition had started out from close by.

Shortly after the Louisiana Purchase of 1803, President Thomas Jefferson commissioned Meriwether Lewis and William Clark to explore the land, and so one of the earliest mapping expeditions set out, and made history. President Jefferson had written to Lewis saying, 'The object of your mission is to explore the Missouri River and such principal stream of it as by its course and communication with the waters of the Pacific Ocean whether the Columbia, Oregon, Colorado or any other river may offer the most direct and practicable water communication across this continent for the purposes of commerce.'

Their route had taken them right across the continent to the Oregon coast. So little was known about the journey they were undertaking that they must have felt a little like Columbus did when he sailed west from Europe in 1492. For example, it was thought that the Rocky Mountains were small and could be crossed in a day. It took Lewis and Clark eleven days and the crossing nearly killed them all. However, during their journey they documented over a hundred types

of animals and drew and described over 176 plants. They also, mostly, made good connections with the Indian peoples they came across on the way – though not all were friendly! All this new knowledge sparked the nation's interest and with that interest, came the real push to 'Go West'.

As surveyors, they also drew maps with great precision and their work has been the basis for many of the routes that we see veining the continent today. However, much of the trail they made is just rough gravel track. In recent times an American called Ed Haley has researched the Lewis and Clark routes by motorcycle and he has written a book called 'The Lewis and Clark Trail, Tracks'. In his book and DVDs he explains all the twists and turns of the trails, and even marks many of the original Lewis and Clark campsites. GPS Coordinates abound. If ever we were lucky enough to be able to return to the US, this would be a book and a DVD I'd want to have, and a ride I'd want to make.

Birgit's old friend Paul and his partner showed us around St Louis, whose size we were just beginning to get used to. And when I looked at the maps, I realised that in comparison to Chicago, St Louis was a pinprick. Did we really want to go to 'The Windy City'? Well yes, a new challenge would be worth having wouldn't it? And logically, it could be considered as a training ground for the riding we were going to have to do in New York. But first, St Louis, land of elegant buildings, the blues, jazz and frozen custard. Frozen custard? (See appendix) Absolutely, one of America's most famous parlours is in St Louis and as Birgit is a keen 'dessertarian', we had to go. It's called Ted Drews and the owner is a guy called Chris Beckemeier, who has long resisted big business attempts to franchise his company.

Chris likes to keep small because he likes his product just the way it is and he fears that a franchise set-up would damage the quality. The building is actually on part of the original Route 66 and when we got there in the early evening the place was buzzing. There must have been fifty cars parked outside, many of them gleaming classics with long, upswept rear fins and radiator grills that made them look as if they were smiling or snarling. There was the usual scattering of SUVs, whose extra suspension was useful on the rugged and potholed streets of St Louis. Many of their drivers were wearing cowboy hats and several of the radiator grills sported impressive cow horns. There were also rows of motorcycles parked at the kerb. Bandanas, leather waistcoats and tattoos abounded. The atmosphere was eager and amiable. The queue for frozen delight was long. But it was worth the wait. Even I had to admit that the frozen custard was very good.

Chapter Seventeen
New York, New York
'The use of travelling is to regulate imagination by reality, and instead of thinking how things may be, to see how they are.'

Samuel Johnson

The next weeks saw us wending our way north from St. Louis along Highway 79, known as the Great River Road because it runs alongside the Mississippi. It was a two-lane highway full of winding turns, lush scenery, warm air, and minimal traffic but with enough straights to give us a bit of a rest between the swooping bends. Tiny towns were scattered along it and the route was well marked by Great River Road signs – all the way to the town of Hannibal. This is Mark Twain country and as you ride through the town itself, you are left in no doubt about whom its most famous resident was. Birgit and I found it hard to decide whether to concentrate on the ride, or the views out over the river. The constant flow of barge traffic made it feel as if the main highway wasn't on land, but on the mighty Mississippi itself. I knew that the next time I read Huckleberry Finn I'd be doing so with the smell and the vision of the land in my mind, as well as Mark Twain's wonderful words.

We finally arrived in Chicago, home of Birgit's old friends, Nancy and Joe who, all those months before, had taken delivery of our African wire model motorbikes, pendants, the Peruvian leather thongs to hang them from, and the silver wire. I liked the leafy suburb they lived in, but felt slightly intimidated by the city itself. Chicago was full of tall buildings, concrete and brick, with the overhead train system, the El, running noisily amongst it all. Jay-walking is a big no-no in the city. If the traffic sign says 'Don't Walk', then for sure you don't. The fine is huge if you are caught by some cop having a bad day. Cops not only drive their beats in powerful cruisers but also ride 'All Terrain Vehicles' with their kerb-eating balloon tyres. These quads seemed to be all over the place. At times it felt a bit Big Brother-ish, but perhaps that was just my imagination, inspired by the threatening feeling I had from the city.

We did what tourists are supposed to do, but we were hungry for the countryside. However, before we left, I did a little deal with a shop that sold ethnic pottery carvings and jewellery. I sold them the last of our pendants at half their retail value, which was absolutely fine. The $200 was in our pockets, the weight saving was as valuable as always, and with some hard dealing we'd actually ended up with $40 more than I'd hoped for.

With our return home now only a month away, we started suffering from 'end-of-holiday' syndrome as the days seemed to pass quicker and quicker, especially since this holiday had lasted over seven years. It was a horribly alien feeling. Life was about to change radically and I did not see the change as one for the better. At times I felt as if we were standing on the edge of another canyon. We had just three weeks left before we were due to hand our bikes over at the docks. I wondered what fate had in store for us when we got back to Europe. All the thoughts I'd been having almost a year ago in Mexico could no longer be put off. This was it. Well, nearly.

But we still had an adventure or two in front of us. There was Niagara Falls to see and the wooded slopes of New Hampshire with its towns and villages full of clapboard houses. We were going to be able to taste some of Maine's famous lobster and ride over covered bridges on a route that would take us zig-zagging across the North East United States on back streets and dirt tracks.

The vibrant late spring landscape encouraged us on through the Adirondack mountains, up in the north of New York state, and that brought us into contact with some chopper riders. I'd always looked at these gleaming, customised works of art with a combination of awe, respect and incredulity. After all, they were beautiful in a bizarre sort of way, and the skill and engineering had to be respected. But I simply could not understand how you could ride something that had such extended forks! It looked decidedly dangerous to me! Perhaps my incredulity should have been admiration for Freddie and his friends. But I sure as hell wasn't going to try to ride one! I felt it would be tempting fate too far.

On the other hand, if I were too cautious I risked squandering the last opportunities of a truly magnificent adventure. I'd be losing out on the last chances to discover, to taste and to try new things. With this realisation I was suddenly riding with my eyes open and my senses sharp again. And, in this part of the USA, they really needed to be. Drivers in rural New York state almost never used their indicators, which meant we were playing a constant guessing game. They also didn't seem to know how to merge from slip roads onto main highways. Confusion reigned.

Some drivers rushed towards the junctions and then slowed right down to a snail's pace to pull out. They were the scariest. Next were those who crept forward really slowly and then at the last second, regardless of whatever was coming, they pulled out with their foot to the floor. Others behaved as if there wasn't a junction there at all, as if they were the kings of the road and everything else had to bow down before them. I realised that I'd been approaching each such junction semi-consciously, but with my knuckles gripping the handlebars so hard that my fingers must have been white under my gloves. I'd been blindly riding with my senses on half power because of the distractions

 in my mind. How stupid to ride like that. If nothing else, I should have remembered being told that half the road deaths in the USA involve drunk drivers. Combine that with sloppy driving practices from them and from me, and a disaster was waiting to happen. A good thing I'd started to concentrate properly again.

Rather than ride all the way into New York City, we decided to take one final boat ride and hopped aboard the ferry from Bridgeport, Connecticut to Port Jefferson, half way up Long Island. (Long Island is adjacent to, but more than sixty times bigger than the island of Manhattan on which New York City stands.) The one and a half hour crossing cost $20 which seemed a fair price to pay for one last watery adventure. That night, we decided to stay on the campsite in the Windwoods State Park. Staying there also gave us the chance to telephone John.

John and I had first met in Kenya, way back at the start of the trip. He and I had travelled together on my bike for a while, but I'd rather ignominiously finished that adventure by tipping him off the back of it. He'd ended up in hospital as a result, but strangely, he still  spoke to me afterwards and we'd remained in loose but warm contact ever since. The last time I'd seen him was actually on the West Coast at Sandi's place in Gig Harbour, near Seattle, 3,000 miles away. When he'd heard we were there, he'd flown over for a few days and we'd done some hiking together and eaten oysters and clams by the handful. The three of us had collected them fresh from the clean waters along the shores of the sounds near Sandi's house.

On returning from his travels overseas, John had followed his career as a teacher, but posts were hard to come by and he'd ended up teaching in one of the roughest schools in New York. I called it a baptism of fire. He was more diplomatic, but we could see that he didn't fancy the thought of staying there longer than he had to. After all, would you like to be sworn at, physically threatened and potentially shot every day you went to work? I'd also found it strange to imagine John living in a city like New York. The John I knew loved the country, hiking, skiing, camping and canoeing. He also had a huge hunger for information and I'd got the feeling that the city really cramped his style. I wondered if these impressions were going to turn out to be true.

Eating oysters with John in Washington State had a quirky connection with our staying with him in New York because the city was founded on oysters, in more ways than one. When explorers had discovered what was to be called the New York bay, the waters were full of the creatures. In those days oysters were one of the main sources of food for the native inhabitants, the Lenape Indians, and for the explorers themselves in their homelands. This readily available and seemingly endless source of food was one of the main reasons that the city survived. Nowadays, oysters are considered to be a prized food and we generally pay through the nose for them, but back then, they were the food for all, in particular the poorer people.

At one time, oysters from the waters around New York had been of an outstanding quality and were exported all over the world. Even today, when new buildings are going up, the foundations are often being dug through layers of discarded oyster shells. In due course the oyster beds were over-fished and over time the waters surrounding New York also became too polluted for the oysters' filtering mechanism to cope with. Their decline was rapid. Yet at one time the oysters were reportedly as large as dinner plates.

That night in the State Park, we were robbed — by furry thieves. The evening on the campsite hadn't started off particularly well when we'd found that the showers were of the timed pull-cord variety, with the cord strangely located outside the shower cubicle. Soap in the eyes and a chilly blast was inevitable, but at least we were clean and the water was significantly warmer than the snowline water on Vancouver Island. We got back into the tent just in time, because the skies opened and a full storm blasted in from the Atlantic. Our tent leaked horribly!

One of the leaks was right where I'd put my boots and enough water collected inside my left boot to keep a goldfish happy. While my boot was filling up, Birgit and I dined luxuriously by the light of a gently flickering candle that both lit up the inside of the tent and provided us with some welcome warmth.

No oysters for us, but the peppery salami in our sandwiches was thick cut, juicy, packed with flavour and topped off with slices of crisp green pickled gherkin. The bread was also thick-cut, fresh, and so full of wheat and oats that each mouthful was a taste bud sensation. The meal was washed down with freshly ground Guatemalan coffee. Outside, the tree branches above us thrashed erratically, and the wind whipped the skirts of our tent like a teenager at a rock'n'roll dance, but we felt quite safe and very much at home.

Then cold water began to ooze inside, in ever-increasing puddles around our sleeping mats. Our old friend and protector was finally giving up on us. The tent had almost made it to the end of the journey, but the east wind had pushed it just that little bit too far. And to cap it all, we discovered that hungry raccoons don't give a damn about stormy weather, and love fresh milk. We'd seen raccoons lurking with obvious intent up in the trees and at some time during the night, one of the raccoons had crept through the rain, snuck under the fly of our tent and purloined our two pint bottle of milk. It must have weighed nearly as much as the wretched animal itself!

In the morning we discovered that our black-eyed neighbours had had a lawn party. The bottle was empty and around it were the muddy prints of more than one furry bandit. Lesson learned. Once again, hindsight is a wonderful thing. We really should have taken notice of the fact that not only were the raccoons in the trees, but their furry bottoms and stripy tails could also be seen sticking out of the tops of the campsite trash cans...

Despite having to have our breakfast muesli with water instead of milk, the day started well and continued that way until we fell asleep tucked up in John's apartment in Queens. The last of the storm had disappeared and the sun was shining. To our delight, we found that the highway into New York City, the 495, had a carpool lane that motorcycles were allowed to use too. No overtaking and undertaking nightmare for us. The carpool lane allowed us to concentrate on the road signs and the city seemed to rise out of the ground before us like some sort of living being. The day got even better when we found our way to meet up with Chris from Motorcycle Sport & Leisure, without getting lost once. To celebrate, we parked Birgit's bike in the backyard of Chris's friend Michael, (he'd very kindly said that we could leave our bikes there until it was time to take them to the docks) and then Chris, Birgit and I meandered off on his bike and Libby, into the centre of New York to take photos.

If you'd asked me the night before about doing such a thing I'd have said, "No way!" But as is so often the case, the fear of the unknown was far worse than the reality and there was something really rather special about riding our bikes along streets bordered with skyscrapers.

Birgit kept hopping off the back of my bike every time we pulled up at traffic lights. She'd run down the road in front of us, turn and be snapping shots of us as the might of Manhattan's traffic bore down on her. I'm not sure if I'd have had the nerve to do that!

John had managed to wangle a couple of days off. "Let's go up into the Catskills," he said. I'm ashamed to say that my first reaction, thought quietly to myself, was "I don't want to ride any more of New York's traffic than I have to". But then John expanded, "There are more than thirty peaks in the area over 3,500 feet high and the Catskills are just a short ride away. It's another world. The mountain range covers four counties: Delaware, Greene, Ulster and Sullivan, and we can find great hiking, forests, waterfalls, beautiful lakes and rivers and there's lots of other stuff to see too."

I got the feeling that the Catskill Mountains were the only reason that John managed to survive his life in the city. With that in mind I put away my lazy thoughts and started to feel inspired by the idea of one last blast on the bikes. And there was another incentive: after almost

eight years on the road, Libby was only a hundred and fifty miles short of clocking up 200,000 miles. What a great opportunity to notch up those final few miles and a fitting way to end the trip.

There was a problem to be dealt with first though. John still had a day's work to do and if we left the city when he finished, it would be dark. As mentioned earlier, Birgit loathes riding in the dark; her night vision is a problem. John could easily come on the back of my bike, so Birgit bit the bullet and set off across New York on her own, in daylight. This was to be the first time we'd ridden separately for any distance, for years. Birgit told me later that riding alone had been a very odd feeling.

But she too was happy to escape from the city. She rode across the Triborough Bridge over the Bronx River and headed North West for the mountains. On the way, just to add yet another layer of spice to the journey, she was pulled over by the police. The cops were quite confused by her German number plate. "Ya need a Noo York plate." They told her. But they were so tickled when she explained that she was riding her bike around the world that they let her off with a laugh and an A-OK sign. The only real battles she'd had then were with the traffic, which still hadn't learnt how to merge, and with the huge potholes in the roads. We'd already become very wary of these. Some of them were big enough to have you off the bike. In fact, we'd not seen many worse than this in the depths of South America! Another surprising and unsettling aspect to many of the roads in and around the city was that they were scored with deep grooves, as if someone had dragged a giant comb through the tar. This may well have helped car drivers in heavy rain and snow, but it made for some buttock-clenching moments for the likes of us. I swear I saw Birgit's bike float sideways on one particularly bad section.

The Catskill Mountains have been a famous resort area for New Yorkers ever since the nineteenth century but during the twentieth century, the land became used to an even greater extent by those seeking fresh air, beauty and exercise. As John and I rode ever higher into the hills I saw signs in the towns and villages advertising skiing, horseback riding, kayaking, and fishing. Many of the shops catered for the tourist trade and the locality seemed to attract some really good artists. There were craft shops and galleries dotted all over the place. One of the things that I thoroughly appreciated was seeing the sight of families all enjoying themselves together. There were an awful lot of smiles going around.

All in all, the Catskills have quite a few claims to fame. For example, they hosted the world famous Woodstock Music Festival in 1969 and have had close connections with or have been locations for such movies as War of the Worlds, Tootsie and Dirty Dancing.

Many of the buildings are holiday homes and after a chance encounter at a petrol station, we were invited to dinner at one of them. The world's a small place. Mikhal, an advertising executive in the city, just happened to know Chris Bright. Sadly, we'd missed the chance to link up

 with Chris again by just a few hours; he was already on his way south at the start of his big adventure. But Mikhal and his friends showed us true American hospitality during the evening. A long evening it was too. They were used to keeping New York time, so we didn't eat dinner until gone 1am, about four hours after our usual bed-time when on the road. But the companionable hours had allowed me the chance to sit quietly back in my chair and to observe my American companions. They were a mixed bunch of people from all sorts of backgrounds but they all had three things in common. They were all sharp-witted, openly friendly and quick to laugh. They were quite happy laughing at themselves too and took every opportunity to poke fun at each other. I let my thoughts meander back to the concerns I'd had a year earlier before I realised that I liked being in the USA. I'd changed my attitude a lot during the twelve months that we'd been here. I'd enjoyed my time in a land that had been inspiring, challenging and very kind to us in so many ways. I hoped I'd get the chance to come back one day. I also hoped that in our own small way, we'd been able to open some eyes to the delights and realities of the world outside the USA. For surely that is one of the most vital things about travel: you shouldn't just 'take' as you pass through; you should try to give something back and to share the knowledge and insights that you have gained.

We spent the next couple of days riding the bikes along some great tracks through the woods, looking out over some magnificent views and hiking some beautiful mountain trails. The weather was perfect, as if nature was happy to give us the best she had.

Our departure from the USA was looming ever closer. The clock had soon ticked round to the day when we had to deliver our bikes to the docks. Our mood was a combination of sadness and uncertainty, along with the sure knowledge that something special was coming to an end. There was a lot to do and much that could go wrong before the bikes were safely on their way to England. Why England? When we'd thought about where to go after the trip had finished it had seemed reasonably logical. We had to start the new life somewhere and as my German was not much more advanced than 'Achtung!', and 'Donner und Blitzen!' as learnt from German soldiers' speech-bubbles in my schoolboy comics about WWII… Birgit told me that when I attempted to speak German, I sounded like an army sergeant major. She was probably right.

The USA had turned out to be a fine halfway house between the road and real life. In many ways it had been a shock to our systems. Though we didn't realise it at the time, this was just what we needed. It was an important foundation stone for what was going to happen next in life.

The USA was sometimes brash and bold, and as we'd been riding in the lands of mañana, in too many places life was much too fast for us, but we'd be returning to the UK. A land where things would have to happen that day, not tomorrow, maybe.

We'd needed to have this transitional time in a first world that was not our own. The USA and all the questions the land had raised in our minds were all an important part of readjusting to 'real life' at home. Often, life on the road feels like it's the version that should be thought of as real life, though perhaps an exotic version of it. The reality is that you are living in a fantasy world. You are living the dream. You can make mistakes and ride away from them. You seldom have to face the consequences of getting it wrong.

Of course, some of the things you get wrong out on the road can actually be life-threatening. You don't have the 'cotton wool' security that being in a homeland gives you. You are out of your comfort zone where many things just happen because of your experience. On the road, little happens without your senses working overtime, except perhaps those moments when you are so in tune with your bike and your environment that you are riding without thinking or planning whatever action is required next.

We'd feared that the USA was going to be horribly expensive and I had worried that this would stifle our adventure. In part I think that this was one of the reasons my instincts had been to head back into the third world. There, we were relatively wealthy. The truth is that we remained wealthy in the USA, but in a completely different way. We might have been 'cash poor' but we were 'time rich', especially when we compared ourselves with Americans. Many had just two weeks of holiday a year, other than public holidays that is. This felt like cruelty to me. How could someone be expected to work for so long every year? What about the time to balance work with the pleasures of life, such as the time to get to and spend weeks in the open air in some ruggedly beautiful place? I sometimes wondered how I would deal with this. I surprised myself with my answer. I would probably not have done a lot with my two weeks vacation. Perhaps I'd have felt burnt out and in need of time to do nothing.

In financial terms, the USA had been horribly expensive of course. With average earnings so much higher than in Central and South America it had to be, but we'd found a way to adapt. We'd managed to counter the 'cash poor' aspect of our journey by not conforming to first world life. All the wild camping we'd done was a significant advantage, as was the fact that we had no need of the things that were being so enthusiastically advertised. TV? No need. A new car? No need? A holiday? No need thanks, we were living one. From time to time the adverts for motels did tempt us though. We'd succumbed on just two occasions. One night was pure necessity born of a rainstorm that looked as if it would never stop, and the other time was because we decided that we deserved a treat.

As if unwilling to let us go, the world slipped into slow motion as we crossed the bridge across to Staten Island where we were due to meet Robert, the shipping agent. A snarly traffic jam reduced everyone's pace to no more than a crawl and relationships began to strike up around us. People leaned good-naturedly out of their car and truck windows to pass the time of day with each other. I'd not seen this in the US before. The last time had been on a winding minor road through the mountains in Colombia when terrorists had blown up a bridge on the main road. The line of traffic along the mountain road had gone on and on, but at the first hairpin bend the problem had become apparent. Much of the traffic from the bigger, faster road was also taking the little country road. If it had been a one-way street it wouldn't have been a problem but the 153 trucks and buses weren't able to pass on the corners in both ways at the same time.

The resulting jam had been twelve kilometres long. The air of Latin 'mañana' and patience had hung gently over the queue. Entrepreneurs were selling empanadas, and soft drinks vendors had strolled through the traffic as groups of truck drivers stood around chatting. We were lucky; it only took us three hours to weave our way through. The truck drivers always had a cheery word for us, and I like to think that we'd provided a little entertainment in what was a very long day for them.

Here in the 'Big Apple' it was as if the bridge had become a giant lounge and the slight irritation we had been feeling soon disappeared. We settled down to chat with our neighbours. "Hey yoo guys! Wherya goin?" called a man whose bulk only just fitted in the driver's seat of his yellow cab. He had a face that reminded me of George and Caroline's boxer dog Heidi. His nose was flattened and almost disappeared into the ridges of his unshaven cheeks. In the corner of his mouth he chewed on a half-smoked, fat black cigar. His jowls wobbled as he chewed a stubbly smile at us. As he wedged his bulk even further through his window to get a closer look at the bikes, I worried that he'd get stuck and then there really would be a traffic jam!

"Nice day for it. You just go ahead and enjoy the ride honeys," called a woman in a brown beaten up old Buick that looked as if it was going to rattle itself to pieces before we got to the other side of the bridge. "Hey, nice bikes buddies," called a gum-chewing youth whose jet-black hair was plastered into spikes on top of his head. A tired looking truck driver looked down at us, nodded, gave a thumbs up sign, and before he could say anything to us his lane of traffic moved and he was off with a smoke-belching roar that had the sooty cap on top of his roof-mounted smoke stack bobbing in time with the pressure of his foot on the accelerator.

The only downside was that as the traffic only crawled forward, we couldn't turn the engines off and they began to get very hot in the sunshine of a June New York day. It was a small price to pay for the surprise of the moment.

After guarding our paperwork for so many years, it felt really strange that this time we had to hand over our original documents to the shipping agent; photocopies would no longer do. Robert calmly took us through the procedure and assured us that there would be no additional charges on top of the $636 cost of shipping the bikes. We weren't entirely convinced but let the point ride. I'd not forgotten the 'additional charges' that the port of Singapore had dumped on me. Would London be the same? If there's paperwork to be done then there's bound to be a cost. At least, we felt, if there were any charges on the UK side they wouldn't be as a result of corruption. Would they...?

With fees paid and paperwork complete, we just had to ride the twenty minute journey to the shipping warehouses at Irvington, New Jersey. There were supposed to be two wooden motorcycle pallets waiting for us there and we'd also been told, "Yes of course, you guys can do your own strapping down."

Life in these last moments wasn't straightforward. The bike pallets were far too small. We hunted around and found some broken pallets, borrowed a hammer, a saw and some nails and set to making our own. The only problem was time. The staff were supposed to finish work at 4pm and it was 2pm already. We weren't going to make it.

We hurried, working on Sir Henry's pallet first. Then we heaved him up onto the wooden slats. Birgit took the front wheel and mudguard off – we'd paid by space as well as the weight of the bikes. To 'shrink' him down to the right size he'd have to sit on his engine bash plate. With the front wheel off, we lowered him forward, and then Birgit slipped. The bike's handlebars whipped round and punched into her ribs, sending her tumbling to the floor with a yell of shock and pain. I managed to keep the bike upright and with Birgit nursing her ribs, she set to strapping him down while I got on with Libby's pallet. The clock was ticking round far too fast. When we looked over our shoulders, the warehousemen Alan, Keith and Nat, were nowhere to be seen. The oily, dusty yard full of containers and packing crates seemed more like a ghost town than a busy shipping warehouse where time was money. I began to wonder if we'd been forgotten about and were going to have to spend the night in the yard.

By 5.50, we'd almost finished. We'd sawed furiously, hammered enthusiastically and strapped cautiously. Those guys couldn't possibly have forgotten about us with the noise we'd been making. Finally, we wrapped the bikes and the dismantled parts in as many layers of discarded bubble-wrap and cardboard as we could find. The guys had obviously been keeping an eye on us from a distance because just as we finished, and were wondering what to do next, Keith rolled over with a fork-lift truck.

Fate had meant that they'd not been keeping up with their own work, and overtime had come into play and they were now due to knock off at 6pm. We'd made it, and the pallets didn't fall to bits as they were bounced across the yard on the prongs of the fork-lift. We breathed a sigh of relief as the bikes disappeared from view, but it felt strange to think that it could be the last time that we'd be doing this.

With the gates to the yard firmly padlocked shut, Keith insisted on giving us a lift to Newark railway station saying, "You guys can't walk there from here. It's far too dangerous!"

'There will come a time when you believe everything is finished.
Yet that will be the beginning.'

Louis L'Amour

What Next?

*'We did not cease from exploration and the end of all our
exploring will be to arrive where we started and know the
place for the first time.'*

TS Eliot

We spent the next week and a half playing tourist in a sunny and
warm New York. This complicated, brash and exciting city, with its
history, glitz, glamour and its harder sides to life, acted as the perfect
exclamation mark at the end of a journey which had covered 200,000
miles, 55 countries and eight years. We had looked for adventure, and
we'd certainly found it.

Then we climbed aboard a Virgin Atlantic 747 to London
Heathrow. During the flight we made the most of the gin and tonics, the
twenty TV and movie channels, the twelve radio stations, and the Virgin
'goody' bag which, amongst other things, contained a yellow plastic
duck. Birgit kept the duck to clip onto Sir Henry – a final souvenir.

This poem from Africa Overland sums up some of the jumble of
thoughts that were tumbling into place in my mind on the flight home:

No one has ever told me why.
No answer ever satisfied this crazy,
bursting, lusting thing that forces me to go away from home.
But I am eager to learn so I must go.
I must go so I can learn

And I will travel around the world.
And I will soak myself with other people's strangeness.
And if I gag on their strange foods,
or turn my nose from their strange smells,
I will learn their foods can be my foods,
their smells my smells.
For I am learning about Mankind.

And if I look in awe upon their sights,
and fill with wonder at their histories,
I will learn their sights were also made for me,
for their histories are my histories.
For I am learning about Mankind.

And if I hurt their pride with clumsiness,
or break their hearts with thoughtlessness,
I will heal them with respect,
and mend them with my understanding.
For I have learned to love Mankind.

For I have learned
That all the world's peoples are my people.
And all the world is One.

I felt the warm glow that having achieved an ambition can give. I'd been gifted with a series of amazing sights, sounds and friendships, and I'd learned that travelling by motorcycle is a spectacular thing to be able to do. I'd also learnt that the vast majority of people in this world are warm, friendly and openly welcome strangers to their homelands.

We landed in the UK with a bump and the rather stunned feeling of finality hit us even harder than we'd expected. We felt decidedly out of place. Birgit recalls, "I'd only been to England a couple of times before and in an optimistic sort of way, I was looking forward to exploring it. But I felt very alien in those first days; I really missed being on the road. Everything seemed so small. The houses were small, the streets small and busy, and everything seemed quite dark after the open road. Everything was so expensive too."

For my part, I'd tried hard to postpone thoughts about the moment when the trip would be over. I didn't know if I'd ever fit in with 'real life' again. Had the road with all its amazing sights and adventures spoiled me for a life in one place doing a nine-to-five job? I was sure it had and couldn't see a way forward. I wasn't happy about being home, but the thought of linking up with our families and friends cushioned the blow and I was really happy that we'd not arrived back totally broke. I had hoped that the excitement of showing Birgit around the UK was going to soften the impact of being back. But that didn't work out; initially I was frustrated.

Many of the roads I knew and had loved were no longer easy to find. Over the eight years I'd been away, a seemingly huge number of 'A' and 'B' roads through towns and villages had been cut off by dual carriageways. They kept the traffic moving, but sadly allowed too many people to get to their destinations without seeing the special things that make up our country. As the first days ticked on by I realised that I'd changed quite dramatically during the time on the road, and the combination of the changes in me and my home country meant that instead of 'just' coming home, I'd arrived in a new land with new sidetracks to explore. I was seeing things in a way I never had before and I no longer whizzed on past things all the

 time, on the way to somewhere else. It felt quite natural to make the time to explore and to appreciate.

Libby and Sir Henry were delayed in New York due to a longshoremen's (dockers') dispute but eventually they arrived safely in the UK. The dispute? Well, they had problems with the admin. The longshoremen simply weren't used to dealing with foreign bikes that had been ridden into the USA from the south. Apparently they weren't sure what to do with the paperwork. At least we had not followed the advice from that oh-so-welcoming blonde immigration officer at the Mexican border into the US. If we had, perhaps we'd not have seen our bikes again. And yes, there was a small fee to pay to retrieve them in the UK, but we didn't care. We had the bikes back and with them, some of our missing sense of freedom returned.

Birgit and I set off to explore together. In this way our journey would go on and with each new adventure I found constant reminders of how fortunate I'd been to be able to travel the world on a motorcycle.

I've never forgotten the thoughts I had on the Las Vegas trailer park. Within a few months of being in the UK, I'd come to realise that the opportunity to live and work in the UK is something of real value. I'd taken it all for granted before. As I started to see my homeland through fresh eyes I also started to really appreciate how good life is in the UK. There's a lot of fun and adventure to be had on my own 'doorstep'.

Yes, it has its problems and yes many Britons, like so many in North America, have no real idea of what goes on in the world outside. But there's a real buzz of excitement amongst so many people at the thought of getting out into our world to explore and to learn. That buzz makes me feel really positive.

I continued to write travel articles for magazines, did odd jobs, and Birgit and I started to build a new life together. The articles also opened up a new opportunity. Readers were asking when I was going to write a book. Until then, that had been the furthest thing from my mind. I wasn't at all sure that I was capable of writing one anyway.

With nothing to lose, and with Birgit acting as my sounding board and proof-reader, I set to writing my first book, Into Africa. It took me two years, part-time, sitting down to write at the end of long working days. It went through thirty full drafts before I felt it was good enough to show to a publisher. Then I spent two more years trying to interest the various publishers who specialised in tales of the road – without success. But the last two refusal letters, from two of the biggest publishers, were personal and encouraging. However, they both pointed out that I was not a media personality and therefore, my book would not sell.

At first, I was very disappointed; those two had been my last hope. But when I sat down and really thought about what they'd said, I saw a new opportunity. They'd liked the book. That was true praise. There was also no disputing the fact that I was not a media personality. But if they genuinely liked the book enough to tell me so, then perhaps I should cut out the 'middle man' and have a go at publishing the book myself.

The 'road' teaches you that there are many people who will say, 'No you can't', but the reality is that you can at least try; you can see what happens. It's like getting to the start of a dodgy-looking dirt road. Do you turn round and go home? No of course not. There's an adventure to be had. Sure you might fall off. So what? You can pick yourself up and have another go.

And so, Birgit and I rode into another new 'country' with new rules, new customs, a new language, new quirks and some very different traditions. When you delve into the world of publishing you are embarking on a fascinating voyage of discovery.

I also discovered a new sensation; the tangible feeling of pride which came from holding a book that I had written and produced. However, wondering, 'am I good enough?' wasn't so much fun. To our complete delight, Into Africa was liked by readers and reviewers alike. When Johnnie Walker invited me onto his BBC Radio 2 Drivetime show, things suddenly began to lift off. Over the next months readers started asking, "When's the next book coming out?" I gambled, left 9 to 5 employment, and sat down to write Under Asian Skies.

I soon discovered that a writer's hours are as erratic and as long as those of a traveller, and like a traveller, when things go well the world is a great place to be. The first months after publishing Under Asian Skies were a tense time. But then the reviews began to come in, and I found that I'd not made the daft mistake I'd feared. The feedback I had from readers encouraged me to write on and I continued telling the story of our travels in Distant Suns. This book takes the reader through the challenging and fascinating months riding up South and Central America and leads up to this fourth and concluding book in the series.

It was very important to us that the books should convey the idea that you don't have to be anyone special to get out into the world and have an amazing adventure. Mostly it's a case of having a strong enough dream, the financial ability (I sold almost everything I'd got) and vitally, the opportunity to take those first few steps into the unknown. For many, the reality is that life's responsibilities unavoidably get in the way of an adventure such as this. So we hope that, at the very least the books have enabled those readers to share in the fun, the dramas and the excitement of the open road.

I'm often asked which part of the world I'd like to travel through again. It's a really hard question to answer as each and every place was packed full of amazing things to discover and it didn't matter where we went, local people always made us welcome. But if my back is put against the wall, then I can only say that if I were able to get out on the road for a year, right now, I'd head for North America. There is so much I wasn't lucky enough to see and to learn from. This time I'd make sure that I had far better bike kit. A decent jacket, heated grips and a heated jacket would allow me to spend more time enjoying the road and the scenery throughout the whole year!

So what is actually going to happen next? Well a recent event has introduced us to a completely new type of adventure.

I've been hit by a kidney disease which has resulted in renal failure. Birgit, my friends and I have debated long and hard about whether to include any mention of the situation here. I wasn't sure if I wanted to bring our problems into the open. My books have always been about the joys, the learning, the people, the observations and the adventures of travel. But Paul Blez, who has done such a brilliant job of editing my most recent books, sent me this emailed comment when he returned the final chapter of 'Tortillas to Totems'. 'Sam, if not yours, then maybe someone else's life can be saved as a result of someone becoming a donor because of what they've read in your book! You have to write about what's going on.'

His words hit home and though my instinct was and still is to keep my problems to myself, and I'm absolutely not after sympathy, I know that we would be wasting an opportunity if I didn't explain. So, knowing that I do feel out of my element or 'comfort zone' with this, I hope you'll bear with me and read on.

As I write this I am very much aware that some people have strong opinions against transplanting. I respect those thoughts, but I hope that you will understand why I have brought some of the issues into the open here. Perhaps my words might encourage a few people who aren't against the idea, to go and sign up to be a donor. In the UK, for example, you can do that at www.uktransplant.org.uk

The learning curve for us is steep. This adventure has an unimaginable set of rules, a new route to negotiate and challenges of a completely different kind. Some of the statistics we have been slowly coming to understand make grim reading. At the time of writing there are 6,882 people waiting for a kidney transplant and fewer than a third of them will get one this year. The rest will survive for as long as they can on dialysis (a mechanical, blood-filtering system) and drugs. Some of the most positive people I've met are going through this ordeal, and are happy to have the opportunity to do so. After all, we could live in some third world country whose medical set up simply wouldn't cope. Self-pitying whinge? Not a chance after a thought like that! But dialysis is far from being a cure, can be painful, it's intrusive and is often an exhausting experience.

There are a couple of things we've learned that are quite successful in bringing a very wry smile to my face. The first is that since motor vehicles have become so much safer, there are far fewer accidents that are severe enough for organs to be available for transplant. Seat belts and air bags are wonderful things too.

The second is that in the UK the law says that people can 'opt' to carry a donor card. The reality is that we are all human beings with busy lives and most never actually get around to registering as donors. Accidents do sadly happen and people die. Every time that happens and the person who dies is not a donor, an opportunity to bring life out of death is wasted.

Mark, a donor card-carrying friend, made a very pertinent point. He said, 'Not carry a donor card? That'd be daft. If I die I want all of my spare parts to be used. If they weren't, well, it'd be like someone coming along and saying that as I had died all my bikes might as well be put in a crusher. What would be the point of that!?'

And yes, I do carry a donor card and have done for a couple of decades. I continue to carry it because though my kidneys are stuffed; there are plenty of my other organs that can be of use. If I'm no longer alive then I've got no further use for my 'parts'.

There have been moves to change our donor system from the opt-in system that we have now, to an opt-out system. In other words, you would carry a card if you didn't want to donate. That way, if you'd not opted out you would automatically be able to save a life or two, or even three, maybe more. The system isn't so weird. Spain, France, Austria and Belgium have now adopted it. Unless we the public ask, we won't be allowed to do it.

Are there any other options? Yes, there is now the living donor scheme. The living donor scheme is a relatively new change in UK law and it could make a dramatic difference. It's now possible to donate a kidney as a living person. The statistics show that more people survive when they are lucky enough to have a living donor transplant – there's less trauma to the organ. Many people are actually born with just one kidney and notice no difference at all.

There is a ton more information that you can learn if you have the desire, but most of it though interesting, isn't important unless you or someone close to you are the ones with a problem. The key issues are as I've just written. Oh and I laughed when I was reminded that my blood group is the somewhat rare B positive. Normally I'm quite happy with being positive! I'm resigned to having a very long wait for the chance of a kidney transplant to come up. It's not a complaint; it's just the way it is.

Of course there is another side to this, and I'm really comfortable ending Tortillas to Totems with these thoughts. Do you remember that old saying about making the most of each day, because you never know what the next one will bring? How lucky I am that I've stumbled into getting this the right way round. I'm one of the fortunate ones.

If you have the dream of living a big adventure, and are lucky enough to be able to make it happen, just do it. Live your life to the full. We live in an amazing world that is just waiting for you to get out into. As Mahatma Ghandi said so wisely, 'Live as if you were to die tomorrow. Learn as if you are to live forever.'

And so this book should have ended, but then something quite amazing happened.

Just a few weeks before 'Tortillas to Totems' was due to be going to print, I received a 4.20am telephone call from the transplant unit at Bristol Southmeads hospital. 'Sam, get here as soon as possible, we think we have a kidney for you!'

Later that morning the transplant went ahead and I am now going through the first recovery period. We are waiting to see if my new kidney will be rejected or not, but so far so good.

The last days have been a complete jumble of emotions. All the feelings I'd tied down, whilst trying to be positive and to look on the bright side of life, came bubbling to the top.

The sheer enormity of the pure gift I have been given is still only just sinking in. Instead of life actually ending, or being years of struggle with significant dietary constraints, discomfort, tiredness and more regulations than I've ever had before in life, I am possibly going to be free. I will never know who had the generosity and the kindly forethought to sign up as a donor, and they are no longer alive so I will never be able to thank them or their family directly. But I can say a huge thank you to all those who have signed up to donate their organs on their death. The feeling of gratitude I have at this moment is almost indescribable.

Birgit and I would also like to thank all those in the Renal teams of the Royal Devon and Exeter, and Bristol Southmeads hospitals. These people have been quite amazing and in many instances their continuing care is far beyond the call of duty.

Appendix

If you want to know more...

This section refers back to Chapter 3. Rather than insert this information within the text at that stage and risk interrupting the flow, I've chosen to insert these facts and observations into Tortillas to Totems as an appendix. You may wish to read Chapter 3 again before continuing.

One of the key reasons I'm fascinated by travel is the constant flow of things we encounter that surprise us. Some observations are fascinatingly different and delightfully quirky, but some are sobering and challenging. I think that such challenges are healthy. Travel brings out the curious in nearly all of us, and riding a long journey is ideal for reviewing the information that catches attention along the way. The road, when I'm travelling in what I call my 'helmet thought bubble', is perfect for mulling things through.

Birgit and I had just travelled up through South and Central America, and had done so scarcely a decade after the Iran Contra affair. As a result, this information was still fresh in my mind as we rode into North America. I'd spoken to quite a few people about the events that the following facts unfold, and had been surprised at how little most people knew. I have no wish to give Americans a 'left hook'! I hope you'll see that I am making a point about humanity as a whole, and our responsibilities.

In Chapter 3 I talked about the effect of foreign government policy on other countries. I referred to actions by the USA, but also to the UK. In particular I had the Central American country of Nicaragua, and the Boer war in South Africa in my mind. Thinking back, my Chapter 3 musings about Nicaragua were also seeded by seeing ox drawn carts, a dearth of new buildings, of markets stalls made of sticks and cloth, bullet holes in walls and a lack of modern cars and equipment. This was a marked difference to neighbouring countries. Though wonderfully friendly, there was an air of sadness, of a kind that we'd not encountered anywhere else in the Americas.

This is a tale of how governments can get out of hand and can cause great damage. Nicaragua has a decidedly traumatic political history, and the USA has had a strong influence in what has happened there for the last two generations. The story also opened my eyes as an example of why many people outside of the US do not respect it, in spite of the fact that there are so many things about the country and its people that should be admired and respected.

The period from the 1960s to the late '80s was a dire period for Nicaragua. The country had a dictator. Anastasio Somoza Debayle had been educated in the USA and was friendly to the West. His family held power in Nicaragua as a sort of evil dynasty, and they led a government that was riddled with corruption; a government out of hand.

A party called the Sandanista Front was set up to oppose Somoza. Partly funded by Cuba's Fidel Castro, this had warning bells ringing in Washington. The US government continued to support the Somoza regime, while keeping a close watch on the country. However, as far back as the early '70s, human rights groups had been making allegations of rights abuses by Somoza's government. In 1975, President Jimmy Carter withdrew the support of the USA, citing human rights abuses observed during Somoza's violent campaign against the Sandinistas, or FSLN. Somoza was subsequently overthrown in a popular uprising, and as part of the new ruling Junta, Daniel Ortega came to power.

In 1981, President Ronald Regan accused the Sandinistas of supporting Marxist revolutionary movements in other Latin American countries. There'd been slim evidence that this had happened. The Central Intelligence Agency was authorised to begin financing, arming and training rebels. These anti-Sandinista guerrillas were basically small groups of malcontents who were united loosely at first, and known collectively as the Contras. Until this time these men were 'insignificant bands of poorly armed and poorly organized ex-members of Somoza's National Guard.' The setting up of the Contras led to one of the largest political scandals in US history, when Oliver North and some of Reagan's administration sold arms to Iran, and then used the proceeds to fund the Contras.

In November 1984, Daniel Ortega the leader of the FSLN and therefore of Nicaragua, called national elections. He won the presidency with 63% of the vote. According to many independent observers, the elections were perhaps the freest and fairest in Nicaraguan history. The general council of New York's Human Rights Commission described the election as 'free, fair and hotly contested.'

Reagan's officials are on record as having stated that this election was a 'Soviet-style sham'. The US government, apparently pressured some opposition parties into boycotting the election, and that enabled Reagan to denounce the election as being unfair. Reagan maintained that he was justified to continue supporting what he referred to as, the Contras' 'democratic resistance'.

You may be thinking 'So what?' That this is typical behaviour for first world governments as they attempt to protect their own borders and interests. Sadly, this was a situation of excess. The USA poured over 50 million dollars into the financing of the Contras. These paramilitaries received training and weapons from the CIA and began to attack the government and the people of Nicaragua. The US sent engineers in to covertly build a secret jungle airfield so that the Contras could be supplied. The Contras destroyed bridges, and planted bombs in Nicaraguan civilian airplanes! They planted bombs in the baggage area of one of Nicaragua's airports. They targeted state farms, grain storage centers and road junctions. Farmers were killed and vehicles destroyed.

The economic damage was huge. Coffee plantations were destroyed, and as coffee is one of Nicaragua's main sources of foreign currency, income and employment, the impact was dramatic. The CIA were directly involved in the blowing up of Nicaragua's only oil pipeline and oil storage tanks. And their personnel were involved in helicopter attacks on a legitimate Nicaraguan army base. They also mined the sea ports.

If you are really hard-nosed then you might still be thinking, 'So what? This is how it's been done for centuries.' Well, to add to the effect and increase the terror, the CIA prepared and distributed a manual called Psychological Operations in Guerrilla Warfare. This guidance included 'use of implicit and explicit terror', and the 'selective use of violence for propaganda effects.' The aim of these instructions being to create a climate of fear in which no one would dare to support the government. The manual also called for the 'neutralization' of Sandinista local government officials. The implication that the officials should be assassinated was clear to many.

The stance of the USA was that the Contras should be used to weaken and destabilize the Nicaraguan government, and so reduce the alleged risk to US interests. It's been suggested that what the US was hoping for, was that the Sandinistas would clamp down hard on the civilian population, and the opposition parties, in their attempt to hunt out the Contras. They also hoped to push the Nicaraguan government so hard that it would take action directly against US personnel based in Nicaragua, and so give the USA every right to intervene openly.

It's been conservatively estimated that 3,886 people were killed and over 4,700 wounded during the main four years of Contra activity. The damage to the infrastructure of the country was estimated to be in the region of $375 million. In the late 80s this was a significant amount. If you can disregard all those whose lives and livelihoods have been ruined, and can ignore those who have lost limbs and family members, then it is worth considering the resulting mistrust of the democratic system in Nicaragua, and of the US government.

But this is history. The realities are that people get things wrong. Paranoia and misinformation are incredibly dangerous, and humanity does have the ability to learn from its mistakes.

I started Tortillas to Totems with a quote from Anatole France. 'What is travelling? Changing your place? By no means! Travelling is changing your opinions and your prejudices.'

After all, aren't these some of the main reasons for going travelling? To experience as many different things and ways of life as possible? To discover new and wonderful things, but also to have preconceived ideas challenged.

I hope that you too can have the opportunity to travel this wonderful, complex and exciting world of ours.

'Every Day an Adventure'

The Bikes

Sam's bike – 1991 R80GS BMW
Bought new from Park Road Motorcycles in Southampton.
200,000 miles – 55 Countries around the world – Africa – Australia –
Asia – Africa (again) – South America – Central America – North
America

Modifications:
WP Rear shock absorber
WP Progressive Fork Springs
Engine protection 'Bash Plate'
Acerbis 43 litre petrol tank
Handguards
Home made luggage rack
Home made aluminium Panniers
Additional brake Light mounted on rear
Sidestand – strengthened and larger area foot added
Additional headlight protector and hand protectors added
10 litre stainless steel water tank mounted in front of right pannier
10 litre fuel jerrycan mounted in front of left pannier
Police spec high output alternator.

Should have put on heated hand grips!

Luggage:
Aluminium panniers, small tank-mounted rucksack, throw-over tank
panniers, roll bag.

Replaced parts due to wear and tear:
1 x wiring Loom
1 x gear box main bearing
1 x set valves

2 x sets piston rings
1 x set brake shoes
4 x sets brake pads
3 x drive Shaft
6 x clutch cables
1 x set choke cables
1 x rear brake cable
1 x set stainless steel brake hoses (replacing standard rubber hoses)
2 x seat covers
2 x driveshaft gaiters
1 set Paralever bearings
1 x starter motor (Bosch)
1 x collector box for stainless 'Y' piece
1 x silencer (Stainless)
2 x fork seals
5 x gearbox output shaft seals
2 x right side switchgear
1 x bevel box seal
2 x sets steering head bearings
2 x sets inlet rubbers
4 x sets carburetor diaphragms
2 x sets carb jets
3 x carb service sets
1 x ignition switch
1 x electronic ignition pickup
2 x sets HT Leads
Frame Powder Coated (at end of trip)

Unusual repairs or replacements (from accidents!):
Jawa mud flap on front mudguard (Egypt)
Rear sub-frame welded (Nairobi)
Speedo replaced - faulty (Nairobi)
Rear mudguard (Brisbane)
Front indicators (Land Rover – Windhoek)

Indicator relay (Harley Davidson - Bangkok)
Fairing panels (Hand made in Rundu Namibia)
Dashboard panel (Hand made in Rundu Namibia)
Fairing cash bars (Hand made in Rundu Namibia)
4 x mirrors (Mbeya, Rundu, Brisbane)
2 x windscreens (Windhoek, Bremen)
2 x centre stand (Repaired in Windhoek, Panama, USA. Replaced in Bremen)
1 x Fairing bash bars (Rebuilt in Rundu Namibia)
1 x Front mudguard (Brisbane, Bremen)

General Servicing items:
Oil Filters – lost count of how many
Air Filters – also lost count
Spark Pugs – plenty! Always NGK or Bosch
Rear shock absorber serviced once.
2 x Battery
Various lights bulbs
10 x In line fuel filters
Inner Tubes – lots!!! (Only 8 punctures in 8 years) Michelin enduro when available
Tyres – Trail - Metzler, Bridgestone, Michelin, Dunlop, Avon – most miles on Avon Gripsters.
Max Mileage Rear = 17,000 Avon
Max Mileage Front = 21,000 Avon

Most useful emergency 'spare parts' :
cable/zip ties and gaffer/duct tape!

Birgit's 1971 R60/5 BMW

No idea how many miles it's done as the bike had seven owners before Birgit got it. Enough to say that it has had an awful lot of miles under its wheels - Birgit took it across Europe, through Africa and up through the Americas.

Modifications:

Complete rebuild – twice prior to the start of the trip.
Converted from 600 to 800cc cylinders with appropriate carbs
Koni rear shock absorbers
Progressive fork springs
Windscreen
Handguards
Engine protective 'Bash Plate'
Home-made luggage rack
Home-made aluminium Panniers
Side Stand – replaced by a Bob Porecha 'Surefoot'
Headlight lens protector grill
Stainless steel brake hose
'Police-style' single saddle
Mud flap on front mudguard
Rubber duck collection.

Should have put on heated handgrips!

Replaced parts due to wear and tear:

2 sets brake pads
1 x clutch cable
1 x set choke cables
1 x rear brake cable
1 set exhaust pipes
1 x starter relay
10 x points
10 x condensers

1 x charging light bulb
2 x batteries
1 x Neutral switch on gearbox

Unusual repairs or replacements:
1 x complete rear wheel (Malawi)
1 x points backing plate (USA)
3 x mirrors (South Africa, USA, Canada)
1 x pair exhaust pipes welded (Colombia)
1 x front brake drum bracket (hand-made in Colombia)
1 x Bicycle gear change lever to replace choke lever
1 x Speedo cable repair (South Africa)

General Servicing items:
Oil filters – lost count of how many
Air filters – also lost count
Spark pugs – plenty! Always NGK or Bosch
In line fuel filters
Various light bulbs
3 x inner tubes – (Only 1 Puncture!) Michelin Enduro when available
Tyres – Enduro's - Metzler, Kenda, Avon – most miles on Avon Gripsters.
Max Mileage Rear = 14,000 Avon
Max Mileage Front = 15,000 Metzler

Most 'useful' spare parts:
Well, it had to be points and condensers!

Luggage:
Aluminium panniers, throw-over tank panniers, roll bag.

General thoughts about the bikes?

They were wonderfully reliable — except for a couple of niggles. Libby's shaft drive had a few worries earlier in the trip and Sir Henry had those points issues. The bikes dealt with very hard lives far better than we could have hoped for. They were very easy to work on and to service. This more than compensated for the fact that they could be thirsty at speed. They were too heavy in very soft sand or thick mud. Those very extreme conditions were about 5% of the journey, though when you are there 'in it' it feels a lot longer! For another 5% they were hard work but perfectly rideable, and for the remaining 90% of the time they were pure blissful fun. Their low centre of gravity was a major advantage off-road. They were both really comfortable to ride. Fun in fact.

Would we use them again? Sir Henry the Hybrid now needs overhauling but afterwards? Why not? The bikes are now like old friends. We know we can rely on them and we know they will be fun to ride. Libby is still my main means of transport.

WWW.SAM-MANICOM.COM
'Every Day an Adventure'

A request from Sam

I hope you've enjoyed the ride with us across these surprising and diverse lands.

The aim of my book is to share the fun, the drama and the unexpected things that are to be found in these three very different countries. If you feel that I have done this well, I would be very grateful if you'd take a few moments to post a review on Amazon.

Independent authors like me really value this help.

Most of us check reviews before we buy something. Your review will help me to share the huge range of extraordinary things that make North America such a fascinating part of the world to explore.

Did you know that you don't have to have bought this book from Amazon to be able to post a review?

Thank you again for reading Tortillas to Totems and thank you for your help.

All the best,

Adverts in a travel book?
Why?

Why are you finding adverts from companies involved in overlanding at this stage of Tortillas to Totems?

These are all companies who are highly recommended as having excellent equipment and quality service.

I'm enjoying the opportunity to guide you in their direction. If you are planning adventures of your own, be they two weeks, a month or two years, I hope you will find some inspiration on these next pages.

You'll also find some worthy causes that I'm happy to help out.

"If you have built castles in the air,
your work need not be lost;
that is where they should be.
Now put foundations under them."

— *Henry David Thoreau*

The motorcycle travellers website.

The definitive guide for planning your motorcycle adventure on DVD.

I expect the unexpected.
I expect things to break.
I expect to need to get my ass out of trouble.
When it happens, your biggest problem
should **not** be your gear.

—Erik

312

Motorcycle Outreach

www.motorcycleoutreach.org
UK Registered Charity 1114675

318

❝ When a person travels they discover
who they really are, what they can
achieve and so much more.
The moment a person's senses are
brought alive, an adventure starts to be
a success. The travel bug bites hard, but
motorcycle travel bites deep. **❞**

Sam Manicom